Media Wars

Media Wars
News at a Time of Terror

Danny Schechter

ROWMAN & LITTLEFIELD PUBLISHERS, INC.
Lanham • Boulder • New York • Oxford

ROWMAN & LITTLEFIELD PUBLISHERS, INC.

Published in the United States of America
by Rowman & Littlefield Publishers, Inc.
A Member of the Rowman & Littlefield Publishing Group
4501 Forbes Boulevard, Suite 200, Lanham, Maryland 20706
www.rowmanlittlefield.com

PO Box 317
Oxford
OX2 9RU, UK

British Library Cataloguing in Publication Information Available

Library of Congress Cataloging-in-Publication Data

Schechter, Danny.
    Media wars : news at a time of terror / Danny Schechter.
        p. cm. — (Polemics)
    Includes bibliographical references.
    ISBN 0-7425-3108-2 (hardcover : alk. paper) —
    ISBN 0-7425-3109-0 (pbk. : alk. paper)
    1. War on Terrorism, 2001—Mass media and the war. I. Title. II. Series.
    P96.W36 S34 2003
    070.4′49973931—dc21   2002153681

Printed in the United States of America

♾™ The paper used in this publication meets the minimum requirements of American National Standard for Information Sciences—Permanence of Paper for Printed Library Materials, ANSI/NISO Z39.48-1992.

POLEMICS

Stephen Eric Bronner, Series Editor

The books in the Polemics series confront readers with provocative ideas by major figures in the social sciences and humanities on a host of controversial issues and developments. The authors combine a sophisticated argument with a lively and engaging style, making the books interesting to even the most accomplished scholar and appealing to the general reader and student.

Media Wars
News at a Time of Terror
By Danny Schechter

FORTHCOMING TITLES

American National Identity in a Post-National Age
By James Sleeper

Animal Rights and Human Evolution
By Steven Best

The Collapse of Liberalism
Why Progressives Need a New Politics
By Charles Noble

Corruption
By Robert Fitch

Freud's Foes
Psychoanalysis, Science, and Resistance
By Kurt Jacobsen

The New Militarism
U.S. Foreign Policy in an Age of Globalization
By Carl Boggs

No Free Lunch
How to Destroy Television as We Know It
By Philip Green

Power and Disruption
By Frances Fox-Piven

Repressive Tolerance, Second Edition
By Herbert Marcuse

Same Sex Marriage and Democracy
By R. Claire Snyder

A Story to Die For
By Judith Kay

Technopolitics and Globalization
By Douglas Kellner

Contents

PART I: Warring with the Coverage of War

Dedication

To Daniel Pearl and the many reporters, correspondents, and photographers, who lost their lives on the front lines of journalism since September 11, 2001.

"The roll call of media casualties provides a tragic reminder of the price we pay for press freedom and democracy."
—*Aidan White*, general secretary of the 106-nation International Federation of Journalists, reporting from Belgium that one hundred news media workers were killed on the job during 2001, the highest toll in six years. The most were twelve journalists and media workers who died as a result of the September 11 attacks; eight journalists have been killed in the Afghan war.

And to all who stand up for truth at a time of "patriotic correctness."

Introductory Statement: On Media Responsibility

Walter Cronkite

I've been increasingly and publicly critical of the direction that journalism has taken of late, and of the impact on democratic discourse and principles. Like you, I'm deeply concerned about the merger mania that has swept our industry, diluting standards, dumbing down the news, and making the bottom line sometimes seem like the only line. It isn't, and it shouldn't be.

At the same time, I'm impressed that so many other serious and concerned people around the world are also becoming interested in holding media companies accountable and upholding the highest standards of journalism.

Corporate censorship is just as dangerous as government censorship, you know, and self-censorship can be the most insidious form of pulling punches. Pressures to go along, to get along, or to place the needs of advertisers or companies above the public's need for reliable information distort a free press and threaten democracy itself.

We have all been supportive for years of dissidents around the world who take great risks to stand up for what they believe in. But here at home, in our own industry, we need to make it possible for people to speak out when they feel they've been wronged, even if it means shaming newsrooms to do the right thing. Journalists shouldn't have to check their consciences at the door when they go to work for a media company. It ought to be just the reverse.

As I've said on other occasions, the strength of the American system is possible and can be nurtured only if there is lively and provocative dissent. In a healthy environment, dissent is encouraged and considered essential to feed a cross-fertilization of ideas and thwart the incestuous growth of stultifying uniformity.

We need to encourage and support those among us who face either overt or covert threats—or even a more subtle absence of encouragement to search out the truth. We all know that economic pressures and insecurities within news organizations have reduced the scope and range of investigative reporting. Sometimes projects are spiked with just a simple phrase: "It's not for us."

We're always ready to speak out when journalists are at risk. But today we must speak out because journalism itself is at risk.

And that's the way it is.

From a statement videotaped by former CBS news anchor Walter Cronkite, a Mediachannel.org advisor, on the occasion of the launch of Mediachannel.org.

February 1, 2000

Foreword

Roland Schatz, MEDIA TENOR

The images of the first attack appeared on the television screen in the midst of an interview I was conducting with Dr. Michael Inacker, chief of the Berlin office of the German weekly *Frankfurter Allgemeine Sonntagszeitung.* As a long-standing expert on terrorism, he refused to believe in the initial presumption that it was an accident. The dreadful confirmation was not to be long in coming: A few minutes later, as the murderers flew the second plane into the World Trade Center, Dr. Inacker said that the former German Interior Minister and Head of Chancellery, Dr. Wolfgang Schäuble, had repeatedly warned of the danger from international terrorism in previous years—but that the media had hardly paid any attention to him.

To us, this was a frightening example of what we call "agenda cutting," the tendency of media outlets to select what stories they will cover and which they will ignore. In the time leading up to September 11, terror threats were stories that were ignored.

Telephone calls to our colleagues at the New York office of MEDIA TENOR and our partners at Mediachannel.org gave us a first impression of the shock and paralysis that gripped many Americans. Only Mediachannel.org editor Danny Schechter immediately reflected on the causes for the attack: What impression have Americans made on those beyond the Atlantic that encourages and drives people into such insanity?

We discussed our impressions of the U.S. delegates' appearance—or should I say their lack of appearance—at the United Nations' racism conference in Durban a couple of days before the attack. The United States left the conference. Both the United States and Israel simply walked away from the negotiations with all the other countries in the world. Their departure left everyone involved with a bad aftertaste, and it provoked particularly bad press. When the American media later ran stories about "why the world hates us," no one referenced this most recent incident.

Extreme and unexpected events are normally a chance to reflect on the past. However, politicians, and especially journalists, did otherwise. Of course, all routines worked perfectly fine: Special editions and special programs came out in no time and helped to raise print runs and viewer shares. Not even the BBC refrained from repeating the "pictures of the day" for the seventy-fifth time on the night of September 12, playing pop music along with them. The subtext: Stay with us, even if we have nothing more to say.

We saw only a few journalists who asked the deeper questions that Danny Schechter and his colleagues at Mediachannel.org immediately raised.

Instead, everybody rushed to talk about the "war" against terror. Any slightly experienced journalist knew that this was nonsense; still, the phrase was repeated all over and disseminated to the audience without contemplation. As our reporting showed, real discussion of the "why" had not even risen to the surface a full month after the attack, because the international community was busy ensuring "unconditional" support to U.S. President George W. Bush and standing ostentatiously at his side. Thus, an impression was shaped: A level of expectation had risen to a point that something at least looking like a war had become inevitable. The war's "success" turned out to be far less impressive than the world was initially led to believe—but this harder and more factual assessment only came out many months later, in the summer of 2002.

As I write, there are many questions yet to be answered. Here are just some of them.

THE QUESTION OF THE RIGHT CHOICE OF WORDS

Are we really in a state of "war"? Many media analysts and communications scientists warned of sloppy rhetoric, if only because strong wording usually provokes strong reactions. Despite the initial rhetoric, the majority of the people in the United States, as well as in Europe, Africa, and Asia, came to realize that after all that had happened, their lives had not changed since September 11—at least not to the extent that President Bush and the global media coverage led them to believe. What's the consequence of all this? A bad conscience on the part of those simply enjoying life? A preventive abstention from consumption with the result that the economic slowdown turned into a veritable recession?

Bin Laden must have been very happy with this outcome.

THE QUESTION OF THE RIGHT BEHAVIOR AMONG FRIENDS

Real friends should be trying to change the focus when talking about Americans: not as ambassadors of Coca-Cola or McDonald's, but rather as a people that believe in values like democracy, freedom, and solidarity. Rarely were such American values put forth in this key context over the past few years. The U.S. delegation's walking out of Durban while the world community was talking about the effects of racism and looking for a solution hardly showed respect for dissent or diversity, two other values Americans say they support.

THE QUESTION OF COVERAGE IN NORMAL TIMES

Foreign news tends to reduce world affairs to terror, natural disasters, and arbitrary shots of state limousines spitting out talking heads. Thus, it should come as no surprise that the Western audience knows little about what is going on in Africa, Asia, or the Middle East. The following pages hold a mirror up to international television newscasters, examining their news selection and contribution to an understanding of international affairs. The findings about the United States and South Africa are especially troublesome. Speaking out among friends might help to improve coverage. The "Initiative Quality Control," organized by the German Journalists' Union, picked up on that idea with the following proposition: Journalists must learn how to say no to bad news stories, no matter how high the production costs involved.

The coverage on the U.N. Racism Conference in Durban gave observers in other parts of the world reason for a reflective pause even before September 11: On the one hand, there was the call for "the deed"—not only to talk about racism in the world, but to pay compensation for past and present exploitations of developing countries by the industrialized world. This demand would cost $999 billion. The United States proved itself as powerless, caught in the contradiction of trying to market the concept of democracy worldwide like a product, but shying away from practicing it when it came down to the basics. Just like Friedrich Schiller wrote in *Demokrit*: "Don't count the votes but weigh them."

The loud and bullheaded U.S. departure from Durban encouraged the rest of the world to stop listening, and that included representatives from totalitarian states who had no interest in the dialogue to begin with.

The MEDIA TENOR analysis shows that due to intensive coverage on the subject, readers and viewers in Africa and Europe did get a chance to evaluate the communication failure at Durban. Their counterparts in the United States did not. As the conference was approaching, the U.S. press and television networks hardly mentioned it. After the conference opened, it was covered mainly from the U.S. government's perspective, ignoring the United Nations' and the nongovernmental organizations' (NGO) points of view.

This pattern confirms a rule: foreign news coverage in the United States is limited to 10 percent of total airtime in prime-time network news; that 10 percent is (again) limited to news stories on crises of all kinds—natural disasters, crime, and terror. It is obvious that this current allocation of time and attention is not the way to encourage respect for other peoples and cultures.

And now? After terrorists declared war on the West, shouldn't efforts be focused on creating an international consensus within the United Nations that could be accepted by all members? It is the media's job to follow this process closely and critically relate it to the people. As the fight against terrorism in Germany in the 1970s and 1980s has shown, refuting the arguments of nonviolent "sympathizers" at an intellectual level helps destroy the breeding ground for the extremists. Constantly repeating pictures of bearded suspects with a turban, however, only stirs up emotions.

The debate about globalization also shows that there is a lack of continuous coverage on the subject. Voters are not willing to learn more about it if they are not provided with information on a regular basis. In the United States, international organizations only rarely make it into prime-time news or on to front pages. Even if that kind of information doesn't make a sensation, important issues are at stake: jobs, education, and health. Yet, these key issues are treated as if they are not newsworthy.

Critics had often warned of the insular attitude of the U.S. media, both as a reflection of and a support for a political agenda that is driven by a simple imperative: "America First."

For the longest time, the Cassandra calls were ignored.

Then, in the wake of the September 11 attacks on the United States, the American television media began to lament the country's "loss of innocence" and "awakening to a more dangerous world." The loss, however, was not of innocence as much as of ignorance to foreign hatred for the United States, and the awakening was not to a more dangerous world but to a world in which the country shared in the catastrophic effects of its own foreign policies. Most Americans were unaware of the political context in which the attacks were planned and executed because the agenda-setting media the public relies on provided negligible overseas policy coverage in the years leading up to them.

Before the attacks, foreign affairs were presented as irrelevant to anyone enjoying the "American way of life." Foreign conflicts and domestic security issues were rarely linked in the news. Accordingly, U.S. foreign policies went largely unexamined, appearing as incontestable extensions of the best in cultural, political, and economic values.

David Fractenberg has written that for an electorate to perform its democratic function, it must be exposed to "reasoned discourse, presentation of policy choices, and open and consequential discussion of moral and social issues," which, in a globalized world, necessarily includes both domestic and foreign concerns. In the period leading to the attacks, the U.S. television media did not present fundamental foreign policy issues to its audience, allowing policies to go unscrutinized domestically, and leaving the public unknowingly exposed to dangerous repercussions.

In 1997, a Harvard University study found that international news coverage on American network television fell by more than 70 percent between the 1970s and 1995. A more recent study by the Tyndall report indicates that the trend has accelerated, with such coverage falling more than 65 percent from 1989 through 2001.

According to MEDIA TENOR research, foreign affairs were the focus of only 22 percent of total network television news reports between May 2000 and August 2001, ten points lower than in comparable British and South African broadcast media and twenty points lower than in German television news. Of this coverage, only about 16 percent of reports (3 percent of all news reports) primarily addressed U.S. foreign policy issues or their effects abroad.

Compounding the scarcity of internationally-focused reporting in general is the infrequency with which such reports have linked foreign affairs to domestic issues. International coverage through the monitored period was dominated by reports on foreign wars, accidents, natural catastrophes, social policies, crimes, and other events that were disconnected from American policies and unrelated to Americans' lives.

Before September 11, the tragically disproved idea that terror would never hit home was clearly projected in some primary news sources. Even when foreign news concerned U.S. citizens and institutions in other countries, the events in which they were involved were rarely linked with home affairs. Terrorist attacks on Americans abroad, for example, attracted considerable coverage in the monitored period but were rarely linked to issues of U.S. domestic security.

After the bombing of the U.S.S. *Cole*, terrorism coverage increased from ten reports in September 2000 to 140 in October, while reports on domestic security remained stable. Again, in June 2001, the sentencing of the U.S. embassy bombers (from the 1998 attacks in Kenya and Tanzania), the suicide bombing of a Tel Aviv restaurant (in which an American was killed), and Timothy McVeigh's execution returned terrorism to the news. Again, the media failed to link the dangers abroad with domestic security issues, which didn't receive more than 3 percent of total coverage in the period.

Although all of the terrorist attacks were explicitly linked to American policy on Israel, the objections were rarely discussed as more than the rantings of terrorists in the television news. This representation was not due to a lack of focus on the region: the Middle East dominated foreign coverage, in fact, comprising 23.4 percent of total internationally-focused reports in the period. Although this might have provided considerable insight into some of the United States' most intransigent critics and most controversial policies, the news instead focused primarily on Israel, which received more than twice as much coverage as the rest of the region's nations combined. Coverage of Israel did little to forge an understanding of the area's political climate either. Images and descriptions of violence largely overshadowed discussion or examination of the Palestinian dispute's foundations or the United States' complex involvement. As with other regions, Middle Eastern countries, including U.S. allies, were presented as dangerous and chaotic, with little reasoned political debate broadcast to help examine underlying causes.

The generally unfavorable topical focus in network coverage of foreign countries was reinforced by the overwhelmingly negative tone in which the reports were presented. Former CNN anchor Peter Arnett's comment that on U.S. television, "there is no international news available anywhere unless there is a major crisis," was clearly evidenced in the news in the period: of the reports broadcast by American networks, foreign countries' negative ratings outweighed positive ratings by 29 percent, a more pronounced disparity than in any of the other countries monitored.

Despite its clearly apparent shortcomings in foreign coverage (prior to the attacks) and although the American public had begun to ask why it was so hated abroad, two of the three monitored networks actually *reduced* foreign-focused coverage in September. Overall foreign coverage fell to just 19.7 percent of reports, with 52 percent of that focused on Afghanistan alone.

Instead of seeking answers to the country's collective "why?" the networks transformed the question into a collective "who?" by presenting the issue as a matter of culprits and victims, rather than an issue of global political conflict. The hunt for Osama bin Laden, the administration's short-lived diplomatic wrangle with the Taliban, potential military approaches to defeating the regime, and the flight of Afghanistan's civilians to the Pakistani border became the primary topics of coverage in the country.

Domestic coverage reinforced a similar "us versus them" polarity, with a dramatic new concentration on domestic security issues that increased from 2.4 percent of coverage prior to September to more than 20 percent after the attacks. Coverage promoted the idea that the United States would overcome the terrible events by finding the individual "bad guys" and by making domestic adjustments so that similar attacks would be impossible to carry out in the future. Any discussion of the government's culpability in attracting foreign hatred, which might have helped answer the country's "why?" and could have prevented increased crosscultural misunderstanding, was conspicuously absent from the news.

Party politics ranked as the second-most dominant topic in the post-attack period, but the question of America's role in the attacks went unexamined in that context as well. Instead, the cultural conceit that the media had projected prior to September 2001 was enhanced through constant patriotic displays, precluding any painful discussion of the country's role in its own suffering and sadly eliminating some hope that the cycle of hatred might have finally been stopped.

According to Nigel Dacre, editor of *ITV News,* the attacks on September 11 were "the biggest story television has ever covered." As the horrific events unfolded, 3.6 million U.K. viewers tuned in to the television news to see the second hijacked plane crash into the south tower of the World Trade Center. Across Britain, and across the world, life was interrupted as the minutes passed as one tower collapsed after the other. Internet connections were slowed due to the massive demand for information, and television became the primary source of information for an estimated 16.4 million British viewers tuned to the live coverage. By 6:00 P.M., almost ten million viewers were tuned to BBC1, and another five million to ITV, watching the apocalyptic images from New York and Washington on the evening news.

Later, the Independent Television Commission praised BBC, ITV, and Sky News for their coverage of the terrorist crisis, writing to the network heads, "The ITC appreciated the care taken to strike the right balance between the sensitivity of the situation and the necessity to inform viewers of the nature of the event." Not all networks struck the right balance in the hours and days after the attacks, however, and many were criticized for misguided musical selections and politically insensitive programming.

The ITC received sixty complaints about a British independent television news organization (ITN) piece that aired the day after the attacks showing a montage of the Twin Towers being hit by the hijacked planes while upbeat music played. The piece was condemned as "tasteless" and "inappropriate."

In another instance, BBC1's *Question Time* received hundreds of calls from angry viewers, stating that the studio audience was heavily biased against the United States and that they lacked respect for the grief of others. Philip Lader, the former U.S. ambassador to Britain had appeared as a panelist on *Question Time,* and he seemed reduced to tears after one audience member explained why Americans are hated all over the world. Greg Dyke, the BBC director general, apologized to Mr. Lader for an error in judging "the mood of the moment" and admitted that "the program had the wrong tone given the scale of the tragedy."

Similar censures of press figures and programs took place in Germany. Ulrich Wickert of the ARD Tagesthemen program was forced to apologize for remarks claiming that George W. Bush and Osama bin Laden were of the same "mind structure," a statement made in reference to George W. Bush's ultimatum that nations would have to choose one side or another.

The attacks caused major content changes in television news programs as well. Terrorism was the main topic of 20 percent and 30 percent of the German and British news networks' content in September. In South Africa, the coverage of the terrorist attacks made up about 9 percent of the overall coverage in the month, still a drastic increase over previous levels. In addition to the rise in terrorism coverage in September, European media noted an increase in security issues.

On BBC and ITV evening news programs, the Northern Ireland conflict and bomb attacks by the "Real IRA" in London dominated news coverage over the previous fifteen months, comprising 53 percent of terrorism coverage overall. During the same period, more than half of German television reports on terrorism focused on a bomb explosion in Düsseldorf and the kidnapping of German tourists in the Philippines. The newly catastrophic level of international terrorism widened the focus of television news on domestic security issues, however, from a national to an international level. Terrorist activities in other countries took on more significant implications for domestic news and individual citizens, and groups within each country came under closer scrutiny for their actions and affiliations abroad.

After September 11, all news programs presented increased coverage of domestic security and international affairs issues. In the aftermath of the attacks, investigations were carried out in Britain and Germany, and legal changes were discussed to improve security and fight terrorism. In Germany, the alleged terrorists' former university attendances in Hamburg and their creation of a prayer group there created a discussion on terrorist organizations taking cover as religious groups, quickly leading to an alteration in the laws governing such clubs and societies.

Civil aviation security, including the introduction of armed sky marshals aboard civil aircraft, resulted in increased coverage of domestic security issues in both German and British news. In Great Britain, such reports were most dominant, comprising 4.5 percent of the overall news content in the analyzed time period. South African television news did not turn to domestic security issues in the period, focusing outward on international terrorism instead.

The international cooperation against terrorism invoked by George W. Bush figured strongly into all international news. It became the most dominant focus of foreign affairs and international politics coverage everywhere except in the United States.

The strong impact that the New York and Washington, D.C., attacks had on the European news media were not just because the deaths of British and Germans at the World Trade Center, but also attributed to the idea that Western civilization itself had been assaulted. Shortly after the attacks, Tony Blair expressed this sentiment by declaring, "We are at war with terrorism—what happened on Tuesday was an attack not just upon the United States but upon the civilized world."

The emphasis on the civilized world's victimization raised the question of who was meant to represent the uncivilized world. This discussion, along with George W. Bush's unfortunate use of the word "crusade" in a public address, began to raise fears that the U.S. retaliation could result in what Samuel P. Huntington called a "clash of civilizations." This newly visible aspect of political affairs was the central focus of only a few reports but was nevertheless an underlying factor in nearly every news program following the attacks. Despite some of leaders' assertions that the conflict was not between religions or civilizations, but rather between the peace-loving world and terrorists, many of the issues raised in the news seemed to point to a different reality.

Immigration and ethnic minority issues were featured strongly throughout the analyzed news media in September, while stories on anti-Arab attacks appeared in several countries. Widespread discussion of a potential battle between Islamic and Christian cultures demonstrated the need for mutual education between cultures, a service that the television media is in a uniquely important position to undertake. The attacks of September 11 demonstrated the futility and danger of portraying foreign countries as isolated and irrelevant in an era when globalization has brought both the riches and the dangers of previously distant economic and cultural realities close to home for everyone.

Meanwhile, the wind has begun blowing from a different direction: the media no longer sees the United States as a victim, but also as an active player. New international trends show that the official America and its media have not learned their lessons—this perception continues to become more and more obvious. Following September 11 and the subsequent international fight against terror—which was not unanimously supported around the world—the country also had to wage a battle against the unremitting disintegration and financial discrepancies of corporate organizations, which started with Enron in 2002 and was followed by Dynergy, Qwest, Global Crossing, Adelphia, Imclone, Tyco, Xerox, and WorldCom. At the time of this writing, the initially scoffed-at Euro has aligned itself with the dollar, with investors from the renowned finance house Goldman Sachs forecasting that, by early 2003, Americans will have to dole out $1.12 for one Euro. According to research done by MEDIA TENOR International, other than the publicity generated by the annual Academy Awards and the Winter Olympic Games in Salt Lake City, almost no positive reports on the United States would have reached television audiences worldwide. The result of MEDIA TENOR's comparative analysis of nineteen television news programs in four countries shows that South African television media broadcasts the only positive images of the United States. This tendency is most probably a result of South African society's view of America as the proverbial land of "milk and honey."

For the rest, reality has set in, and sympathy for the United States has waned since the attacks of September 11. MEDIA TENOR's results show that before this event, coverage on the United States was relatively frequent and on a continual basis, peaking during certain events. The rating of the U.S. government, economy, and society remained fairly balanced in both negative and positive statements. Notably, prior to the attacks, the South African media was slightly more critical than the German and British media, with the latter focusing on issues pertaining to the United States' domestic policy as well as general interests. In a similar manner, the United States focused on domestic policy, party politics, and business. This created an illusory image of a "safe world." To a greater extent, issues dominating overseas media related to human-interest news or gossip. These stories were mostly reported on by the respective private broadcasters. Sports, especially in South Africa's media, were largely responsible for positive coverage on the United States, with a primary focus on African American golfer Tiger Woods.

If only for two months, September 11 (understandably) shifted the world's attention to the United States. While the U.K. and U.S. media turned their attention to the act of terror committed against the United States, German and South African television focused on the foreign affairs response following the attacks.

However, in the United States, foreign affairs action followed in fourth position after crime, business, and general interest. South African and German television news programs mainly focused on—with a similar share—foreign affairs, sports, general interest, and crime. However, with 20 percent of reports on foreign affairs, German television was far less critical than its South African counterpart, with 60 percent of reporting on this topic. Similarly, the United Kingdom was "tentative" in its reporting with only 18 percent of the U.S. foreign affairs coverage found to be negative. While negative statements on business-related issues increased across the board, the rating of the U.S. government and President Bush remained the same in the United States, Germany, and the United Kingdom.

However, following late 2002 reports on the Bush–Cheney involvement in corporate scandals, it is doubtful whether it will stay this way for much longer. In conjunction with foreign policies and business (possibly), Bush should be focusing on both his own personal media image and that of those surrounding him. Even previously U.S.–supportive magazines such as *Time* are starting to change their stance on the United States. Perhaps the forerunner in this trend, South Africa was the single exception, actually increasing both its criticism of the government of the United States and its president. This slight backlash is despite Bush's promise of extensive aid to the country. Rumors of Bush's possible no-show at the U.N. World Summit for Sustainable Development in Johannesburg in August 2002 did not assist his shaky image. Ultimately, Bush did not attend. He sent Secretary of State Colin Powell in his place, who was booed by many delegates.

Responsible for the largely negative reporting on business issues were reports on the U.S. stock market. In both the U.S. and South African television news, market reports were top of the agenda. U.K. television focused intensively on the Enron investigation while German television highlighted the scandal around Ford's use of Firestone tires. Quite disparate is the reporting on the U.S. foreign affairs' issues. While the bulk of reporting in the United States focused on the attack on the United States—as well as the direct reaction to the attacks— coverage on international cooperation in the conflict was reduced to only 7 percent in South Africa, 5 percent in the United States, 9 percent in the United Kingdom, and 4 percent in Germany. While a mere 4 percent in South African media repeated footage of the actual attack, every fifth report on the U.S. foreign affairs' issues showed planes crashing into the World Trade Center. As if the United States had not had enough negative coverage in business and foreign affairs reports, the accusations of pedophilia committed by individual Catholic priests resulted in an intense debate on this subject in international media. Internationally, the image of the United States suffered a further blow following the frenzy that resulted from the anthrax scares and attacks after September 11.

Issues previously prevalent on the agenda were reduced to marginal positions. For example, such topics as research and science were reduced to the tenth position in the United Kingdom, the ninth position in Germany, tenth in South Africa, and in the United States research and science did not even break into the top ten. Previously, this order of priority was different. Between July 2001 and September 2001, coverage in the U.S. media on its own scientific research was—although not the top priority (seventh position)—an issue that received the highest positive share of reporting and simultaneously the lowest negative share of reports. South African television saw U.S. research in seventh position, with no negative statements. In the United Kingdom, research used to be the second most important issue relating to the United States.

Thankfully, there is still sports. Since April 2002, South African television media found Tiger Woods and golf tournaments a source valuable enough to devote every second report on the United States. Besides golf in South Africa, the Olympic Games in Salt Lake City have contributed greatly to a positive image of the United States. However, this event remained unique in this respect, and it has been shown that the United States' image cannot be carried on sports-related issues alone.

Even the initial support by Britain has come into doubt, with the *New Statesman* headlining that "America is spitting on Britain" and further stating that the "Bush–Blair Alliance is ending." African media are already becoming extremely critical of George W. Bush after it surfaced that the promised aid to Africa was significantly smaller than expected and that support for its Nepad development plan was not as concrete as initially promised. MEDIA TENOR's research also indicates that despite negative issues surfacing (and therefore negative reports slightly increasing), the number of positive reports remains stable and is in fact even improving. But with its business, foreign affairs, and ostensibly its president's image in the international media in shambles, and other critical issues not featuring in the media, the only hope seems to rest in sports.

This sanctity alone is not much, one year after the attack. Initiatives like Mediachannel.org, with its global networking and daily quality control in journalism, offer a reliable tool, even as it swims against the mainstream.

Roland Schatz, Bonn
August 2002

Introduction

Many of us have been here before. Watching our world go to war, watching through the lens of a mainstream media system that in far too many instances functions as a megaphone for official views and sanitized news. In America, it was like that in the early days of the Vietnam conflict and later, in much of the coverage of the Gulf War. And now, once again, with some distinct differences, in Afghanistan and other fronts in the still-expanding "war" against terrorism. The difference is that today, despite all the new technologies, hundreds of news channels and diverse views instantaneously available through the Internet, the information situation is even more grave.

We have more media and less understanding. Yes, I know how imprecise the term "media" has become, since we are all exposed to information of all kinds, online and offline, analog and digital, broadband and satellite, in the traditional press and conventional television newscasts, as well as in a proliferating array of magazines, websites, webzines, videos, and films. What is called "news" pours into us and through us, mediated through yet more technologies and platforms than I can keep up with. And, yet, at a time of deepening crisis, when responsible media is needed more than ever, so much of it is failing us all the same.

There were even instances in this time of terror that the media seemed to terrorize us more than enlighten us. News about terror often became distancing and frightening, with alarmist reporting of an often unsubstantiated (if not misleading) kind of journalism, which resulted in a panicked response in which millions of Americans said that they were ready to sacrifice their basic freedoms for security. In many instances, the first stories and "breaking news" bulletins that forecast new attacks proved wrong. They were based on either skimpy evidence or no evidence at all.

Millions of people ended up relying on such reports, often believing that they were being well served by them. Many of our minds and attention spans quickly became tethered to a flow of bulletins, headlines, and buzzwords, floating cryptically as text at the bottom of television screens, endlessly presenting a parade of headlines about wars and deaths and celebrity divorces. All of these items were treated with the same sense of urgency—as if they all shared the same gravitas.

Much of the public became hooked, even addicted, to this ever-flowing digital news stream, tuned in and zoned out by the endless and repetitive chatter of the twenty-four-hour news channels, with their nonstop, wall-to-wall imagery and "breaking news." Far too many viewers then believed they were in the loop, in the know, and getting the "real" story. Ironically, much of the entertainment programming on the air is now called "reality television," so distinctions between "faction" and fiction are often elusive. At the same time, television news looks so authoritative and comprehensive. It is packaged to be perceived as "credible" and then delivered with well-honed and well-tested techniques designed to be believable. How are most viewers to know what is left out? Or that the sources are often limited and skewed? Or how partisan politics fuses seamlessly into a genre of patriotically correct but one-sided perspectives that aim to manipulate emotions and encourage more viewing through constant promos of what's next.

Cumulatively, this image-driven approach often supplants information. Today's picture-driven mediums conceal as much as they reveal. The problem is worse than ever, because all but a few journalists have effectively been barred from battlefields from the east of Afghanistan to the West Bank of Palestine. Government sources increasingly set the agenda and help frame the issues from which the news is constucted. Access to documents and details are limited by policy and practice.

News coverage of this conflict is worse than ever as well because many media institutions have confused jingoism with journalism. Truth telling tends to be degraded when American flags start flying in the lapels of newscasters and in the graphics surrounding news sets. In this red, white, and blue environment, voices of dissent quickly disappear like some dissident priest in Argentina during the days of that country's "dirty war." It took *The New York Times* almost two months to discover and report that news management techniques were orchestrating what television newscasts were covering and that the television reporting and pundit shows were leaving out dissident voices once the war was up and running. Ironically or not, in a war against a Taliban condemned for its treatment of women, most of the pundits on American television remained men (according to *The Washington Post*), with only twelve women experts interviewed against seventy-eight men on the weekend shows in the month after September 11. The writer mocked this clear pattern of bias by repeating "men, men, men," as if we needed a reminder of the macho ethic that takes over when media discussions on the use of military power get underway.

We live in an age of media politics, governed not just by politicians but by what is in effect a "mediaocracy," a mutually dependent relationship between media and politics, a nexus of power in which political leaders use media exposure to shape opinions and drive policy. Political candidates increasingly rely on their media advisors and spend small fortunes to buy airtime to broadcast ads to get their poll-tested messages across. Governments don't have to buy time, but their media operations have big budgets to hire small armies of strategists, spinners, and speechwriters. This mediaocracy then sets the agenda and frames what issues get the focus, and which do not.

The events of September 11 introduced a new player in our media-dominated political culture. The attacks on American targets were staged for their dramatic effect, as a variant on what revolutionaries once called "armed propaganda," an attack orchestrated to achieve maximum media attention by extremely media-conscious terror groups. And yet, with few exceptions, their media strategy and sophistication was rarely explained in the media.

Understand this well. Osama bin Laden and his al Qaeda cadres were very media savvy. They used computer games to train for the assault on the World Trade Center. They relied on the Internet for communication, and they had their own video unit to make training tapes for their internal use and video messages for external transmission to receptive outlets like Al-Jazeera, the Qatar-based, Arabic-language satellite station. Those staged videos were then reported on and rebroadcast by media outlets worldwide. All were image-conscious communiqúes, skillfully exploiting the symbols of their jihad politics and top leader just as consciously as U.S. presidents do when staging photo ops and press conferences in the Rose Garden.

In our new high-tech age of connectivity, media wars are increasingly fought alongside armed conflicts. Today's warriors fight along the grids of technology: economic interdependence and ideological combat. Information wars have become central to war fighting. Their messages are targeted in equal measure to different audiences—both to their respective constituencies and adversaries. The war on terrorism builds its own strategy of countermeasures, as influenced by playbooks used by their enemies. While cats fight rats and the martyrs of the mujahideen take on the "kafir" (nonbelieving) infidels, the White House attacks "evil doers" and their "axis," as the two sides become more alike than they realize, with an almost shared polemic. Bin Laden denounces "crusaders" while

President Bush calls for a crusade. Caught in these crosshairs are ordinary people, citizens at risk with a need to know what is going on and how to survive a frightening new situation in an era that has "changed forever."

I write as a media maker cum media critic who is convinced that the media role in this conflict is central to understanding it, although it is mostly ignored. Media rarely calls attention to its own role, and yet the media's impact in this crisis is at once total and at the same time elusive. It needs to be understood more deeply, to be dissected as it were. And it also needs to be challenged.

In the aftermath of the attacks of September 11, it was common to hear journalists and pundits alike say we (all of us) were at a turning point, as in "the world will never be the same." The media are part of the world. We must ask, how has the media changed *in* this crisis, and how much has it been changed *by* this crisis? Has it changed for better or for worse? Many believe there has been a fundamental shift in its overall focus. Some see an improvement, a new dispensation. How true is this impression? For the news media, especially in the United States, the unexpected catastrophic events of September 11 represented a wake-up call, like an injection of adrenaline coursing through veins that had spent a summer slumbering through coverage of sex scandals and shark bites at the beach. Covering those dramatic terror attacks gave many outlets a heady *gravitas,* with the incidents themselves representing a dramatic megamedia challenge, underscoring the key role and keen responsibility media outlets now assume in every national crisis. As we will see, some media outlets acquitted themselves well at the outset, but quickly reverted to precrisis mode.

In this book, the term *media war* is used on three levels. First, it examines the role media plays in covering (and miscovering) the many conflicts that have escalated since September 11. This book explores that coverage from different angles, with analysis, commentary, and reports on the terror attack and the retaliation it sparked. It examines the mainstream news coverage and the U.S. government's approach to managing it. This content analysis also shows the use of media as a tool of modern war fighting and as an instrument of propaganda and spin, the key dissemination belt for often carefully managed "official" information, much of it from U.S. government sources.

Second, the term looks at the many roles media outlets play at a time of terror, and it looks at war as both an information resource and a unifying force. Critics who view media itself as a "weapon of mass distraction" also recognize its use as a tool in the arsenal of mass mobilization. There is no better way of rallying the public.

Third, the term examines how media often becomes a battleground in the war for public opinion, as a competitive arena in which media outlets are often at war with each other, at war for market share and what is now called "mind share." The scramble for ratings, profitability, and competitive advantage used to mean a fight driven by whoever is the first to get the story or present a scoop. Journalists used to compete over who would get there first and who would be first to send out the exclusive interviews and break news. That was then. Today, news gathering is far more corporate and formularized. It involves targeting demographics and using tried and tested methods for marketing news programs to build audiences for advertisers. In the "old days" (or what some now call *the golden era*), hard news ruled. Today, the focus is on human-interest features, often with a sleazy tinge, storytelling, and sensationalism.

As I write, it is clear but rarely noted that this conflict manifests in more than content terms. The coverage has been deeply inflected with a worldview. It is thoroughly ideological, and rarely crude in its delivery, despite being one-sided in form and content. Its biases are found in its orientation, in the choices made daily on what to cover (and what not to cover), and in how to cover news. As newsbiz fuses with showbiz, those biases are now built into the very structure of media presentation. Hard-edge, formula-driven discussion programs become "shout shows" that increasingly resemble wrestling matches. (Wrestling, a form of violent entertainment that is often staged to simulate a sporting event, is the most popular program format on cable television.) Heat (not light) drives formats that thrive on offering a clash of extremes with polished sound-bite specialists hurling often-simplistic arguments (not information) at each other. No participant in this theatrical spectacle really listens to the other. There isn't time. It is all about who dominates the discourse and makes an adversary look silly or stupid. Many of these shows lean politically to the right with often demagogic conservative commentators taking the lead on television and radio. They are skillful operators in a predesigned, preconstructed world of fast talkers and put-down artists whose trade craft is cynicism, cliché, and conscience-free verbal gymnastics. A whole network of "media trainers," often former television producers and journalists, hire themselves out to teach the tips and tricks of the trade.

These entertainers posing as commentators became the frontline troops in the media war for eyeballs and ratings. This is a bitterly fought contest pitting competitive news outlets against one another. These news organizations are constantly raiding each other's personnel and cloning each other's graphics and look. That conflict is most visible as Rupert Murdoch's new raucous Fox News Network challenges more traditional broadcasters like CNN with polarizing programming and right-wing polemicists slamming a nonexistent "liberal media." Increasingly, journalism itself, which once claimed to be balanced if not "objective," is itself taking a backseat to hot-button opinionizing by all the channels. This all becomes an exercise in the deliberate but artful management of perception.

Media Wars also discusses the coverage of some cultural responses to September 11. It offers an assessment of global media reporting, which all too often followed the U.S. lead or relies on Western news agencies and television outlets like CNN. It looks at coverage of the Israel–Palestine conflict as an ongoing global crisis that deserves attention in the context of responses to terrorism. Like any examination of an ongoing story, it is incomplete and still tentative in many of its formulations. There is some unavoidable repetition since this is a collection of pieces on similar themes assembled with some haste. If journalism itself is still spoken of as the first draft of history, then *Media Wars* is an early assessment of how the media *system* serves and fails to serve us in this ongoing crisis.

There is also another media war in these pages, a personal battle that goes back to reporting I did during the Vietnam War and its aftermath. It reflects one journalist's war with media institutions fought out in the media and with media. This is a war hardened by years of outrage and personal experience. It expresses itself in these pages and on the Mediachannel.org website, which I edit as a "war of words."

It is a war fought out within the pages of this compilation as a self-proclaimed "news dissector's" crusade against media distortions, simplifications, and government propaganda. This fight is admittedly subjective and tilted toward critical perspectives. As a media watcher, I believe I am as much an eyewitness to these events as those who see it all firsthand in a foxhole or through the back seat of a tank or a Pentagon press briefing. I have a right to speak and a duty to speak out as an outsider, turned network insider, turned outsider again. And yes, I know that many of my colleagues don't share these views or reflect much on the questions I have raised. Media is, after all, a business, and for most of us, it is just business as usual. Why agonize over practices you feel powerless to change? Promotions and job security are often tied to keeping your head down, not by opening your mouth.

Modern media no longer just covers wars; it has become a player within them. Media organizes populations to rally behind wars and at rare points in history to actually question them. I believe I am certainly, if not uniquely, qualified to discuss these issues, since I have been writing about military-press tensions for over thirty years. Some of that time was spent reporting from the "field" in Southeast Asia, South Africa, and Beirut. Far more time was spent writing about war and its coverage since the 1960s.

Most books about wars tend to be I-was-there accounts by participants focusing on what happened on the battlefield. This book is not. It is written in an age where perception often trumps reality. It is, instead, a view through the sometimes-foggy lens of media analysis that was sharpened by thirty years in the industry as a writer, reporter, correspondent, producer, director, newscaster, and editor. It brings together daily reports, a weekly column, longer articles, research studies, and other commentary. It seeks to assess the performance of journalism, news companies, and television channels, as well as the role of government agencies in trying to influence the way the terror story has been reported and the spin it has been given.

This book also reports on the work of the media-monitoring world, with accounts that have appeared on a global media website I oversee, Mediachannel.org, and includes more systematic decoding by our colleagues at MEDIA TENOR, an international company. It was that company, led by a communications scientist named Roland Schatz, that not only analyzed some of the coverage but also arranged for the publication of this book after a number of U.S. publishers "passed," on grounds that the media story was a sidebar. We, however, believe it is central.

A "NEWS DISSECTOR'S" APPROACH

It was in the immediate aftermath of the events of September 11 that I began somewhat obsessively tracking the news coverage, and its consequences in all of its variation and conformity, on a daily basis. Ever since the 1970s, I have used "News Dissector" as a *media nom de guerre*, a humorous moniker given to me during a decade of newscasting at WBCN radio in Boston. I have revived the nickname as the title of a column for the online media issues network I edit. Because I am also a principal in the Globalvision News Network (gvnews.net), a global syndication service that provides access to other perspectives from every region in the world, I am exposed to news from 375 news providers worldwide. As a result, I am able to read, watch, and monitor coverage across borders and mediums, online and offline, on a daily basis.

Soon after the attacks, I began writing about the media's differences and similarities, omissions and errors, as well as attitudes and outlooks in a daily column, or *blog* (from the word *weblog*), posted on Mediachannel.org (Mediachannel.org/weblog). These columns, reviews, rants, raves, and cites draw from and comment on what colleagues worldwide are writing. They ranged between 2,500 to 3,500 words a day, almost every day, seven days a week. Obsessive maybe, but taken together, fairly comprehensive. This focus on news coverage also tracked the progress of the ongoing war for more than a year and still counting.

I took on this project out of a sense of duty and out of a self-defined mission to become a witness, in real time, to what various media outlets were telling us about this "BIG" story and (inadvertently) about themselves. I brought to this effort an approach to writing about media's reporting on war that goes back thirty years.

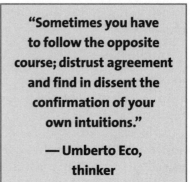

"Sometimes you have to follow the opposite course; distrust agreement and find in dissent the confirmation of your own intuitions."

— Umberto Eco, thinker

I had just published a collection of some of that coverage in my book of pieces, passions, and polemics called *News Dissector* (Akashic Books) with some of my stories from Vietnam and about the Gulf War and Bosnia. I had cut my eye-teeth on this type of "between the lines and behind the scenes" analysis. I felt like I knew what questions to ask, and as a former network television producer at CNN and ABC news, I knew what to look for in terms of network formats and formula.

After September 11, while much of the media mantra spoke of a changing world, I observed an unchanging media. There was more news, of course, but much of it stuck, repeating itself like a needle on a record, in the *As* (airplane attacks, anthrax, and Afghanistan), never reaching the rest of the alphabet, except for a few *Os* (Osama, Omar). At year's end, *The New York Times* devoted a major story to "Headlines from the Cutting Room Floor," referring to "key stories that were overlooked, that might have played out differently had the world's gaze not been fixed on terrorism." (The *Times*, of course, helps fix the gaze.)

Their "news NOT in the news" included the Florida presidential election returns, a watershed moment in American democracy. That story disappeared as "the debate shifted from 'Who won' to 'Who cares,'" acknowledged the "newspaper of record" that was, institutionally a member of the consortium of news organizations behind a mysteriously delayed media review. Imagine: the most disputed election in U.S. history became a footnote, receiving just a few headlines, as a larger question about the substance of our democracy was being swept under the rug. There were many more underreported stories that weren't pursued at all in the nonstop news stream that I reported on in my column. (While I was writing this column, I was also directing a film about the missing votes in Florida called *Counting on Democracy*; see globalvision.org for more info.)

As the current public consensus behind the war on terror begins to fracture and fragment, I anticipate more demand for independent media perspectives in much the same way U.S. bookstores were overwhelmed with demands for books on Islam, Afghanistan, terrorism, and the Taliban. Clearly, our own survival depends on consulting more diverse news and information than we are currently receiving.

Our own experience mirrors this trend. In the aftermath of September 11, Mediachannel.org experienced a surge in traffic, as did virtually every major news outlet and site. According to National Public Radio (NPR), international news sites like the BBC and CBS reported a 50 percent increase in traffic from Americans, presumably dissatisfied with U.S. news coverage.

On September 11, Mediachannel.org had 750 affiliates; one hundred days later, more than one hundred new media sites joined. Six months after September 11, there were nearly one hundred more. As I write, there are over 1,000. Traffic reached four million hits monthly. My own "News Dissector" columns were picked up and posted on other sites, and reprinted in magazines and newspapers. Because of the column, I was interviewed on CNN, by NPR programs and stations, and heard on more than fifty radio broadcasts in the United States and worldwide including radio outlets in Singapore, South Africa, New Zealand, Slovenia; and television outlets in Greece, Japan, South Africa, and Sweden. I published pieces in Italy, Spain, Germany, and the United Kingdom, and I spoke at many conferences and journalism symposiums from Boston to Bonn, Washington, D.C., to Seattle, Washington. I was also quoted in the *New Yorker, Vanity Fair, New York,* and *The Nation.*

But in the end, it is up to you as a reader to find this book of value or not, and to decide whether to join us in doing something about the media, challenging its inadequacies and encouraging its reform.

This book seeks to shine a light on media practices and its coverage limitations. Clearly, at the moment, only a few national outlets in the United States give regular voice to the types of perspectives I am calling for. There are media reviews like the *Columbia Journalism Review* and the *American Journalism Review*. There are many media watch groups and websites on the margins. There are still many magazines and some newspapers that offer a regular diet of critical journalism. On television, two new channels—Free Speech TV and World Links— are seen on satellite stations. There are 500 public access channels nationwide, some of which carry shows like Amy Goodman's *Democracy Now*. The Pacifica radio network offers dissenting voices that cannot easily be heard elsewhere. Independent (indy) media videos and websites reach audiences worldwide, but they lack the means of promotion and marketing, as does most of progressive media. Professional organizations, like the Project on Excellence in Journalism and their media reviews, report on these issues in depth. You can find many of their websites on Mediachannel.org, which includes links to Mediatenor.com, FAIR.org, Alternet.org, and ZNET.org—all of which offer dissenting views, along with hundreds of other websites. I consider myself just one voice in a growing community of concern.

Special thanks for help in this project to my "brother" Roland Schatz of MEDIA TENOR, who first published this book; to Vidhura Ralapanawe, a reader who began corresponding with me and later volunteered to help edit the book; to my daily weblog editor, Jeanette Friedman, with whom I quarrel almost daily, mostly about coverage of Israel, but whose professionalism comes through; to our readers worldwide who send in items and perspectives to enrich the discourse; to my weekly "News Dissector" editor and old friend, Elinor Nauen, who also loses patience with me on political and grammatical grounds but knows how to cut me down to size; and to Catherine Borgman Aboleda, Aliza Dichter, Doug George, Murad Ryani, Andrew Levi, and many others, especially the funders, who keep Mediachannel.org alive and cooking. To Polar Levine, also known as Polarity l, editor of popcultmedia.com, who designed the cover; and to Jeffrey Ladd, who donated the cover photo taken in Cairo on September 11. And, *por supuesto,* to my colleagues at Globalvision, Globalvision New Media, its news editor Tim Karr, and my running mate in this adventure, Rory O'Connor. And like my other books, it is dedicated to Sarah Debs Schechter, now a creative executive in Hollywood, with hopes that her media imprint will soon be seen. I admire all these folks and couldn't have pulled this off without them.

> **"We're giving you, as television so often does, a very limited view."**
>
> **— PETER JENNINGS, ABC News anchor ("Where more Americans get their news than from any other source"), on the night of the World Trade Center/Pentagon attack (9/11/01)**

The point is this: love the media or hate it, we all have a responsibility for our own media choices. We need to look more deeply at it, to "read" media and see its corporate incarnation as a problem to be examined and ultimately confronted. As my old friend and newscaster "Scoop" Nisker used to advise on San Francisco radio, "If you don't like the news, go out and make some of your own." And, you can. Yes, you can. If not, you can at least develop the critical skills needed to find truths buried in news.

The book itself is divided between a catalogue of what happened, what was reported, and what was often "news not in the news" (at least in the United States). It offers some detailed analysis of specific stories and commentaries about gaps, omissions, and outright distortions. Throughout, I have sought to incorporate some ideas about how the coverage might be improved. This is not a work of media bashing because it comes from a media maker who believes deeply in the vital role that a free and independent press must play to preserve democracy.

In the months that have gone by in this first year of the terror wars, we have learned much that we did not know about what happened on a day that will forever be enshrined in our history. We have learned about missed signals, intelligence failures, and a national defense that did not (and perhaps could not) defend us in this instance. Those of us who delved more deeply learned about a history of collaboration between covert U.S. warriors and armed Islamic groups. Closer to home, there were disturbing stories to come about structural flaws in the World Trade Center and an uncoordinated, poorly run rescue effort by police and fire units.

We learned that some of our heroes were anything but. We learned that our great victory in Afghanistan was anything but. We learned that much of our news was, sadly, anything but. We were inundated with content but shortchanged on context. I hope we learned that there is still much to learn. Too much has not been covered, and too much has been just plain covered up. We still do not have answers to many urgent questions, and we need a vigilant media worldwide with the guts to ask them.

Danny Schechter, The News Dissector
New York City, January 2003

Opening Salvo

On July 4, 2002, an over-the-top patriotic fireworks display lit up the skies over New York City's East River like "the rockets' red glare" that Americans sing about in the national anthem. In the song, the rockets reassured the soldiers fighting the War of 1812 that "our flag was still there." The holiday spectacle was paid for by a department store, and it was intended to reassure New Yorkers that life was back to normal and that patriotism is an appropriate national pastime. While part of this colorful display was underway, I was escaping the one-hundred-degree heat in a movie theater watching Steven Spielberg's *Minority Report*. It is a story set in the future, about a "precrime" program built around the "previsions" of three damaged but human "precogs," who visualize crimes that are about to happen. Their mental images and nightmares are recorded for analysis by a police unit that is then dispatched to prevent the crimes before they occur.

The movie is a bit absurd, but it prompted me to think back, as Americans are constantly reminded to do these days by the media and government officials, to September 11, a day that the discourse in America changed, even if the world didn't. I wondered about what "precogs" in that period were "previsioning." As it turns out, there were former senators and other experts, including an ex-soldier turned security chief at an investment bank based in the Twin Towers, who warned that a terrorist attack was imminent. The U.S. president was actually given a top-secret report to the same effect, but it too was ignored. We would later be told that the "dots" were not connected.

In the months that have passed, millions of words have commented on the "bubble" that America lived in before its sense of invulnerability was punctured in such a deadly and dramatic fashion. We have since heard the reports about signals that were overlooked and warnings that were ignored at the highest—and I mean the highest—levels of the administration. We know for sure that there is so much more to be revealed, even when we dismiss the many conspiracy theories that swirl around our body politic like malarial mosquitoes feeding on the national unease.

Looking back, like some "postcog," I wondered why I expected the media response to be any different. After all, to assess the performance of the news media on "The Day," we need to be reminded of what it was and wasn't doing before the attacks, in the period leading up to it, and, in fact, during the years before. A July–August 2002 *American Journalism Review (AJR)* survey of journalists in the hinterlands of America found editors quite candid about the deficiencies of their own coverage after a decade of closing foreign bureaus and limiting global reporting in what is supposed to be an age of globalization.

AJR quotes Edward Seaton of the Manhattan (Kansas) *Mercury,* who says, "The duties of newspapers are to keep readers from being surprised by major developments." The media review concludes, "By that measure, *almost every American paper* failed its readers" (emphasis added). Others were also self-critical. "I think all of us are asking why we didn't see this coming in greater dimension," laments Ron Martin, until recently the editor of the *Atlanta Journal Constitution*. This survey significantly shows a bigger reader demand for international news than most news outlets offered either then or now. It also notes that not one of the newspapers surveyed have opened a foreign bureau since September 11, 2001.

That was pre–September 11. What has happened since? That's the terrain this book explores.

THE WAR IN THE MEDIA

After the September 11 attacks on the World Trade Center and the Pentagon, millions of people worldwide glued themselves to their television sets and every means of available media to keep informed and stay in touch. Media outlets were soon disseminating an alarming and often alarmist global conversation in the aftermath of unexpected shockwaves and trauma. At a time of unprecedented alarm and anxiety in the United States, people shared what they heard as well as all the latest rumors they worried about. The U.S. networks went wall-to-wall with a twenty-four / seven, commercial-free "newsathon." It was easily the biggest story of the new century.

"All of our lives have been changed today," said Aaron Brown of CNN. Many in the media were eyewitnesses. One CNBC reporter in the vicinity of the

World Trade Center said she saw the second plane crash into the office tower and ran for her life. "It was like a movie," she said. Most of the all-news channels went into commercial-free mode as soon as the disaster began to unfold. Remarkably, CNN Headline News aired a spot for Boeing, which made some of the planes that were hijacked, at approximately 10:20 A.M., according to the Electronic Media website, which retitled itself, "America Under Attack." (Boeing, one of America's top military contractors, would become the first company to sponsor a network television special on the first anniversary of September 11.)

Throughout much of the news media, there was soon a self-congratulatory undercurrent about all this comprehensive *stop the presses* coverage. "For all that we lost on September 11 as Americans and human beings," enthused Tad Bartimus in *The American Editor*, the official organ of America's newspaper editors, "we journalists regained our relevance and credibility. . . . All media outlets became information clearinghouses, every journalist became a storyteller. . . . Collectively we rededicated ourselves to informing, reassuring, and comforting a transfixed nation holding vigil in a communal living room."

True enough, that is how many journalists felt. And it is true to a point, but hardly the *whole* truth. There was indeed a well-justified sense of pride among the journalists on the scene, but it turned into exhaustion, as the news media pushed itself to keep up with the flow of breaking news. At the same time, the acres of print and hours of television programming also showcased institutional flaws and shortcomings that made journalism (in some instances) a limited and not totally trustworthy guide to understanding the meaning of rapidly unfolding events.

Soon, on television, the coverage moved from recycling information about the damages suffered to focusing on the response. Graphic packages under titles like "America Under Attack" soon turned into "America Rising" to "America Fights Back." In some ways, this format evolution was an attempt to calm and reassure a worried public. At the same time, the networks and the written press began forging a consensus about the need for mobilization, offering an ideological framework that was later described as "patriotic correctness."

Almost nine months later in an interview on the BBC news program *Newsnight*, CBS news anchor Dan Rather—who in the immediate aftermath of September 11 wrapped himself in the flag, telling late-night CBS program host David Letterman that he was waiting for the president to tell him what to do next—was more reflective about the tension between jingoism and journalism that played out in the media and inside the souls of many viewers and some journalists.

To the surprise of those who saw him as a voice of the Establishment, Rather blasted the media coverage and his role as one of America's best-known television newscasters in the *Newsnight* interview. He even made a comparison that he himself called "obscene."

"It is an obscene comparison—you know, I am not sure I like it—but you know there was a time in South Africa that people would put flaming tires around people's necks if they dissented. And in some ways the fear is that you will be necklaced here, you will have a flaming tire of lack of patriotism put around your neck," he said. "Now it is that fear that keeps journalists from asking the toughest of the tough questions."

Rather lashed out at self-censorship, beginning with himself. "It starts with a feeling of patriotism within oneself. It carries through with a certain knowledge that the country as a whole—and for all the right reasons—felt and continues to feel this surge of patriotism within themselves. And one finds oneself saying: 'I know the right question, but you know what? This is not exactly the right time to ask it.'" (Apparently it was not the "right time" for sustained coverage of the world either. A few months later, on the eve of the first anniversary of September 11, Rather shifted his critical gaze from his colleagues to his audience. He told *TV Guide* that "the public has lost interest in international reporting. . . . They would much rather hear about the Robert Blake murder case or what's happening on Wall Street. . . . A feeling is creeping back that if you lead foreign you die." Without citing any real evidence, he asserted that the "public has lost interest.")

Rather's initial assessment of the self-censorship in broadcasting made big news in leading newspapers in England, but not in his own country. The interview conducted by BBC's *Newsnight*, a program similar to ABC's *Nightline* was not rebroadcast by any American network. His remarks were not covered on CBS or on any other U.S. network. Only one major newspaper, the *Los Angeles Times*, reported on his comments, and only in its soft news calendar section, known for celebrity coverage.

Rather's honesty may have been calculated since it was not directed at his own viewers. It was also a bit late in the day, as the British say, because by then, patriotism had long fused with punditry. By then, alternative perspectives had few platforms. The news programs were dominated by the think-alike speculation and hawkish sentiments of "terrorism experts," who serve the national security agencies and conservative think tanks. (Let's not let the British media off the hook. Many media outlets there have functioned as outlets for Prime Minister Tony Blair and his Foreign Office. Academics and NGOs in Britain have compiled detailed and irrefutable studies showing a vast cutback in documentaries about the world, as well as a lack of critical programming overall.)

An American president, whose own legitimacy and competence was in question in a country still divided along partisan lines after the 2000 presidential election (Bush's popularity was below 50 percent on September 10), used the crisis to his advantage. On the strength of one well-delivered speech to Congress, he suddenly had a televised makeover, becoming the symbol of leadership for a nation united as never before. His approval ratings skyrocketed. Media coverage then stoked his approval ratings, massaging support for the administration's newly proclaimed global war against terrorism that followed. Sounding like a sheriff in the Old West, he vowed to "smoke out" the terrorists and show them they can't mess with America (or Texas). There were cheers in the bar where I saw his well-managed and carefully prepared performance. That speech, in a prime-time media environment, was a turning point.

As public opinion legitimized Bush's stance, it also depoliticized it, because as polls later showed, most Americans do not view national security and defense as a political or partisan matter. Nine months after September 11, a *Los Angeles Times* survey found that with the exception of the war on terror, Americans clung to the sharply divided opinions on issues along a fault line that was almost identical to the attitudes recorded on election day, positioning the terror war beyond politics or even debate.

This was not, in any sense, unique as a phenomenon. Nations always rally together when attacked, and media often becomes an echo chamber for national leadership in moments of crises. While many media outlets had spent years assessing, and even in some cases admitting or decrying manipulation by the government in earlier wars, many of those lessons and the skepticism they produced seem to fall by the wayside this time around.

After the debacle in Vietnam, and years of debates over foreign policy, many media outlets had come to see themselves, perhaps mythically to some degree, as an independent voice, a fourth estate, and even a watchdog to keep government as transparent and accountable as possible. The tendency of the Pentagon to blame the media coverage for their loss in Vietnam encouraged this belief even if it was false.

This relationship is always put to the test in times of war, when "truth" is often the first casualty. Governments often make demands on the media to serve what they define as the national interest. They classify information and withhold access. They stage media events, frame the issues, and articulate positions that are, in essence, pure propaganda.

A virtual merger between the military and the media was evident early on in this war, and with the exception of a few stories here and there, it is still in place at the time of this writing. The White House and the Pentagon have successfully framed their coverage and worked hard to influence its spin. The spin machine worked overtime. And the media visibly pulled in its horns.

One example we know about: CNN's president and former *Time* editor Walter Isaacson issued a memo warning news executives not to "get out in front of the audience" and to downplay reporting civilian casualties for fear that some segments of the audience might question the media's patriotism if it took a critical tack. Months later in August 2002, London's *Press Gazette* reported that an executive of CNN International admitted in a talk to *News World* in Asia that CNN had self-censored the news so as not to get ahead of what it perceived to be public opinion. She said that other networks did the same. This admission was not intended for U.S. consumption. To my knowledge, it was not reported in the press, and it certainly was not admitted on the air. Market pressures were blamed for a news network's deliberate massaging of the message.

For the first time, an aggressively conservative national cable news network, Rupert Murdoch's Fox News, was on the scene, terrifying more mainstream outlets who didn't want to be outflanked on the right or challenged by a president who was dividing and polarizing the world into a "you are either with me or bin Laden" worldview. A noisy patriotism was the preferred response.

In what objectively *was* a confusing situation, dumbing it down and providing a platform for government views was a far safer tack for media outlets to take. No wonder, key nuances and critical commentary tended to disappear from view.

Behind the scenes, there was another, more pressing economic worry driving media coverage at a time of economic downturn and a soft advertising market. The media was fearful of alienating the government for its own corporate reasons. As Joan Konner, the former dean of the Columbia University Graduate School of Journalism, wrote in *Newsday*: "Despite ongoing giveaways to them, the media industry wants more: relaxation of cross-ownership rules, tax rebates, and final burial rites for the requirement—some would say the patriotic requirement—that it serve the public interest, convenience, and necessity in exchange for the license to broadcast. In other words, the corporate owners of the news networks are looking for favors from an administration they are covering. In journalistic circles, this is known as a conflict of interest and a breach of ethics. . . . " This book offers an assessment of these issues in more depth.

Much of the mainstream media reporting was carefully contained within a narrow discourse. The events of September 11 personally affected many journalists. It was hard for many media people to keep a professional distance from a story that seemed also to be an attack on their own way of life. (This sense was inflamed when anthrax spores were sent to news organizations, harming employees who came in contact with it.) The September 11 attacks were also seen as a blow to a symbol of, and center of, a business system of which media companies form a part. Journalists in Washington felt attacked when the Pentagon, the symbol and center of national military power in their city, was targeted; and for those sent to Afghanistan to cover the war there, journalists saw the U.S. government's enemy as their own when they too began to be targeted. Journalists were as frightened and infuriated as all Americans. It is hard to maintain a sense of professional detachment in such a climate.

At one point, more journalists had been killed than soldiers in Afghanistan or Pakistan. As a result, journalists who began interviewing victims and reporting on that catastrophe were quickly no less involved or angered than the people who were the subjects of their stories. Suddenly, much of the arrogance and hubris often associated with the media was gone as media workers felt as vulnerable as everyone else.

But there was another fear in what soon became a climate of intimidation. In the immediate aftermath of September 11, both the host of and a guest on *Politically Incorrect*, a nightly news satire show, made some comments that were interpreted as unpatriotic and insensitive. A conservative radio talk show host called for an advertiser boycott, and some advertisers actually pulled their ads. This sent a shockwave through the television business.

Next, many conservative media pundits (and there are now as many news talk shows as news reporting programs on the air) began to suggest that the media was willing to compromise national security and secrecy. This fueled the anticipation that any "wrong move," wrong statement, or wrong guest could lead to the tarnishing of media credibility and reinforce the oft-repeated but rarely proven view of a liberal bias. Journalists who began asking "why they hate us" or who sought to look for deeper explanations of the violence in a way that might call American policy priorities into question were lambasted as part of a "hate America" crowd. A split on the left fueled this tension as well, with many progressive voices nervous about appearing to rationalize the terror attacks. The Democratic and Republican parties united behind the president. Only one member of Congress voted against a resolution uncritically giving the administration a blank check. She would later have her reputation tarnished.

In an industry often given to amnesia, some media executives no doubt remembered what happened at CNN during the Gulf War when Peter Arnett's reports from Baghdad were characterized as pro-Iraqi by veterans' groups and other Desert Storm boosters. Reporting Saddam Hussein's response to U.S. charges was defined by many right-wing talk show hosts as the equivalent of justifying them or, worse, an act of treason. CNN added an army of former military officers as analysts to undercut any such impression. No media company wanted to stir any angry hornets' nest of this kind during this war that could "blow back" in their direction.

The result: dissent virtually disappeared, as even magazines like *Vanity Fair* confirmed, in a media that began to sound increasingly alike in its slant and selection of stories. Six weeks into the crisis, *The New York Times* reported that their monitoring of television shows found no war critics on the air. (Mediachannel.org found very few in the *Times* itself). Some intellectuals who questioned the policy—the "usual suspects" like MIT professor Noam Chomsky and writers like Susan Sontag—became targets of abuse and press baiting. Their voices were quickly marginalized (Chomsky was heard about again months later when his pamphlet *9/11, A Collection of Interviews and Essays*, rocketed to the bestseller list. You would think that would have lead to his getting mainstream media attention. It didn't.)

When journalists from other countries—particularly Britain, where more critical voices were heard (which no doubt helped fuel antiwar activism with polls reporting a majority opposed to U.S. bombings)—criticized Americans, their views were simply not reported here. One example that will be explored in this book revolved around coverage of the dramatic Mazar-I-Sharif prison revolt. Four major outlets in Britain cited evidence of war crimes with U.S. complicity. Those charges were muzzled, and where they were heard, they were downplayed.

When the Washington-based Brookings Institution held a panel on the media and the military, Victoria Clarke, the Pentagon official who manages media relations, boasted how successful she had been in *embedding* journalists alongside U.S. military units. (All the coverage was positive.) She praised the media as responsible and supportive. Michael Getler, ombudsman of *The Washington Post,* didn't take her on, but noted that there is still a great deal that we don't know. "We don't even know what we don't know," he said and then complained that no one was standing up for the press' right to gain access to the story.

This book stands up for the rights of the media because all of us have a right to know and a duty to act on what we do know. We know more than we think, and we need to think about what we do know far more than we do.

Read on.

Warring with the
Coverage of War

The Attack—September 11, 2001: From the News Dissector's Weblog

September 11–October 13

L ike everyone in New York and like most in the media world, the events of September 11 galvanized me into a flurry of activity. Most of us wanted to contribute something to help a shocked public make sense of the cataclysmic events. Everyone on the television networks talked about how the world had changed forever. But as I watched the coverage in as many outlets as I could keep up with, I quickly saw that for the most part, the news media did not change in its fundamentals. What became clear on many of these outlets had not prepared us to understand the quickening pace of a global threat. Suddenly, we all realized that we needed to know more about issues that had been barely and badly explained.

Yes, suddenly, there was more coverage, dramatic coverage, commercial-free news, and round-the-clock reporting. But was it necessarily better coverage? Certain problems began to surface: tensions between jingoism and journalism became obvious; government information management asserted itself; and a failure to offer context and background disappointed many who had hoped that the coverage would illuminate the *whys* as well as the *whats*. I decided to try to write about the coverage every day. Our weblog technology made it easy to post information and analysis in a timely way, sometimes even as the events were unfolding. I was at my computer

3

in our Times Square offices when we heard via a radio report about the first plane's crashing into the Twin Towers. (Our building gets terrible television reception!)

I went online and started writing as the first news came in. I am still doing it.

September 11

Reports of disaster pumps adrenaline throughout the news business.

Here we are, in the morning in New York, listening to reports on planes crashing into the World Trade Center, as if they were coming from Edward R. Murrow during the blitz in London. Unconfirmed reports. And then rumors. And then more alarming news. First one plane, pictured initially as an accident, then another. Not an accident. A tower collapses. Then another. The Pentagon is hit.

This is what we call a developing story.

This is a catastrophe.

The consequences are not known.

Watch how it develops.

Remember that truth tends to be the first casualty in war.

We need accurate information. And we need truth.

The BIG MEDIA are in action with graphics, music, and a drumbeat of urgency.

News ratings are up at last.

Walking home through empty streets, as New York shut down early on the day of the World Trade Center Towers' apocalypse, one was struck by how dazed and stunned people seemed. There was an eerie silence punctuated by ambulances and police cars as they raced from place to place. Cops were dispatched to guard post offices, police stations, and the bus terminal, as if the terrorists would be back. The mayor gave press conferences from "a secret location" as if the Osama bin Laden brigade had targeted him, clearly a conceit wrapped up as a security consideration.

I had spent the morning following events on the web and the radio. At home, I was finally able to experience the day's turmoil that many media outlets were saying had "changed America forever" the way most Americans had—on television. It was, of course, wall-to-wall coverage, with each outlet featuring its own "exclusive coverage" of the same scene—that jet plane tearing through the World Trade Center. And when we weren't seeing that horrendous image being recycled endlessly, used as what we in the television business used to call "wallpaper" (or B-roll), other equally compelling images were on the screen: the Pentagon on fire, smoke coming out of the buildings, buildings collapsing, people jumping from high floors, and panic in the streets. It was on for hours, over and over again, awakening outrage and then oddly numbing it by overexposure.

The reporting focused first on the facts, the chronology of planes hijacked and the national symbols attacked. Then the parade of "expert" interviews began, featuring virtually the same group of former government officials and terrorism specialists on each show. Even Ronald Reagan's favorite novelist, Tom Clancy, was given airtime to bang his own drum for giving the military and CIA everything it says it will need to strike back.

You could imagine the show bookers all working overtime from the same Rolodex, shuttling these pundits-for-all-seasons from studio to studio, from CNN to Jim Lehrer's *NewsHour,* to CBS and back again. How many times have we seen these soundalike, wind-them-up-and-let-them-prattle, sound-bite artists—such as former ambassador Lawrence Eagleburger and television generals like H. Norman Schwartzkopf—waxing tough for the cameras?

Unfortunately, there was no one to say that violence breeds violence or that a massive retaliation may only invite more of the same. Likewise, few questions were raised about why there had been no response for so long by the media or the government to so many official predictions about imminent terrorist threats. These concerns were raised, but then they were quickly sidelined by discussions of national complacency and naiveté about the world. How the U.S. intelligence apparatus could have missed this was taken only as evidence that it needs more money, not a different policy to serve. No mention was made (of course) of the cutback in international news coverage that keeps Americans so out of touch with global events.

Suddenly, we had moved from the stage of facts to the realm of opinion and endless speculation about what America would do and, then, what America *must* do. The anchors were touched when members of Congress spontaneously erupted into a bipartisan rendition of "God Bless America" on the Capitol steps. They paused reverentially to go live to the White House for a presidential address, which turned out to be five minutes of banalities and rally-'round-the-flag reassurances from the national father figure.

Who was it that called patriotism the last refuge of scoundrels? The news anchors certainly never used that line.

Missing in all of this was any discussion of possible motives of the alleged terrorists, why would they do it, and why now? What was their political agenda? There was no mention of September 11 as the anniversary of the failed Camp David accord, or for that matter, the anniversary of the death of Chile's Salvadore Allende. There was certainly no mention of the fact that state terrorism by countries like the United States and Israel often trigger counterterrorism by guerilla forces. There was virtually no international angle offered except for a few snatches of file footage of Osama bin Laden fondling an AK-47, with "Exclusive" stamped on it. He looked like a cartoon figure. It must be said that most of the journalists I saw were cautious about this, perhaps because of what happened in Oklahoma City when the bombing of a federal building turned out to be the work of an American.

NBC carried the only real report I saw on why Palestinians consider America complicit in the attacks against them. They mentioned that Hamas and bin Laden denied involvement, and they even featured a condemnation by Arafat. That was reported by the always-excellent Martin Fletcher, a non-American who is as informed about what is happening on the ground there, as most of the anchors and reporters are not. I saw one other sound bite from a Middle Eastern politician, but that was the only one on all the channels for hours. CNN carried videophone footage of an attack on an arms depot in Kabul, Afghanistan, but it turned out not to be connected. Some on-air reporter thought it may have been an outgrowth of that country's ongoing civil war. Another replied, "Oh, are they having one?"

As the coverage wore on, boyish-looking George Stephanopolous, now an ABC commentator and former advisor to then–President Clinton, popped up with Peter Jennings to suggest that in situations like this, governments need a scapegoat and someone to demonize, and he predicted they'd find one. Jennings, to his credit, reminded viewers that in the past, our counterattacks against terrorist incidents were hardly triumphant. He and the other national anchors were far more restrained and cautious than their counterparts on local stations.

It was only back on PBS, in one of Jim Lehrer's interminable "snooze hour," beltway-blather sessions that one got an inkling of what the Bush administration may actually be planning to do, once the final fatality count sinks in and once the sadness of the funerals and the mourning begin. Then, as everyone knows, Americans will go from shock to outrage. One of Lehrer's mostly conservative experts, Bill Kristol of Rupert Murdoch's *Weekly Standard,* passed on an official high-level leak—namely, that the United States will link bin Laden to Iraq's Saddam Hussein.

Recall that Dubya (George W. Bush) said he would "punish" states who harbor terrorists. No one really spent much time discussing what that meant. Now Rupert's emissary was predicting that the game plan might be to ask for a declaration of war against Iraq to "finish the job." There was, of course, no discussion of any evidence implicating Iraq, nor was there an explanation of the economics of the oil supply there, which U.S. companies currently tap in abundance. You can bet that once this incident is formally cranked up into a national crisis, there will be calls for war. Failing economies often need a good one to get back on track.

So, is another Gulf War in the offing? Will the Son of Bush finish his father's desert storm? That is a fascinating possibility, naturally suggesting, for sure, that more media manipulation is on the way. The coverage on that Tuesday night whipped up the outrage to such a degree that no alternatives to war were even discussed, much less offered.

This possible "Let's get Iraq" scenario, however, wasn't discussed in any depth, perhaps because there was no footage to show yet. But you heard it here first: the road to revenge may just take us back to Baghdad, guilty or not. Will international terrorism be wiped out then? It was a bit frightening to hear many of the on-air wise men speak of the next steps as a long difficult struggle that will take national resolve and that may lead to restrictions on the freedoms we have long prized. This line of thinking will lead to the antiterrorist campaign's targeting domestic protesters as well.

Will God then bless America? I thought only the bad guys spoke in terms of a holy war.

Stay tuned.

P.S. I must admit that I share much of the popular emotional outrage at the carnage. If we could afford it, our own company might have had an office there. In fact, I used to work out of CNN's bureau when it was based at the World Trade Center, and I have been in an out of those towers over the years. It is terrifying and traumatizing to realize that it is gone, like one giant bloody amputation from the body of the city. This was not just an attack on symbols but on real people, not just at world capitalism but also at urban culture, not just on some remote "them" but on "us."

I woke up to the sound of more sirens. I admit it: I am in shock as I write.

September 13

ABC and others have already packaged the disaster as a sitcom called "America Under Attack." Conjuring up: "America Held Hostage." Conjuring up: "America Wins in the Gulf." And reminding me of all the trivialized packaging of so many important stories in the past. (At last, a break from Gary Condit stories!) In the bar around the corner, workmen guzzle beer and stare at the television. All you see is smoke billowing. The same shot is shown over and over. Disbelief is the dominant emotion. Cut here, cut there. This cavalcade of horror and paralysis and fear and tears is on every channel, and it will be for weeks. In these first minutes, reactions of all kinds are flooding my e-mail in-box along with expressions of concern from friends and family all over the world. Crises like this make us realize the importance of community and friendship. And yes, life!

Today, we can see the abyss. Can we find the light?

September 14

One issue not getting the attention it deserves involves how this painful moment of national crisis is being maneuvered politically to the point that Congress gives the president a blank check and the authorization to do whatever he and his "team" decide. The *New York Times* headline this Friday leads with a Bush aide's call for "ending" states that harbor terrorists. R. W. Apple's front page analysis says "No Middle Ground." No dissent on page one is cited this morning.

This is not unusual in mainstream media, report Russell Mokhiber and Robert Weissman of (respectively) the Corporate Crime Reporter and Multinational Monitor. Open The *Washington Post* to its editorial pages, and war talk dominates.

Henry Kissinger: Destroy the Network.

Robert Kagan: We Must Fight This War.

Charles Krauthammer: To War, Not to Court.

William S. Cohen: American Holy War.

There is no column by Colman McCarthy talking peace.

From 1969 to 1997, McCarthy wrote a pro-peace column for The *Washington Post*. He was let go because the column, he was told, wasn't making enough money for the company. "The market has spoken," was the way Robert Kaiser, managing editor at the *Post,* put it at the time. McCarthy is a pacifist. "I'm opposed to any kind of violence—economic, political, military, domestic." But McCarthy is not surprised by the war talk coming from the *Post*. He has just completed an analysis of 430 opinion pieces that ran in The *Washington Post* in June, July, and August 2001. Of the 430 opinion pieces, right-wingers or centrists wrote 420. Only ten were written by columnists one might consider left of center.

The Day Video Cameras
Were Everywhere

Newsday, September 18, 2001

News took a dramatic turn last week, as broadcast journalism became a participatory process, with footage from a thousand sources providing us with every imaginable video angle of the attack on the World Trade Center. The widespread availability and use of low-cost video cameras transformed news gathering. Anyone can be—and now, often is—a reporter.

Coverage of the terrorist attacks on the Twin Towers and the Pentagon was enhanced dramatically by amateur video shot via digital cameras, with pictures every bit as good as those from the cameras used in my days as a producer at ABC's *20/20*. In fact, one ABC producer bought a camera from a tourist on the scene and captured images of the collapse of one of the buildings. Even newer technologies emerged.

Last week, CNN showed fuzzier images of an arms dump burning in Kabul, Afghanistan.

As it turned out, the explosion resulted from an internal military conflict, but those pictures initially suggested a U.S. retaliation that hadn't actually occurred. The experimental footage was transmitted without satellites or expensive hookups. It was shown over a state-of-the-art videophone. The networks love these cameras and gadgets because freelancers are always cheaper than professional and unionized staff crews. The material they produce gives editors a lot more to choose from, too.

People's video often provides more intimate, even diverse, points of view. That's welcome, because as every television watcher knows, there's a sameness in approach, language, sources, style, and even guests. We may have many channels and choices, but we still have too few voices.

The constant recycling of footage of those hijacked jets slicing through the Twin Towers ended up cheapening its impact. It was numbing after the twentieth viewing. At the same time, what distinguishes news from those tabloid video "reality" shows is that editorial decisions are still made about what to run and what not to run.

On the entertainment side, the more exploitative, gut-wrenching, or extreme, the better. In news, discretion is still thankfully exercised, more often in the editing room than live. But images can too often substitute for analysis. We need smarter coverage, not more graphic home videos. Missing from much of the news is analysis of why these killers did what they did, and what they hoped to gain.

Pictures alone also don't explain why our nation was so unprepared for the attack, especially in light of the billions of dollars spent on defense and antiterrorist intelligence. They didn't tell us much about the history of the Mideast, or past U.S. support for Osama bin Laden. The videos also offer no clues on how President George W. Bush's "Star Wars" plan might, or might not, safeguard us from future attacks by knife-wielding hijackers.

Sadly, it may be that a lack of pictures in exchange for more in-depth angles on the story makes less compelling television, even if such angles are essential to the entire understanding of the story.

Flashback: Before September 11
What Was in the U.S. Media?

MEDIA TENOR: Quarterly Journal, No. 1, 2002

The country's leading weeklies began 2001 with a decidedly soft focus. Coverage informed readers as consumers of popular culture and products, and it de-emphasized significant domestic and foreign political issues, despite a new presidency so precarious at its inception that the state of American democracy itself seemed at risk.

Nine of the top-ten topics in the country's leading news weeklies prior to September 11 (which together accounted for 36 percent of total coverage) were various brands of human-interest stories, consumer-product reports, or entertainment reviews. The only hard news reports to make it into the magazines' top-ten topics were court cases, making up 2.5 percent of total coverage and focusing overwhelmingly on U.S. crises.

The positive treatment of the United States prior to the attacks was arguably linked to the softness of the news in the period. Before the attacks, the nightly television news lineup seemed consumed by shark attacks, entertainment reports, and the Gary Condit scandal. Meanwhile, CNN remade itself in the younger, flashier image of its competitors, a signal to many that the "dumbing down" of the news media was no longer just an option for certain broadcasters, but the emergent, operating principle for the country's profit-driven television news organizations.

News content might have continued its rapid slide from information to "infotainment" in 2001 had the September 11 attacks on New York and Washington never occurred. Journalists reported that the attacks "changed everything," a description intended for the American political and cultural landscape but equally descriptive of the media environment. News outlets began to focus on serious domestic and international affairs and to play catch-up concerning a few issues that it had previously ignored.

Americans looking for illumination in the most popular mainstream news outlets in 2001 were left largely in the shadows. Foreign coverage, which has steadily declined as a percentage of total news reports since the 1970s, made up about 25 percent of total coverage in the first period of 2001, allowing for very little sustained attention to American foreign policy and an extremely limited view of most current events abroad.

The lack of coverage was coupled with a topical focus that might well have compounded ignorance with fear of foreign nations: the Israeli–Palestinian conflict, various accidents and tragedies, demonstrations, and natural cataclysms were all among the most covered foreign news topics.

The topical focus was reflected in the ratings in foreign coverage, which were much more negative than the ratings in domestic reports. Previous to the attacks, the net difference between positive and negative ratings in foreign-focused coverage was 12 percent negative while the same calculation applied to U.S. coverage showed a 10 percent positive rating (although the attacks and the weakened economy would have seemed to indicate a less rosy picture).

HUGE BOOST FOR THE PRESIDENT

Although there was a new weight in the top-ten topical issues, the seriousness of focus only extended as far as the scope of the attacks. After September 11, United States unemployment rose, increasing the numbers of uninsured and the burden on an already selectively effective health system; a rickety stock market demonstrated the dangers of handing Social Security over to private investor accounts (as Bush had proposed in the 2000 campaign); and the education system continued its decline, especially in the country's poorest areas.

However, America's most popular media allotted less than 0.5 percent of coverage to any of these areas, seeming to shy away from issues that might be difficult for the current administration in its new role as the savior of "civilization." Entertainment and product reports maintained their lead, perhaps both a comforting distraction from the political realities the attacks underscored and an effective promotion of the idea that America could shop its way out of the economic burden the attacks had helped to create.

The media not only indirectly protected the Bush administration from troublesome policy issues, but it gave Bush himself a huge boost in ratings after the attacks. His coverage during the first period of the year was only lukewarm, with a net rating of 12 percent negative, driven down by his handling of the stem cell research debate, his budgetary policies, and some of his personal qualities.

He received a meteoric boost after September 11, however, as the media repeated a campaign-era practice, which was to attribute greatness to his speeches (or his debate performances, in the case of 2000), as long as he simply made it through them. For the remainder of 2001 following the attacks, his ratings shot up to 41 percent positive, indicating a dangerous willingness to act as the mouthpiece for the administration, instead of as the voice of the people and the agenda setters for a precarious democracy.

Political protestors appeared as the main actors in only twelve reports (less than 0.3 percent of the total) and environmentalists appeared as the focus of only two.

On September 11, the country and the media shifted their focus to the attacks and the U.S. government's likely response. Directly related topics—including the attacks themselves, the clearing up efforts at the World Trade Center and Pentagon, domestic security measures, and the war in Afghanistan—made up over 40 percent of coverage in the weeklies and about 54 percent of television news through the end of the year. The anthrax assaults that began in October were the next most-covered issue on television, with 255 reports. The debate over stem cell research, the Israel–Palestine conflict, and the state of American education each received just under 1 percent of coverage, putting them ahead of all other political topics in terms of volume during the period, if perhaps only barely on the public's radar screen. The top-ten people and organizations in the news weeklies also emphasized a culture of consumption, either personal or vicarious, with celebrities accounting for more than 800 of the protagonists (18 percent of the total) and companies appearing as the focus of more than 500 reports (11 percent of coverage).

On the other hand, protagonists who represented contrasting worldviews or specific political issues received very little focus (all spiritual and religious representatives combined).

The Global News We Ignore Can Be Fatal

Sometimes it takes a catastrophe to force cultures to undergo self-examination. Today, as American missiles target shadowy figures in the mountains of Afghanistan, many Americans—indirectly spurred by our media (and despite the flags waving on the sets of newscasts)—are doing some rethinking about their country's role in the world.

The September 11 tragedy sent a shock through a society that has for many years been isolated and insulated from the rest of the world, especially the countries now in the crossfire. That estrangement has been media-fed and media-led, as public attention was often deliberately diverted by a television system that Larry Gelbart of *M*A*S*H* fame labeled a "weapon of mass distraction." We lurched from one big scandal to another—O. J. to Monica to Gary Condit—as sleaze replaced substance and as news was dumbed down into a diet of tabloid sensationalism. The majority of humanity began to disappear from television view, glimpsed only through the prism of cutesy features like "The World in a Minute," short blips of footage that convey images of chaos, not people with problems, to whom we might feel empathetic.

Network executives defended this format on grounds that they were "giving viewers what they wanted." In fact, as ratings for exploitative programs went up, the share of those watching television news went down. News programs actually lost viewers as newsbiz and showbiz fused. For many who hungered to understand the world, to quote myself quoting others, "the more you watched, the less you knew." As we have since discovered, ignoring the news can be fatal.

Now that more lethal weapons are being deployed in what CNN brands "America's New War," mass audiences are back, drawn by a need to know in an environment of fear, alarm, and outrage. Initially, after September 11, the spectrum of mainstream television coverage was narrow and devoid of context, as Michael Massing noted in *The Nation*: "As the nation prepares to go to war, the coverage on television—the primary source of news for most Americans—has been appallingly superficial. Constantly clicking my remote in search of insight, I was stunned at the narrowness of the views offered, at the Soviet-style reliance on official and semiofficial sources."

You saw many scenes of journalists' turning to maps to show where Pakistan is and trying to explain who lives in Afghanistan. On many television outlets, there were confusing explanations of Islam, with little attention paid to the history of U.S. support for fundamentalist forces in Afghanistan or why Washington's alignments in the Middle East stir so much opposition. Few voices from the region itself were heard.

The reasons for this failure of information sharing are found in the structure and orientation of our media system and its abandonment of international news. This style of journalism has fueled two cultures, each virtually segregated from the other. One culture is a small elite that operates globally with "a need to know." The second includes most people, who are in effect told that they do not "need to know." In an age of globalization, global news has declined—and not only in the United States. It may be because as power shifts away from governments to multinational corporations, ordinary people have a shrinking role to play in decision making . . . hence, the emphasis on consumerism over citizenship . . . hence, that media mantra to the masses, "Shut up and shop." This line of thought is rationalized with the conventional wisdom that no one cares.

Another shift has kept us in the dark as well. As media analyst David Shaw reported in the *Los Angles Times,* "Coverage of international news by the U.S. media has declined significantly in recent years in response to corporate demands for larger profits and an increasingly fragmented audience. Having decided that readers and viewers in post–Cold War America cared more about celebrities, scandals and local news, newspaper editors and television news executives have reduced the space and time devoted to foreign coverage by 70 to 80 percent during the past 15 to 20 years."

He quotes prominent journalists who say these cutbacks might have contributed to the uncertainty and confusion among many Americans about why terrorists committed so heinous an assault on September 11. "I think most

Americans are clueless when it comes to the politics and ideology and religion in [the Muslim] world and, in that sense, I think we do bear some responsibility," says Martin Baron, editor of the *Boston Globe,* "in consequence, we are not only less informed about what's happening in the world but about how others see us."

A NEW PERSPECTIVE

Now, a month after the attack, some outlets are slowly opening up to perspectives that acknowledge that the media system has failed to promote a sense of global citizenship, even as globalization binds us closer. Skeptical and iconoclastic writers like Michael Wolff in slick publications like *New York Magazine* now say, "International news, cast aside by almost every media outlet, at best a nostalgist's beat, is a life-and-death issue. Big media had clearly gotten its priorities wrong."

You can see a tremor of a trend in a flurry of stories that ask "why," as in "why would they do this to us?" and "why do so many around the world seem to hate us?" The events clearly promoted questioning, although non-American journalists have had a field day putting down what they see as American ignorance of the world. One example: a piece in the *Guardian* in London titled, "Americans Just Don't Get It."

The fact is, many of us don't "get it" because most U.S. media companies won't do their job and give us a nuanced view of the world. While, thanks to the Internet, many diverse sources of information are available, mainstream media is still the main source of news and explanation for most citizens.

There are any number of crucial issues swirling around the current world situation. The problem is that these debates are still flying below the radar of those mainstream media outlets. This is a time when all views should be reported, discussed, and debated. We need to deepen our global conversation. We need more investigations.

The media has a major role to play in reminding us all of the many ways in which our lives are entwined and our futures interconnected worldwide. Ostriches can put their heads in the sand; people no longer can.

Death and Civic Renewal: From the News Dissector's Weblog

September 15

It is Saturday, September 15, a day that started for me with more sirens out the window and with my walk to the newspaper stand delayed, as the four cops at my corner stopped traffic to let a few police cars escorting a giant truck get through the intersection. There was only one word on the side of it, and it got me teary: MORGUE.

A few avenues over and a few blocks north, an armory is open for business as family members of the missing are asked to bring their toothbrushes over or any other personal items that might retain residue of their DNA. While the rescue effort continues at what is now being labeled "Hell's Half Acre," only body parts are surfacing, making it hard to sustain hope for survivors. My friend Glo tells me of a finger that has been recovered with a wedding ring still on it. She's been volunteering as a keypuncher to keep tabs of all the volunteers, who are told to list their special skills. One young woman, whose application touched her, wrote: "I have no special skills. But I am very small. Let me crawl into small places."

These small stories help define the response of so many people in our city, and they speak volumes about how this disaster is bringing people together, connecting us in ways that tend to be forgotten in busy urban centers like New York. It is humanizing and inspiring to hear these stories, but so far they are rare in most of the coverage that keeps so many people riveted to their televisions. My friend Polar comments about the irony that the towers that housed the financial elite are being cleaned by the nonstop dedication of working-class people who are honored everywhere as heroes—but soon, to be replaced no doubt by warriors.

Worried

I am worried about what is to come, but believe me, I share the outrage and the anger, too. I want to get back at the bastards who did this. The streets where I live are plastered with posters and pictures of the missing. At the same time, it is precisely at a time of such emotion that critical discussion is needed. I am trying not to be righteous or insensitive, but some have challenged me on those grounds. A friend writes:

> The tone of your column is a bit insensitive. We've just been attacked and have had thousands of innocent people killed. Forty-eight percent of Americans are mainly angry, and lots of people, in the face of a coming war, are waving the flag. Why are you snickering? . . . You're raising important issues that are ignored elsewhere. But don't lose touch with the fact that a couple hundred million people here who aren't as "smart" as we'd like them to be are traumatized and terrified. Lots of folks are scared shitless about possibly losing their kids in the mountains of Afghanistan or the subways.

Another reader goes further: "While I know that the United States and U.S. citizens have a long way to go in dispelling their reputations as 'ugly Americans,' I hardly think that beginning some verbal attack on American foreign policy is appropriate at this time," he insists. "I have no intention of defending capitalism, but I will defend my country and its right to declare war on those people."

Without debating politics, I do think that this is precisely the moment for us all to begin to try to understand just who "those people" are, and then, to assess the role of the media—for good and bad in all of this. The "America United" and "God Bless America" flag waving on the air may not necessarily reflect the sincerity, pride, or even the need for a sense of national purpose that individuals now feel. These images and themes are being used by companies who know how to market and position themselves. They are not agenda-free; they know that they are shaping public opinion. They are readying the country for a war with implications and impacts that no one (especially them) is discussing in depth (as if ignoring the issues will make them go away). I was pleased when another e-mail reminded me, "There's nothing 'unfeeling' about being analytical. It sure beats being hysterical."

A Question

The question about the media is this: are these powerful instruments of communication helping us make sense of the crisis with all the many options that may exist? There is no shortage of up-to-the-minute "breaking news," headlines, and the endless accretion of details. And there's plenty of off-the-cuff opinionating, including my own, which admittedly may not always come off as intended or be as thoughtful as I would like. But where can we find other perspectives? Often, in the media in other countries.

What follows are a few international perspectives, which I offer here only to underscore what is missing in most mainstream media accounts. I begin with Pakistan, the country at the center of this crisis. How many Pakistanis have we heard on this issue? Here's one that I know well. His name is Tariq Ali, and he lives in London, where he warns that too much pressure on Pakistan can lead to a mutiny in the army there and a further turning to militant Islamic groups.

Pakistan

"The United States is whipping itself into a frenzy. Its ideologues talk of this, as an attack on 'civilization,' but what kind of civilization is it that thinks in terms of blood-revenge? For the last sixty years and more the United States has toppled democratic leaders, bombed countries in three continents, used nuclear weapons against Japanese civilians, but never knew what it felt like to have your own cities under attack. Now they know.

"To the victims of the attack and their relatives one can offer our deep sympathy as one does to people who the U.S. government has victimized. But to accept that somehow an American life is worth more than that of a Rwandan, a Yugoslav, a Vietnamese, a Korean, a Japanese, a Palestinian ... that is unacceptable."

Israel

What about Israel, the country led by Ariel Sharon, a general many consider a war criminal, who has been waging war against terrorism for fifty years. Here's a voice I would like to see on *Nightline:* Uri Avnery, an Israeli who asks us to recognize what a war on terrorism implies. His comments appeared on the gush-shalom website (gush-shalm.org):

> After the smoke has cleared, the dust has settled down and the initial fury blown over, humankind will wake up and realize a new fact: there is no safe place on earth.

A handful of suicide-bombers has brought the United States to a standstill, caused the President to hide in a bunker under a far-away mountain, dealt a terrible blow to the economy, grounded all aircraft, and emptied government offices throughout the country. This can happen in every country. The Twin Towers are everywhere.

Not only Israel, but the whole world is now full of gibberish about "fighting terrorism." Politicians, "experts on terrorism" and their likes propose to hit, destroy, annihilate etc., as well as to allocate more billions to the "intelligence community." They make brilliant suggestions. But nothing of this kind will help the threatened nations, much as nothing of this kind has helped Israel.

There is no patent remedy for terrorism. The only remedy is to remove its causes. One can kill a million mosquitoes, and millions more will take their place. In order to get rid of them, one has to dry the swamp that breeds them. And the swamp is always political.

A person does not wake up one morning and tell himself: Today I shall hijack a plane and kill myself. Nor does a person wake up one morning and tell himself: Today I shall blow myself up in a Tel-Aviv discotheque. Such a decision grows in a person's mind through a slow process, taking years. The background to the decision is either national or religious, social and spiritual.

No fighting underground can operate without popular roots and a supportive environment that is ready to supply new recruits, assistance, hiding places, money and means of propaganda. An underground organization wants to gain popularity, not lose it. Therefore it commits attacks when it thinks that this is what the surrounding public wants. Terror attacks always testify to the public mood. That is true in this case, too. The initiators of the attacks decided to implement their plan after America has provoked immense hatred throughout the world. Not because of its might, but because of the way it uses its might.

Canada

On to Canada where Michel Chossudovsky of the Center for Research on Globalization accuses the U.S. media of parroting official statements, like threats made by former secretary of state Lawrence Eagleburger who said on many news programs, "I think we will show when we get attacked like this, we are terrible in our strength and in our retribution." Meanwhile, mimicking official statements, the Western media mantra has approved the launching of "punitive actions" directed against civilian targets in the Middle East. In the words of William Safire, writing in

The New York Times: "When we reasonably determine our attackers' bases and camps, we must pulverize them—minimizing but accepting the risk of collateral damage—and act overtly or covertly to destabilize terror's national hosts." Meanwhile in Quebec City, Lyle Stewart, who writes for the *Montreal Gazette,* had a column pulled "for reasons I don't fully understand." It said in part:

> Just last week, the *Gazette* reported on former U.S. senator and presidential hopeful Gary Hart's speech in Montreal warning of a major terrorist attack that would kill thousands and wreak major changes in American society. Hart forecast a massive outcry for the government to act, and an unprecedented crackdown by the authorities. "We will be spied on, our privacy will be gone; that will have a huge impact on our society." To be sure, Hart gave all this a fairly loose timeline of the next "twenty-five years." He likely didn't expect to have to shorten it to six days. The president will now, no doubt, get his extra billions for whatever military program his lobbyist friends deem necessary. Civil liberties will be stepped on, probably in permanent fashion. And more misery will be inflicted on populations that have already been driven to startling desperation, in turn producing more motivated martyrs willing to die for their cause.

Why do you think this column was dropped? By the way, had anyone else reported on Gary Hart's speech anywhere? In fact, when was the last time we saw Gary Hart on television?

September 17

Pro-war cheerleading in the tabloids is reaching new heights. If their words could kill, everyone in Afghanistan would be dead already.

September 19: Not Much Truth from David Letterman

The late-night talk show host was applauded last night when CBS newsman Bryant Gumbel praised him for being on the air to restore "normalcy." Letterman confided that he had wished for "mayhem" to be the U.S. response to the attacks on the World Trade Center. He asked if the attitudes of the terrorists should be considered a form of mental illness. During the 2000 election, it was revealed that as many as a quarter of young people were getting *all* their news from late-night television shows like his.

October 8: Simulate This!

On Sunday morning, ABC *News* trotted out one of its state-of-the-art, made-for-this-war graphic simulations. It was like a video game, showing the shape of a bomber gliding over the brown and rocky topography of what is supposedly Afghanistan. Anchor Peter Jennings described what the graphic was illustrating, then paused. You could almost see his brain clicking away. "You know," he said, "I don't really trust simulations like these even though you are supposed to use them in television." He had clearly deviated from the script by commenting on his own presentation. He reminded viewers that when the Reagan administration first proposed its antiballistic missile-defense system, every television station ran a simulation that showed a rocket knocking out an incoming missile. It worked every time. Of course, that was totally deceptive, and no test the Pentagon has done since has demonstrated that the system is quite so infallible. Thank you, Mr. Jennings, for a rare moment of candor and appropriate skepticism. I first learned about this bit of graphic trickery from Cathe Ishino, then the art director of the *McNeil-Lehrer NewsHour* and Globalvision. She actually made a presentation exposing the issue at a conference of broadcast designers. Sadly, many networks continued to use such expensively produced flimflams.

October 11

Today is the one month anniversary of the tragic events of September 11. A moment of silence and reflection is in order to mourn for the dead and the missing, and to mark that catastrophe, and the catastrophes that seem to be unfolding. We live in scary and dangerous times. An independent media is more important than ever to help us all know what is happening, why it's happening, and what it means.

October 12: There Is at Least One "Media Hero" in the Madness

Yesterday, I was given a dose of media hope in an unusual place. To get there, you had to walk through a National Guard checkpoint in the "exclusion zone" not far from Ground Zero, where the stench of death can still take your breath away. There, in what was once a firehouse, is the home of veteran television producer Jon Alpert's Downtown Community Television Center, which for a quarter of a century has housed independent media in New York. The firehouse is now hosting a radio studio and ancillary cable television operation for the radio program *Democracy Now*, anchored by the tenacious and super-committed Amy Goodman. Along with a team of dedicated volunteers, Amy is offering a daily two-hour "War and Peace Report," which is unrivaled on radio anywhere in the world, to my knowledge.

October 13: Anthrax Aimed at Media

So far, there have been no articles in the U.S. media about "why they would attack us (in the media)," but judging from the many inquiries I am getting from overseas, I am concluding that many journalists elsewhere don't seem to see much of a distinction between the U.S. media and the U.S. government—a challenge that we in the media must take seriously.

A Blow to the City
New York City, September 11:
An Attack on Urban Culture?

Urban Culture Magazine

The September 11 attack on the World Trade Center was an attack on urban culture. Many cultures that oppose Western culture perceive urban development as a threat. For example, the Serbs who attacked Sarejevo attacked a mixed society in which Muslims were very deeply integrated. This was an attack on a cosmopolitan culture, an attack on the idea of people from different backgrounds living together. It was a blow from a traditional, rural-based culture against the power of the city and the power of its ideas.

Likewise, the Islamic fundamentalists—if that's what they are, the people presumed to be behind the attack on the World Trade Center—saw these buildings as the physical manifestation of a globalized economy and society. Benjamin Barber wrote a book called *Jihad vs. McWorld,* arguing that this holy war pits the forces of Islamic fundamentalism against a different fundamentalism, the forces of market capitalism. McWorld wants to concentrate power in global corporations, symbolized by the size of the World Trade Center. The World Trade Center represented the power of the people on top of the world, a power that people from other cultures resent. They resent the arrogance associated with it; they resent the fact that these people are looking down and don't really see them. Hence, the buildings and their occupants become the target in a war of symbols and icons. The 1993 bombing and the September 11 attacks were strikes against these symbols of financial power and of America as a dominant cultural force in the world. If they knocked down those buildings, they believed, they would show the society's vulnerabilities and its weaknesses. Knocking the World Trade Center down was also a way of striking a blow against the values that underlie it, which are, in many ways, urban values, values of modernity.

New York represents an incredible diversity; the old and the new coexist dramatically. An energetic business culture coexists with the arts in some sort of ongoing dialectic. The counterculture—*The Village Voice* culture, if you will—coexists with *The New York Times* culture. If you believe in rule by mullah, in one traditional set of values, this is very threatening. The law of God is violated by this lack of respect for tradition, the lack of order, the emancipation of women, the sexuality of the city, the energy, and the music. New York in particular and urban society in general represent an obscene pole of culture to the more traditional societies. These societies have been able to coexist with ours for many years, but increasingly, there's been an encroachment by our culture into other cultures. There's been a reverse penetration as well—more Muslims than Episcopalians live in the United States—but by and large there's a much more overt intrusion of American movies, lifestyle, dress, and consumer products into other cultures.

On a psychological level, these attacks have brought all New Yorkers together. Suddenly, the heroes of the new post-September 11 New York—the firefighters and the police officers, are working-class people. People who are digging out the city and rebuilding it have gained a level of respect in the culture that they never had before. People became aware of the bus boys at the Windows on the World, who were Mexicans and were probably working illegally. Will their families be taken care of? These questions began to get asked. You go to any dinner in New York City—I went to one the other night, at the Creative Coalition, a celebrity function—there were firefighters and cops there as part of the family of New York.

Week Seven: From the News Dissector's Weblog

The newscasts blare on day and night with constant updates, but what I sense is a growing fear and frustration among viewers. The impression much of this news conveys may also be false, or at least one-dimensional. That's why I have been devoting a chunk of my day to watching as much of it as I can and feeding it back in a timely manner. I try to include reports from different countries, diverse sources, and a variety of vantage points. Fortunately, I have the space, but I am not sure how many readers have the time or attention span to read all of it. (Later, we learned that our readership tripled post–September 11.)

October 19: "We Will Not Flinch, Bend, or Swerve."

You could hear the echo of Franklin Delano Roosevelt as CBS news anchor Dan Rather virtually recycled the World War II president's famous line "We have nothing to fear but fear itself." Rather, known for grand eloquence and gushing hyperbole, may have been trying to top FDR with his declaration at a CBS news conference held yesterday to respond to reports that his assistant—still unnamed, but "British born," according to London papers—has been infected with the milder form of anthrax. The anchor said fear, not anthrax, is what worries him. "We will not flinch, we will not bend, we will not swerve," was his fighting phrase, uttered in a white, short-sleeved shirt while sitting next to his similarly attired boss, Andrew Heyward, announcing that the news, a "classy newscast" as he called it, would go on. "Just two regular guys in white shirts and ties," quipped *New York Post* columnist Adam Buckman, who also pointed out, "They were even on multiple channels—Fox News, MSNBC, CNN—but, curiously, not on CBS." CBS, you will recall, refused to preempt a rerun of the *I Love Lucy* show years ago for an important Senate hearing on the Vietnam War. Observers also noted with praise that unlike network colleagues who also suffered anthrax exposure, there were no PR flacks present at CBS's media event.

Why Is the Media in the Crossfire?

Why? Because we live in "one nation under television," where the news anchors are national symbols and the television news screen is like the church we all worship in. Terrorists know that the media has more power than most politicians, especially the power to reinforce a national mood. And that's also why politicians want the media to play the role of megaphone and rally the people to support their leaders in this hour of need. The late media writer Ed Diamond, an old friend of mine, wrote about a colleague of the political columnist Walter Lippmann (1889–1974), who he accused of "always dredging up basic principles." Noted Diamond in his book *The Tin Gazoo*: "'That won't do in daily journalism.' The colleague explained and offered this metaphor: A piano has eight octaves, a violin three and a bugle only four notes. 'Now if what you've got to play is a bugle,' the friend concluded, 'there isn't any sense in camping down in front of piano music.' 'You may be right,' Lippmann replied. 'But I am not going to spend my life writing bugle calls.'" Let's hope that more voices in the media understand that they have a duty to play more than bugle calls, too—especially in wartime, when bugle calls rouse warriors and silence critics. One of the problems, given the lack of international coverage over the years, is that you can't blame most people for not being critical. As longtime propaganda analysts Ed Herman and David Peterson write: "Thanks to the effectiveness of the U.S. propaganda system, U.S. citizens by and large are caught within the epistemic bind of not knowing that they do not know."

October 20: When Networks Become Crime Scenes

NPR's *On the Media* show this morning reports on the difficulty most networks have had in covering the attacks on themselves. Reuven Frank, a former NBC president, says the network should respond like a company, not a news organization. Media monitor Andrew Tyndall says that NBC's coverage on the issue was initially wrong, reporting that the infected letter to Tom Brokaw was postmarked Florida when it turned out to have come through New Jersey and that the network relied on unnamed sources, without corroboration from its own security people.

October 22: The Latest Dispute on the Battlefield

On the war front, a dispute is making news as I write on this Monday morning. CNN is reporting that the Taliban, with parts of aircraft debris in hand, claim that they shot down a U.S. helicopter. The Pentagon insists it is not true. Surely, controversies like this matter very little in the scheme of things. A war usually implies the presence of two armed forces, each with the capacity to cause damage to each other and each with claims that require independent verification. The blow-by-blow coverage and tit-for-tat claims reported from afar are not always very helpful in reaching any deeper understanding or in getting distance from the nonstop cycles of constantly updated info. What should we be asking? I received a notice of an upcoming military and diplomatic briefing that poses more basic questions of the kind that media outlets themselves need to be asking:

"Is the war in Afghanistan a winnable war?"

"What regional and global impact might we see?"

"What are the domestic costs of ensuring safety?"

"What are the root causes of terrorism?"

"What are the long-term obstacles to this fight?"

October 23: Pilger Attacks "Lobotomized" Media's Coverage of War

Britain's veteran campaigning journalist John Pilger has accused sections of the Western media of behaving like "government lackeys" during the current war against the Taliban. Pilger told a meeting of Media Workers against the War: "There is already a long list of 'intelligence' and 'diplomatic' lies that emerged after the Gulf War and other conflicts. But we are seeing the same thing over again. It's as if there is a traditional lobotomy that journalists seem to have to undergo every time the political leaders feel they want to go out somewhere and bomb people." Is this true? Is he exaggerating? Increasingly, U.S. media outlets are reporting on the media restrictions but without, to my knowledge, any official complaints or aggressive protest lobbying by media companies.

Censorship Is Back—In China

Add this item to your file on how much the world, and media, have *not* changed since September 11. *The Washington Post* reports that blocks on Internet websites of foreign news organizations—including CNN, BBC, Reuters, and *The Washington Post*—were reinstituted in China after the end of the Asia-Pacific Economic Cooperation

(APEC) meeting earlier this month in Shanghai. While Western sources are blocked in China, Chinese propaganda news is being welcomed in the United States by AOL TimeWarner in an "exchange": They get "Miami Vice"; we get the thoughts of Jiang Zemin on CCTV broadcasts.

October 26: Reality Television Runs into a New Reality

When *Survivor* debuted in the summer of 2000, it was a tremendous success, spawning many imitators. Now after more than a year has passed, reality shows are on the schedule of most broadcast and cable networks. But, with the new reality ushered in by the events of September 11, these shows haven't been doing well.

Al-Jazeera to Go Online in English

The *Online Journalism Review* reports that the controversial Arabic language satellite television station will go online in English within a year. Since more than 40 percent of the site's visitors are from the United States, I would welcome critiques of Al-Jazeera's coverage from Arabic-speaking readers. As we all know, the Qatar-based broadcaster is called the "CNN of the Arab world." Yet, as a former CNN producer and occasional critic, that's not a great recommendation in my eyes. In fact, the people at Al-Jazeera say their channel was modeled on the BBC. But the U.S. media is so self-referential that they seem unwilling to acknowledge that a media outside the United States might prefer not to compare itself to a U.S. media brand. In principle, I welcome more perspectives in the media mix, but all need higher levels of transparency and accountability.

The "Turbanators" and the Terrorists—War Crimes and Media Omissions: From the News Dissector's Weblog

December 7

My late and great friend Abbie Hoffman used to open his lectures with a bet, what he called the "Journalist Challenge." He offered one hundred dollars to any reporter present who could file a story on his talk with less than three errors. He was a chronic gambler all his life, but he told me that this was one bet he never lost.

Mistakes by reporters are common as we go about the rush of making deadlines with what is often acknowledged as "the first draft of history." But sometimes it is more than the facts that get messed up. Sometimes a whole story gets botched or half-told. When that story involves hundreds of dead people, as the one I am about to tell you does, it becomes essential to try to understand why some in the media avoid or fail to fully investigate odious war crimes. American news outlets all reported the Mazar-I-Sharif prison revolt, but virtually none deviated from Washington's view of it. Many questions went unasked: What led up to it? What was the U.S. role? Was the Taliban suckered into a trap? Was there a massacre?

A deeper question: How can so much of the world press, now covering the Afghan war, miss so much of the forest for the trees? I am talking about the apparent slaughter of 600 prisoners in late November. I will revisit the details in a moment, but permit me a flashback—to another war, the one in Vietnam, and an infamous hamlet called My Lai, set off in the rice fields of the countryside.

"Q: Babies? A: Babies."

My generation won't forget what happened there, how American soldiers, pressed by their commanders to escalate their "enemy kill rate," shot down civilians in a ditch, even as other U.S. soldiers in a passing helicopter landed and, at gunpoint, forced the unit, under the command of Lieutenant William Calley (later pardoned by the even more criminal Richard Nixon), to stop the massacre. There was a famous antiwar poster about the event that was briefly plastered in the subways of New York. It featured a color photo of the dead bodies of the victims, men, women, and children sprawled in a ditch. Designed by activist/writer Lee Baxandall, the poster was memorable for its simplicity. Above and below the grisly picture was a short question and answer: "Q: Babies? A: Babies."

That massacre did not go unreported, thanks to an American soldier, the late Ron Ridenhour, with the help of a young journalist, Seymour Hersh. Ron uncovered the story; Sy wrote it up, but no one would run it. They had to set up their own news agency, the Dispatch News Service, to disseminate the story, after it was first suppressed by most news outlets when the Pentagon initially denied that there had been an atrocity. Most U.S. media ignored it until they no longer could. To this day, U.S. military commanders hate most journalists because of embarrassing exposés like this one, even though the military did prosecute these crimes later. The truth is that war-making doesn't always look very good in the light of independent scrutiny. Significantly, a year ago, CBS's *60 Minutes* went back to My Lai with some of the soldiers who witnessed what happened, and who now say their own government deserves to be tried for war crimes. (Back in the 1960s, CBS was scoffing at well-documented charges of war crimes raised by philosopher Bertrand Russell and other war critics, who conducted a much maligned War Crimes tribunal.)

Where Are the War Crimes Reporters Today?

Where were the U.S. mainstream media outlets when crimes of similar moral gravitas were being committed right in front of them today? I am talking about that so-called prison revolt in the old Afghan fort called Qalai Janghi in the town of Mazar-I-Sharif, which was only fully extinguished by the end of last week. To be sure, these men were not civilians, but armed combatants. But once in custody, they must be treated according to the Geneva Conventions. A fuller probe is warranted.

Thanks to the British press, the story has received more than the usual episodic treatment, with a story here and there, but with no cumulative impact. While *Time* and CNN covered it, the U.K. media offered in-depth analysis, not only of the horror but its meaning in terms of possible war crimes. The BBC, *Times of London, Independent,* and *Guardian* were all over the grisly story in graphic detail, while most American outlets played it only as more bang-bang.

Justin Huggler wrote in London's *Independent* last Friday about its gruesome aftermath:

> "Those guilty of Tuesday's attack should pay. But hunting monsters is risky business. The danger isn't that the monster will catch you, but that you won't know when you have become one yourself."
>
> — ROBERT KIRBY, columnist, 9/16/01

They were still carrying the bodies out yesterday. So many of them were strewn around the old fortress. We saw one go past whose foot had been half-torn off and was hanging from his leg by a shred of flesh. The expression on the face of the dead man was so clear that it was hard to believe he was dead until you saw the gaping red hole in the side of his forehead. The stench of rotting human flesh had become overpowering; at times, it was hard to breathe. But questions remained as they cleared away the bodies of slaughtered foreign Taliban fighters believed to be loyal to Osama bin Laden.

The Media and the Massacre

Let's turn to those questions in a minute since this column is more about media than massacres. And it is also about how some journalists performed like modern-day Ridenhours and Hershs, while most did not. For one thing, few journalists explained the run-up to the prison outrage, as in how the Taliban prisoners got there in the first place. There was allusion to it but little investigation. On November 25, *The New York Times* carried a front page photo showing members of the Northern Alliance and the Taliban shaking hands in Konduz and appearing to peacefully resolve a showdown that U.S. Defense Secretary Rumsfeld had predicted would be a bloody fight to the finish, an eventuality he seemed to relish in the sound bites I saw. At that time, the Northern Alliance, advised and outfitted by the United States and Britain, had the town surrounded and was moving in for the kill—until, that is, talks broke out and a peace of sorts was brokered.

As I discovered from the Sunday *New York Times,* the two sides had worked out a deal. The Taliban forces believed they would be treated fairly if they gave up. A photo underscored the point. The caption: "Northern Alliance troops near Amirabad watched as a convoy of surrendering Taliban soldiers from Konduz passed through the front lines." These men were on their way to the Northern Alliance fort at Mazar-I-Sharif as part of what the *Times* called, "a script for surrender." The *Times* correspondent also reported that General Rashid Dostum had promised to turn them over to the United Nations and international courts.

This information was reported without clarification. What "international courts" they were to be taken to were not specified. I shook my head. The *Times* knew there were no international courts in place. They also knew the United Nations had no standing in the conflict and made no provisions to accept prisoners. Why didn't the newspaper of record mention this? Was this some scam? Had the Taliban's feared foreign troops been suckered? The *Times* then added, rather obliquely, "It was unclear if his (Dostum's) view would hold." The next sentence seems to reflect the "catch 'em and kill 'em" orientation of the Alliance and the Pentagon, which was cheering them on: "Other Northern Alliance Leaders say they want to try the men in Afghan criminal courts and possibly put them to death." Again, the *Times* failed to point out that there were no such courts in place.

That was Saturday. The foreign troops surrendered, presumably with the expectation that they would be turned over to the United Nations. Maybe they didn't know better. Maybe they believed Dostum, a war lord who has fought on every side over the long years of combat in that country, with the Russians against the mujahideen and then with the mujahideen against the Russians, with the Taliban and now against it. He is known as a killer par excellence. His forces slaughtered 50,000 people between 1992 and 1996 in Kabul, leading many Afghans to welcome the Taliban as saviors. Now he was wheeling and dealing with the Taliban, cajoling them to stop fighting. Those fanatical fighters believed they had a deal. The next day, when they discovered they didn't, the world would find out that it had a problem. A deadly one.

A Revolting Revolt

What happened next? Here is the reconstruction by the *Independent's* Huggler, published five days later:

> Bound to one another, the prisoners were taken in pickup trucks to Qalai Janghi, the 19th-century mud-walled fortress that Dostum had used as his

headquarters after the fall of Mazar-I-Sharif to his Northern Alliance forces three weeks previously.

It was on Saturday that what started as the relatively peaceful surrender of the northern Afghan Taliban stronghold of Konduz suddenly started to go out of control inside the fort. Before the eyes of Western reporters, two foreign Taliban prisoners, in the process of being registered by the Red Cross, detonated hand grenades, killing themselves and two senior aides to General Dostum and slightly injuring the ITN news reporter Andrea Catherwood.

It was not the first time that we had heard of bin Laden's "foreigners" committing suicide rather than be taken alive. The Northern Alliance claimed that a group of around 60 of them jumped into a river and drowned themselves. Another group were found kneeling in positions of prayer, each with a single bullet wound from behind. A Northern Alliance commander alleged that one of them had killed all of the others in a suicide pact before turning the gun on himself.

But there were always fears that the stories might have been invented to cover up Northern Alliance massacres of the foreign fighters. Nor was it the first time that surrendering Taliban had not been properly disarmed. Over the past few weeks, journalists in Afghanistan have watched repeatedly as Taliban who had surrendered were allowed to head into Northern Alliance-held towns, waving their Kalashnikovs and rocket-launchers triumphantly in the air. This time, however, defiance grew into mayhem, culminating in the scenes of trucks piled high with human bodies that we saw heading out of Qalai Janghi yesterday.

The Plot Thickens

OK. So far, we have two Taliban prisoners, allowed to take arms into a prison—how crazy is that—and then attack their jailers. *Time* magazine reported that they were outraged when they saw Western reporters present. Perhaps they thought the United Nations would be there. But that was just the first incident.

Huggler continues:

The next day, Sunday, the prisoners—many of them with their arms tied behind their backs—were being herded into a room for interrogation before two CIA agents [Mike Spann and one identified only as Dave]. Did they fear retribution for the previous day's murder of the two Northern Alliance commanders? Or was it, as another account suggests, the mere sight of two Americans—from the foreign fighters' point of view, sworn enemies of bin Laden—that provoked the bloodbath that followed?

The incompetence of the Northern Alliance soldiers—who, guided by the United States and British special forces, failed to search the prisoners properly and thus allowed them to smuggle in knives and grenades hidden in their clothes—must be seen as a key factor in the disaster. The men were also housed next to the fortress's well-stocked armory.

Enter Mike Spann, the CIA agent, now being celebrated as America's first dead hero by many U.S. media outlets. Why is he there? Not to hand the prisoners over to a nonexistent U.N. presence, to be sure. He is there as an interrogator, and you can perhaps imagine what interrogation means in these circumstances.

Now we have an account from the Taliban side. One of those feared "foreign" troops turned out not to be so foreign. He is twenty-year-old American citizen John Walker Lindh, also known as Abdul Hamid, now in a military hospital as a prisoner of war in U.S. hands. He told *Newsweek*'s Colin Soloway, "Early in the morning, they began taking us out, slowly, one by one into the compound. Some of the majahdeen (Taliban) were scared. They thought we were all going to be killed. I saw two Americans there. They were taking pictures with a digital camera and a video camera. As soon as the last of us was taken out, someone either pulled a knife or threw a grenade at the guards and got their guns and started shooting." (My hunch is that the fight in the prison will be nothing compared to the fight by agents, studios, and television companies for the rights to his story.)

Who Fired First?

BBC's *Newsnight* interviewed Oliver August, correspondent for the *Times*, London, in Mazar-I-Sharif, who said that Spann and his CIA colleague Dave were thought (by reporters on the scene) to have set off the violence by aggressively interrogating foreign Taliban prisoners and asking, "Why did you come to Afghanistan?" This really pissed off the Taliban captives, who probably wanted to ask them the same thing. August said their questions were answered by one prisoner jumping forward and announcing, "We're here to kill you." The *Guardian's* Mazar-I-Sharif correspondent blamed the CIA for failing "on entering the fort to observe the first rule of espionage: keep a low profile." Rashmee X. Ahmed of the *Times* of India reported that "August said Spann subsequently pulled his gun, and his CIA colleague shot three prisoners dead in cold blood before losing control of the situation." This report was carried in a Murdoch-owned outlet, which is hardly sympathetic to Islamic militancy. Meanwhile, other would-be observers like Amnesty International and the Red Cross, which has a duty to ensure that prisoners of war are treated according to law, asked to observe. They were denied entrance.

According to Ahmed, "Spann was then 'kicked, beaten and bitten to death,' the journalists said, in an account of the ferocity of the violence that lasted four days, leaving more than 500 people dead and the fort littered with 'bodies, shrapnel and shell casings.'"

The fort was later bombed, when U.S. air strikes were called in by the Northern Alliance's U.S. advisors. One of them killed Northern Alliance troops. All of this action was detailed on British television and in the media there. But not in the United States. On December 3, the *New York Post* reported that "Northern Alliance forces slaughtered more than 600 prisoners." Somehow the U.S. role was omitted in a blatant rewrite of the incident. The possibility that these men had revolted because they feared execution without trial—a not unreasonable fear given the Northern Alliance's track record in the past and as recently as their bloody "liberation" of Mazar-I-Sharif with hundreds killed—wasn't cited anywhere. I am not rationalizing their fanaticism, just noting that their motives and the larger context needed more explication. The Western media had already demonized them, but the circumstances of this incident, while reported, went unexplained.

What We Saw

On Tuesday night, we saw the bodies on ABC's *World News Tonight* and other outlets. We saw front pages stories in the *New York Post* and *Daily News* honoring Spann, but no details of why this revolt started. As news of this incident—without any reference to the fact that massacring prisoners is a violation of international law—started getting airplay on CNN, it triggered my memory of an atrocity closer to home, the massacre at Attica Prison in upstate New York in 1971, which I covered back in my radio days. It was also initially blamed on the bloodthirsty prisoners who slashed the necks of the guards. That claim was later disproved when it was shown that prisoners had been executed by the New York state police. I wondered if Qalai Janghi would become known as the Afghan Attica. (Incidentally, last year, almost thirty years later, New York state was forced by the courts to pay compensation to the survivors.)

But issues of responsibility and allegations of war crimes had still not become a major U.S. media focus as of Friday. *The New York Times* downplayed the suggestion that this was a war crime by reporting, "No major human rights group has its own monitors in Afghanistan, and their officials agree that in a war with few credible witnesses, and with some of the Taliban soldiers clearly fanatical, the exact circumstances of such killings are murky."

Later, Amnesty in London would call for a full probe but Human Rights Watch in New York was more wishy-washy: "Any summary execution of prisoners is a clear violation of the Geneva Convention, but there are a lot of gray areas," said Sidney Jones, the Asia director for Human Rights Watch. "For example, there has been a lot of concern raised that dozens of the dead prisoners in the fort had their hands bound. But that doesn't mean they were summarily executed, and we have nobody on the ground to investigate." I saw reports of men with bullet holes through their heads, execution-style, and later, I heard an account of at least one Northern Alliance soldier prying gold teeth out of a corpse's mouth.

The lack of careful, thorough coverage by the U.S. media is a crime in its own right—a crime against the public's right to know. The failure to condemn this outrageous conduct infuriated the *Independent's* veteran Middle East watcher Robert Fisk, who was equally scornful of the media and the military. His words deserve more than brief quotation:

Are We War Criminals?

We are becoming war criminals in Afghanistan. The U.S. Air Force bombs Mazar-I-Sharif for the Northern Alliance, and our heroic Afghan allies—who slaughtered 50,000 people in Kabul between 1992 and 1996—move into the city and execute up to 300 Taliban fighters. The report is a footnote on the television satellite channels, a "nib" in journalistic parlance. Perfectly normal, it seems. The Afghans have a "tradition" of revenge. So, with the strategic assistance of the USAF [U.S. Air Force], a war crime is committed.

Now we have the Mazar-I-Sharif prison "revolt," in which Taliban inmates opened fire on their Alliance jailers. U.S. Special Forces—and, it has emerged, British troops—helped the Alliance to overcome the uprising and, sure enough, CNN tells us some prisoners were "executed" trying to escape. It is an atrocity.

The Americans have even less excuse for this massacre. For the U.S. Secretary of Defense, Donald Rumsfeld, stated quite specifically during the siege of the city that U.S. air raids on the Taliban defenders would stop "if the Northern Alliance requested it." Leaving aside the revelation that the thugs and murderers of the Northern Alliance were now acting as air controllers to the USAF in its battle with the thugs and murderers of the Taliban, Mr. Rumsfeld's incriminating remark places Washington in the witness box of any war-crimes trial over Konduz. The United States was acting in full military cooperation with the Northern Alliance militia.

Most television journalists, to their shame, have shown little or no interest in these disgraceful crimes. Cozying up to the Northern Alliance, chatting to the American troops, most have done little more than mention the war crimes against prisoners in the midst of their reports. What on earth has gone wrong with our moral compass since 11 September? . . .

The Need for Continuing Coverage

What indeed? Eventually, this atrocity may come to stand for this war that the United States seems to be "winning" (if wars are ever fully won) in the same way that My Lai came to symbolize the war we lost. At My Lai, there was a soldier on the ground with the courage to blow the whistle. Only the British press has done so this time. As Amnesty International and U.N. Human Rights Commissioner Mary Robinson demand an investigation, let's hope this incident will receive better coverage here in the States.

There are laws governing the treatment of prisoners. Imagine the outcry in the United States if U.S. prisoners in a Taliban jail had revolted and been bombed or fired upon. As Human Rights Day approaches on December 10, Washington must be held accountable for its abuses, just as we demand that the Taliban and the terrorists be punished for theirs.

Let me be clear: In upholding the primacy of international law, I am not excusing Taliban crimes. Scenes of splattered bodies of men in captivity make better recruiting videos for bin Laden than all his in-cave pronouncements combined. They erode the idea that somehow America's technologically advanced campaign for "justice" is morally superior to the Taliban or al Qaeda's cruder terror tactics.

Trying to Kill the Survivors

What is amazing is that despite all the bombardments and the killings, sixty prisoners survived in the fort's subcellar. When they were first discovered, *Newsweek* reported, "Alliance soldiers poured diesel fuel into the basement and lit it, on the assumption that any remaining Taliban would be killed by the fire and the fumes. When this incineration strategy failed, they were washed out when their basement bunker was flooded with freezing water." (Now Defense Secretary Rumsfeld says that the United States may use gas to "smoke out" bin Laden if U.S. troops find him hiding in any of the caves they are blasting, amidst fears of significant collateral damage from folks living in the vicinity.)

Coverage of these attacks and crime is trickling out, largely because an American was among the captives. Today's "Turbanators," as one satirist recently characterized President Bush in a mock movie ad modeled on Schwarzenegger's "Terminator," might play more by the same international rules of war if they knew that the media would hold their feet to the fire if they didn't. The lack of government information about the war is bad enough. The U.S. media's failure to fully investigate this alleged war crime makes them complicit in a cover-up.

Postscript

In the months that followed this incident, the John Walker Lindh case remained in the public eye and the subject of ongoing press attention, much of it hostile to Lindh. Most of the defense motions filed in his behalf were rejected by a court in northern Virginia, picked by prosecutors because it is considered a rubberstamp for administration contentions in almost all national security matters. In late June, reports surfaced that an independent film was being shown in Europe that purported to document the claim that war crimes were committed by American military personnel in connection with the suppression of the prison uprising. At the time of writing, it has yet to be seen in the United States.

Jim Ridgeway reported in *The Village Voice* on July 3, 2002, after stories had appeared in the *New Scotsman* and in the German press:

The film, *Massacre in Mazar*, was made by Jamie Doran, a former BBC producer. The film tracks what happened after Kunduz, the last Taliban stronghold, fell on November 21, 2001, to Northern Alliance commanders with considerable assistance from U.S. Special Forces. Various people in the film claim to have seen U.S. troops participating in the torture and killing of thousands of Taliban prisoners near Mazar-I-Sharif. Doran includes footage of John Walker Lindh on his knees being interrogated in the desert. One witness claims he saw an American soldier break the neck of a Taliban prisoner, and Americans supposedly collaborated with their Islamic allies in cutting off Taliban soldiers' fingers, tongues, and ears.

The Pentagon has dismissed the allegations as the work of a commie propagandist," a conclusion apparently drawn from the screening recently arranged by the PDS, a left-wing political party in Germany. "Frankly, I didn't even know who the PDS were before I went—I haven't a clue," Doran told the *Voice* in an interview last Friday. The movie has not been shown in the States, although Doran said he hopes the film will air here on television, perhaps in the fall.

Since there is little footage of actual events, the film's credibility depends on witnesses. Among the six eyewitnesses were two drivers from hostile regions who separately took the crew to the same place in the desert where they'd been forced to dump the evidence of summary executions. One taxi driver said he had gone to a gas station when he wondered what the horrific smell was, and he asked the attendant and he [the attendant] said, "Look behind you," Dolan related. "And there were three containers with blood pouring out from them."

In late August 2002, nearly ten months after these events, well after the public's impression of what happened in Afghanistan and the heroic role played by U.S. forces was deeply ingrained, American complicity in war crimes finally became a cover story in *Newsweek*. The magazine did not advance the story of the prison revolt, but it did add new and grisly details about the torture and incarceration of prisoners held by American allies, many of whom perished by deliberate starvation in containers. Many suffocated and were buried in mass graves, as later confirmed by U.N. investigators. *Newsweek* asked why so few media outlets had ignored practices like these, and indeed, they hadn't carried a more critical assessment of the U.S. campaign in Afghanistan. Why indeed?

On August 27, 2002, *The Washington Post* reported that Pentagon authorities found no evidence that American soldiers were aware of the "alleged" deaths. Note the phrase "alleged deaths" in *Newsweek's* sister publication. Marine General Peter Pace said his units reported "zero reported cases of human rights violations." Reported by whom? General Dostrum, who commanded the U.S. troops with U.S. advisors, remains in control of the region. He fought alongside Mohammad Fahim, now defense minister in the U.S.-supported government of Afghanistan. The *Post* reported that that government "stopped short of pledging to organize an investigation, promising only to cooperate."

The Week of the Skeptics: From the News Dissector's Weblog

October 28: When the News Is Uncritical, Columnists Are More Outspoken

While the news seems to strain to hit an upbeat tone, editorial columnists like Maureen Dowd and Frank Rich of *The New York Times* are growing more skeptical. A Pundit Watch is in order, because wherever the editorial section goes, the tone of news reporting often follows.

Dowd: "After one of the worst weeks in the capital's history, the question was suspended like a spore in the autumn air: Are we quagmiring ourselves again?"

While Dowd doubts the war on one front, Rich was spraying sarcasm yesterday on progress in the war at home:

> Of the more than 900 suspects arrested, exactly zero have been criminally charged in the World Trade Center attack (though one has died of natural causes, we're told, in a New Jersey jail cell). The Bush team didn't fully recognize that a second attack on America had begun until more than a week after the first casualty. Given that this is the administration that was touted as being run with C.E.O. clockwork, perhaps it should be added to the growing list of Things

That Have Not Changed Forever since Sept. 11. But let's not be so hasty. Not everything changes that fast—least of all Washington. The White House's home-front failures are not sudden, unpredictable products of wartime confusion but direct products of an ethos that has been in place since Jan. 20.

A Call to Journalists to Speak Out

Veteran *Washington Post* writer Ben Bagdikian, author of the classic exposé, "Media Monopoly," is the first to sign a petition to protest the growing press restrictions in the United States. It was initiated by San Francisco's Media Alliance, and it will be passed on to the powers that be in the administration, presumably including the White House and Pentagon. Here's an excerpt:

> It is during times of war and crisis that the importance of freedom of the press is most vital. During such times there is increased government pressure to restrict press freedom.
>
> We join together to remind the public that the media must report the truth—even when that truth challenges assertions that are made by the U.S. government.
>
> We, the undersigned journalists, editors, and media producers, call on publishers, owners of media outlets, and our colleagues to resist government intimidation, restrictions on information, and direct censorship, and to reject "loyalty tests" and other actions which restrict media workers' ability to act in the interest of the public's right to know.
>
> We also call on the Bush Administration to cease its overt and covert interference with freedom of the press.

October 29: Government News Management

Yesterday, I was on Larry Bensky's *Sunday Salon* program on KPFA, the Pacifica station in Berkeley, talking about government media strategies. Larry's other guest was Jacqueline E. Sharkey, a well-informed University of Arizona journalism professor who has written on the way the media was used in the Gulf War. She claimed that the media is being subjected to the same playbook in this one, too. She has written about her findings on TomPaine.com:

> The techniques used by the government to limit and shape news coverage— which have included prohibiting access to military operations and releasing

misleading data about U.S. successes and casualties—bring up issues that go far beyond the obvious need to balance military secrecy requirements with the public's right to know. This information-control program has distorted accounts of what occurred during the military operations in Grenada, Panama and the Persian Gulf, has led to false perceptions about the operations' short- and long-term impact on these regions and on U.S. policy, and has threatened the historical record.

October 31: A Failure to Communicate

Germany: On the flight over, I caught up with some newspaper stories I had missed. Most notably, there was a front page *International Herald Tribune* reprint of a *Washington Post* story on twenty secret talks over three years between the Taliban and U.S. representatives. The last took place just days before September 11. One was held in Washington and involved a Taliban emissary bringing a rug as a gift for President Bush. I learned that the American representatives now feel that they blew it by not being willing to find an "aabroh," which is Pashto for a face-saving formula to induce the Afghan regime to hand over bin Laden. The United States kept demanding his arrest, and the Taliban kept insisting on evidence first. The outcome was a stalemate. "We never heard what they were trying to say," said Milt Bearden, who ran the CIA's secret operations that supported the mujahideen with their war against Russians in Afghanistan in the 1980s. "We had no common language. Ours was 'give up bin Laden.' They were saying, 'do something to help us give him up.'" It is failures of communication like this that so often lead to wars.

November 2: African Success

The MEDIA TENOR organization, which is arranging the conference I am attending in Germany, gave its international television prize this year for media diversity to the South African Broadcasting Corporation (SABC), a clear sign that media makers in other countries are not just looking to Western broadcast models as their paragons of excellence. Media monitors from this group based in Bonn, Germany (but also in New York; Pretoria, South Africa; and three other cities), rated broadcasts by a variety of criteria. In their view, the SABC outclassed and outreported two prime-time BBC news programs and all the U.S. networks. When Matatha Tsetu (a veteran and respected editor turned television journalist) accepted the award, he spoke of his network's efforts to give voice to the poor and voiceless in his country.

He later told me about the war he is most worried about and that it is not in central Africa. He explained how his country's soldiers and former President Nelson Mandela were engaged, at that moment, in helping to promote peace in the central African nation of Burundi. Burundi had also had a genocidal ethnic conflict. It was his hope that if its new transitional government works (as supported by soldiers from his homeland), it may provide a model for neighboring Rwanda. Let us not forget the million who were massacred there while most of the world fiddled and looked away.

I tried to remember the last story I had seen about Burundi. CNN International, the global news service broadcast from Atlanta to the world (but not to the United States), did devote one of their world news minutes to an image of Mandela on the scene there, while BBC World gave it slightly more time. Tsetu stressed that African news barely makes it onto our radar screen, so I was happy that the MEDIA TENOR conference made Africa a part of its agenda. Albina du Boisrouvray, the campaigner for AIDS orphans through her FXB Foundation [Francois Xavier Bagnoud Foundation, named after her son who was killed in a helicopter crash] was here too, discussing how hard it is to get the plight of forty million children onto the news agenda. She explained why so many oppressed and forgotten children are already becoming child soldiers and terrorists in training.

November 4: Support Independent Media!

Feeding back to the media was part of my message here in Boston, where I spoke today to the Alliance for Democracy confab at the Boston Public Library. I called on the assembled minions to stop bashing "The Media," as if they are one seamless monolith, and to start seeking out more diverse sources. I also called on them to support independent media with their wallets as well as their mouths, and I requested that they reach out *to* the media and *through* the media, rather than just talk to themselves.

What was welcome this week was a chance to sample coverage in Europe, where more diverse voices are being heard than here. Getting out of New York offered a respite from the hothouse of Yankee fantasies, battles between the Bravest and the Finest, and a mayoral race in which media mogul Mike Bloomberg spreads millions of dollars like manna from heaven in an environment that is increasingly depressed economically and now, psychologically, by the loss of the World Series. It makes you worry about the efficacy of bombing when you see the mighty Bronx Bombers go down in defeat.

And finally, a word to honor the memory of Kathy Nguyen, who died last week in New York of inhalation anthrax, although she has no known link to post offices or media companies. What tragic irony. She was a refugee from the Vietnam War, plucked into a new life from the roof of the U.S. embassy in Saigon in 1975, only to perish as an innocent casualty in America's newest war. She fled South Vietnam's final media moment for the South Bronx, only to be driven into the glare of media attention in death. For me, she became a human link between the two wars, leading me to hope anew that history will not repeat itself.

The Role of CNN

Danny Schechter and Aliza Dichter, Mediachannel.org and Globalvision News Network

There is no denying CNN's enormous impact on world events and the global news agenda. Many governments and news organizations have its electronic face on twenty-four hours a day. CNN virtually enjoys country status because when an issue is not on television, it doesn't exist for most people in the world. But at the same time, CNN has inspired a network's worth of criticism.

On certain websites, critics micromonitor CNN coverage, especially on the Middle East, adding up the time Israel gets as opposed to other players. Former CNN employees have sites like "Turner's Turnovers" blowing the whistle on abusive treatment and other practices they don't like. As a former CNN producer in the heady start-up year of 1980, I worked inside its news "bunker" in Atlanta. I later wrote about my experiences in a chapter of my book *The More You Watch, the Less You Know.* The chapter offers a spin on the networks former slogan, quieting a CNN colleague who dubbed it "The Word's Most (Self-Important) Network."

CNN sees itself as the global news "brand." People around the world think of it as America's number one network for news, not always aware of the existence of look-alike ABC/NBC/CBS. CNN went from a fledgling operation to a multichannel news machine, available in airports, hotel rooms, and now on cell phones. As CNN started to go global, many people all over the world began to think of CNN as the real "Voice of America." CNN correspondent Wolf Blitzer once revealed that the Pentagon had leaked a story to him, rather than hold a press conference, because they knew that when people saw him standing in a suit and tie in front of an American flag they assumed he was a spokesman for government policy.

"We are not naive. We do know that people seek to use us as a player," admitted Chris Cramer, president of CNN International in a June 1 interview with Agence France-Press (AFP), but "we don't have an agenda—we are not exporting an American viewpoint." But onetime television news exec David Klattel of the Columbia School of Journalism in New York told AFP that he believes CNN does broadcast a U.S. perspective. "It has made the world of politics and media much more American because of the dominant impact of American television and the American economy," Klattel says, noting particularly the evolving style of the news media in the many less-powerful countries. "When there is a scandal or a war, even smaller countries try to approach it the way the Americans do," he says.

I asked Mediachannel.org editor Aliza Dichter to scour our many media sources and affiliates for articles about CNN. She writes:

> Ten years ago, CNN became a major television force when it had the only correspondents on the ground in Iraq. But while Gulf War coverage helped launch CNN as a leading U.S. news outlet, it also led to widespread criticism that the network was simply a mouthpiece for the U.S. government and military.
>
> CNN is not only a global media brand but a powerful player in a small world. Live, international broadcasts of breaking news can shape foreign policy—it's called the "CNN effect." Former U.N. Secretary General Boutros Boutros-Ghali once described CNN as the sixteenth member of the U.N. Security Council. The global Arab station Al-Jazeera, the only network with a satellite uplink in Kabul, has been called the "CNN of the East."
>
> But as millions watch CNN and CNN International worldwide, many are increasingly skeptical of the network. A rumor, since debunked, that CNN had used old footage of Palestinians celebrating after the September 11 attacks flew around the Internet with amazing speed, so ready were people to accept that the network would actually fabricate a story.
>
> In this new conflict, the U.S. government promises tight information control while U.S. media speak of their "patriotism" and "duty." President

Bush and Osama bin Laden appear on television as part of a propaganda war to win hearts and minds (and international military support) in what both promise will be a long, fierce, and borderless war. Should we expect that CNN will simply repeat official U.S. views? Is it bias or just sensationalized, shallow journalism? In August 2002, the executive in charge of CNN International admitted that CNN censored the news so as not to inflame public opinion.

During the Gulf War, CNN was run by maverick mogul Ted Turner and since then was often accused of not only serving U.S. government interests, but also reflecting Turner's liberal biases. Now Turner is out, and CNN is owned by AOL Time Warner, the largest media company in the world. CNN news is not only broadcast by cable and satellite around the world, it is pushed to AOL's millions of users, through web browsers, in airports and in *Time* magazine, and every other corner of the AOL Time Warner empire.

In many ways, CNN has become a symbol and reality of the global information imbalance where Western media are the loudest voices. Osama bin Laden's charismatic hatred has appealed to many who resent America's massive global footprint, its dominance of world culture. CNN is part of this dominance. But perhaps we shouldn't expect that to be explained on the twenty-four-hour news network.

Here are some comments about CNN coverage from journalists and observers:

> CNN advertises itself as the world news leader, but its true spots have been showing during the past one month. Since September 11, it has virtually reduced itself to a local channel obsessed with only American news. What's more, it has assumed the role of an official American broadcaster. In fact, it's not lack of news sense or general journalistic incompetence we are talking about. CNN's problem is of bias.
>
> Rajeev Shukla, *Indian Express*

> CNN has been changing the brand name of its coverage of the terrorist attacks and the aftermath—from "America Under Attack" to "America's New War" to "War Against Terror." In all this, the television networks and their brand name correspondents have found it convenient to show and tell only one side of the story.
>
> S. Raghotham, *The Hoot,* India

TEN WAYS TO LOOK LIKE A CNN CORRESPONDENT

By Ayeda, in the *Friday Times*, Pakistan's weekly independent paper.

10. Pretend to be in grave danger while reporting from the roof of the Marriott, Islamabad.
9. Never learn how to pronounce "Pakistan."
8. Get a U.S. marine escort to help you do your groceries.
7. Bond with the locals by hanging out at Muddy's Café.
6. Carry big black cameras with CNN stickers pasted all over them.
5. Always wear a safari jacket (esp. when in big cities).
4. Wear a CNN t-shirt.
3. Wear a CNN hat.
2. Wear CNN underwear.
1. Hunt for the biggest lunatics to put on air.

CNN is becoming slicker and slicker and decidedly mainstream, offering cookie-cutter news, driven by the agendas of the powerful. The news world today, with its lingo and frames of reference, is a world of its own. "It hasn't done much to improve the way we get our news," Tom Rosensteil, of the Committee of Concerned Journalists, wrote in the *New Republic* a couple of years back. "In certain ways, the network has even had a pernicious effect on the rest of journalism; it has accelerated the loss of control news organizations have over content, which in turn has bred a rush to sensationalism and an emphasis on punditry and interpretation at the expense of old-fashioned reporting. . . . The constant clatter of its 24-hour programming is more flattening than deepening."

Perhaps that is one reason why much of television news reporting itself is often more distancing than involving. The classic journalist—someone with ideas, values, and interpretative skills—has been replaced by the "post-journalist" packager, who imposes a standardized format on news programming. David Altheide and Robert Snow call this "information mechanics" in their book *Media Worlds in the Post Journalism Era*. "We are post journalism and very much in the age of media talent, performers and actors," they write. With some notable exceptions—reporting by Aaron Brown and Nic Robertson in Afghanistan—it is no longer the individual, creative work of journalists that gives us news of the world, but rather standard templates, routines, and typical courses of action. No wonder so much news looks the same, no matter where it comes from.

In August 2002, I had a chance to hang out with a CNN correspondent who confirmed that the network was deliberately softening the news, with daily meetings to reformulate its news flow so as to better compete with Fox News. It also became controversial, especially for its Middle East coverage that both Israelis and Palestinians found "biased." Israeli cable stations temporarily dropped CNN, replacing it with the more overtly supportive Fox News. (CNN was reinstated after it agreed to pay a higher fee.) When I was in South Africa in late August 2002, I saw Islamic groups carrying signs that read "Boycott CNN." CNN was spelled with a *C* with a cents marker on it. A local columnist in the *Star* in Johannesburg blasted the network for giving the notion of "dumbing down news" new meaning. She singled out Connie Chung's overheated broadcasts, which specialize in milking emotional moments out of tragic situations.

I would only note that CNN does offer some serious and well-considered coverage from experienced correspondents like Charlayne Hunter Gault and Garrick Utley (who is known by insiders as "Mr. Context") and commentators like Jeff Greenfield and others. (Utley and other senior correspondents were fired in January 2003 to bring in younger reporters.) CNN is a well-known news brand designed with a "look" that is instantly recognizable and, at the same time, often instantly forgettable. Its sameness can deaden as often as enlighten. CNN's "revolution" turned out to be fusing the most innovative technology with the most conventional programming. Ted Turner was not always known as a news lover. Back in 1976, four years before the advent of CNN, he once actually replaced a news anchor on the local television station he owned with a dog, a German shepherd. "I hate the news," he said back then. "News is evil."

Now, the team he created promises to keep us informed until the world ends. I am watching you, CNN.

Looking for Light at a Time of Darkness: From the News Dissector's Weblog

New Year's Eve, 2001

New Year's Eve is a time for assessing where I have been and where I want to go. It is a time for resolutions. I am an optimist by nature, and so, at the start of a new year, I would like to take singer Bobby McFerrin's advice to heart: "Don't worry, be happy."

After all, unlike thousands of Americans, Afghans, and others, we at MediaChannel.org are alive to fight another day in what feels increasingly like a war between media competitors and those of us who want to change the media. As this crisis in communications both takes on permanency and seems more urgent than ever, I want to rededicate myself to the battle—a battle that seems to have taken longer than Mao's Long March.

For decades now, I have been marching, as the late German activist Rudi Dutschke once put it, "through the institutions." From student publications to maverick magazines. From the Liberation News Service to alternative radio. From dissecting radio news to local on-air television reporting and producing. From local television to cable news networks. From a fledgling CNN to ABC's news magazine *20/20*.

And then, the insider became an outsider again in the mid-1980s, when I "defected" into the volatile world of independent production. Ever since, along with making television shows and films, I've been writing books, making speeches, panelizing and columnizing, and for the last two years, Mediachanneling. At heart, I am a media maker, committed to covering underreported stories and offering more diverse perspectives.

I want my work to be read and seen, and I want my often-dissident voice heard. At first, it seemed like "cool running" (a Jamaican Rasta expression), as I became part of clubs that I was surprised would have me as a member. I worked my way into the media, but getting heard was a bit harder. Wouldn't you know it? There was more than just a little barrier in my way.

It's called the media system, a consolidating and interwoven ganglia of big corporate combines that tend to be at each other's throats but who also tend to think and act the same way. They seek to monopolize the means of communication and along with it, the marketplace of ideas. Fifty of them controlled the U.S. media ten years ago. Now it's down to ten. Nine. Eight. Seven. Six....

My system-questioning instincts were at odds with their largely uncritical system-supporting mission.

I wanted to make change and a difference. They believe if it ain't broke (in their terms), why fix it?

I identified with the aspirations of media heroes like the late I. F. Stone, who defined his goals in these terms: "To give a little comfort to the oppressed, to write the truth exactly as I saw it, to make no compromises other than those that are demands of quality imposed by my own inadequacies...."

That's one agenda. But by its very nature, it challenges the ethos and values of many of those on the inside of the media system. They want to make money more than they want to make media. For them, making media is primarily a means to making money.

Impossible Dream?

To give these devils their due, these companies and their networks often disseminate engaging programming while in pursuit of their bottom line. And they know how to build and hold audiences. Mass audiences. They excel at marketing themselves and those that sponsor their programming. They know how to package "product" in ways that are often seductive and influential, even illuminating. They also offer us a window into the world they want us to know about. The problem is that their world is often worlds apart from the one I want to live in, know about or tell people about. It's simple: we need to change the media system, but *how* we do that is not so simple.

To add broader views requires building a constituency for holding media accountable. It means lobbying for regulation in the public interest and the validity of the idea of the public interest itself.

Is this some impossible dream?

My feelings about what's achievable go back and forth like alternate sides of the street parking in New York City. On

> **"Big calamities of this sort make you think about things, and I think that is something that people have to do, is just think more."**
>
> **— JOHN SAYLES, filmmaker**

Mondays and Wednesdays, I am on the left side, tilting at the windmills, trying to speak my truths to power. On Tuesdays and Thursdays, I am on the other side, realizing the limits and justifying the time spent in terms of a larger duty, but without feeling I have much of a chance of breaking through. My hunch is that most wannabe media reformers feel this way. We are driven by our anger and our values. Fortunately, many of us don't get disillusioned because we have few illusions to start with.

On the other hand (always that other hand), history happens, and nothing stays the same. In my career, I covered and was supportive of movements that toppled segregation, ended apartheid, and helped end a war. All of those outcomes seemed impossible at the beginning. And so it is with this media war. Power always seems permanent—until it fragments, cracks, loses credibility, and arouses opposition. And so I ask:

Who determined that ten companies should control the media?

Who elected Rupert Murdoch? (The answer is 126 banks!)

Who decided that AOL Time Warner has a right to control the Internet?

Who gave NBC/CBS/VIACOM/ABC/DISNEY the means to decide what we should and shouldn't know?

Not I.

And not you either.

What will it take for folks to realize that programming is a verb as well as a noun and that all around the world there are overlooked people with lots to say, lots to report, and lots to propose. Today's central story line is a global one and one that is still unfolding.

Mediachannel.org started with twenty affiliates. We now have 1,000. The hits are multiplying. Interest is growing. Three years ago, Mediachannel.org was just an idea. Now it is a vibrant resource for research, diverse views, suppressed news, advocates, activists, and journalists.

Can we keep going? Can we learn how to be effective and prevail in our war of ideas? Can those of us who want change and a just, public interest work together across boundaries and borders to create a media that is worthy of a just world?

This is a dark time. It is a time of terror, of political pessimism, and for many, of personal paralysis.

It is also a time to look for light.

In that pursuit, I am comforted and inspired by the empowering truth in these words of the late James Baldwin, an American writer of color and consciousness: "One discovers the light in darkness; that is what darkness is for, but everything in our lives depends on how to bear the light. It is necessary, while in darkness, to know that there is a light somewhere, to know that in oneself, there is a light waiting to be found. What the light reveals is danger, and what it demands is faith."

Return to Normalcy?

How the Media Has Covered the War on Terrorism

Project for Excellence in Journalism

JANUARY 28, 2002

The news media reacted to the terrorist attacks of September 11 with great care, worried about not getting ahead of the facts. Over time, however, the press is inching back toward pre–September 11 norms of behavior, according to a new study of press coverage of the war on terrorism, conducted by the Project for Excellence in Journalism with Princeton Survey Research Associates. (The Project for Excellence in Journalism is a journalism think tank affiliated with Columbia University Graduate School of Journalism and is funded by the Pew Charitable Trusts.)

The study involved a detailed examination of 2,496 stories contained on television, magazines, and newspapers in three phases of the crisis: September 13–15, November 13–15, and December 10–12, as well as the closest weekend Sunday shows and news magazines. For the purpose of the study, the following were examined: four newspapers (*The New York Times, The Washington Post,* Cleveland's *Plain Dealer,* and *The Fresno Bee*), two news magazines (*Time* and

Newsweek), four nightly news broadcasts (ABC, CBS, NBC, and PBS), the three main network morning shows, the Sunday talk shows, three weeknight talk shows (*Larry King Live, The Charlie Rose Show,* and *Hardball with Chris Matthews*), *Nightline,* and relevant segments of three prime-time network news magazines (*Dateline, 20/20,* and *60 Minutes II*). The study also included an examination of two cable nightly newscasts (Fox's *Special Report with Brit Hume*[1] and CNN's *NewsNight*).

The study claims that at the beginning of the crisis, solid sourcing and factualness dominated the coverage of the bombings and their aftermath. A full 75 percent of what the press reported was a straightforward accounting of events—but here is what happened afterward.

As the story moved to the war in Afghanistan, analysis and opinion swelled—so much so that the level of factualness declined to levels *lower* than those seen in the middle of the Clinton–Lewinsky scandal. The early coverage may help account for why we saw the first measurable upturn in public approval of the press in fifteen years. But the changes in coverage offer a caution about why that approval has started to fall again. Has the news media become jingoistic in covering the war amid intense Pentagon restrictions? Or is there either a liberal or negative tilt to the coverage?

The study found that during the periods examined, the press heavily favored the viewpoints of the administration and the viewpoints of U.S. officials—as high as 71 percent early on. But over time, the balance of viewpoints has broadened. Even then, what might be considered criticism remained minimal—below 10 percent.

TABLE 12.1 Coverage of the Crisis[1]

	Sept.	Nov.	Dec.	Total
Fact	75%	63%	63%	69%
Analysis	14%	21%	22%	18%
Opinion	9%	11%	10%	10%
Speculation	2%	4%	4%	3%
Total	100%	100%	100%	100%

[1]For all tables, totals may not equal 100% due to rounding.

After the press earned high-approval marks from the public and praise from critics for its coverage, the study set out to probe why. To that end, it looked at a cross-section of the news media to examine the sourcing, verification, and range of viewpoints in the coverage. Among the findings were the following:

- In the earliest days, the news media tended to avoid interpretation. Just 25 percent of the coverage was analysis, opinion, and speculation—including even the talk shows and the opinion pages.
- By December, that percentage had swelled to close to 36 percent of all the reportage.
- The number of sources cited as evidence in stories also declined over time, though it is still relatively high. The level of on-the-record sources has remained consistently high—75 percent of all sources.

On talk shows, journalists often seemed to luxuriate in sounding not like knowledgeable experts on television stages, but like anyone else standing in a barroom. For example, the death of Osama bin Laden's third-in-command for CNN's Margaret Carlson on December 17 was "another reason to be cheerful." Or, "Having Osama bin Laden on trial in the United States of America is a nightmare," Cokie Roberts declared on ABC's *This Week* November 18. "With any luck, you know, he is—he is found dead."

One reason for the decline in sourcing and factualness as well as the rise in interpretation over time may be the restrictions the government is imposing on journalists' access to information. "The restrictions are unprecedented and they are successful," ABC National Security correspondent John McWethy told a panel at Columbia University Graduate School of Journalism last week. The evidence strongly suggests that coverage is more factual when journalists have more information and that it becomes more interpretative, perhaps ironically, when they have less.

OTHER OVERALL FINDINGS

- It is an oversimplification to suggest that since the United States has won the war against the Taliban, the press has returned to a so-called normal diet of softer news. Even on programs that often have less in the way of traditional hard news, such as morning television, the coverage of the war on terrorism actually increased from the November-to-December periods, after a significant decline from September to November.

- Even if news of the war was easy to find, what Americans know about it varies drastically, depending on what medium they get their information from. Television news, for instance, is measurably less likely to include criticism of the administration than the print media.
- Contrary to the suggestions of Fox News executives, there is no evidence that CNN is less "pro-American" than Fox or has some liberal tilt. To the contrary, there is no appreciable difference in the likelihood of CNN to air viewpoints that dissent from American policy than there is Fox. This may not be anything to boast about. Both channels tended to favor pro-administration viewpoints more than most other newscasts—even most talk shows.
- Just as the Project found in the Clinton–Lewinsky scandal, those who know the least may be the most prone to offer their opinions. As a rule, the weaker a story's sourcing, the more likely it is to be interpretive. The better the sourcing, the less likely it is to interpret.

The three phases of the crisis examined in the study each offered distinct story lines. The first phase, September 13–15, began with the day the television media returned to regular news programming. The press focused on a nation in shock. Airlines remained grounded. President Bush was still five days from addressing a joint session of Congress to outline the U.S. response. The coverage focused on four themes—the potential war on terrorism; the September attacks and rescue efforts; personal connections stories; and citizen, community, and state response.

The second phase of the study examined the media two months later, from November 13–15. The Northern Alliance was making major gains in the north. The Taliban was fleeing the Afghan capital of Kabul, but it was still unclear whether this was a collapse or a strategic regrouping. The press coverage focused on the action in Afghanistan, the war on terrorism in general, and the international response.

The third phase of the study examined December 10–12. The Taliban had fled Kandahar to the mountains around Tora Bora. The U.S. military focus had turned to the hunt for bin Laden, Taliban leader Mullah Omar, and other al Qaeda leaders. The coverage focused on action in Afghanistan, the fight against terrorism in general, and continuing community and civic response to the September attacks.

Public reaction to the coverage was initially extremely positive. By November, indeed, the Pew Research Center for the People and the Press found the first upturn in broad public support for the press in fifteen years. More Americans suddenly considered the press accurate, professional, moral, caring about people, and patriotic—after years of steady decline. Newspaper circulation and television audience numbers spiked.[2]

What exactly was it that people liked? "Timeliness," "comprehensiveness," and "informativeness," were the reasons survey respondents most often volunteered. Few people complained of bias and sensationalism. They liked the coverage, even though they found it tiring and depressing. In short, researchers concluded, people craved the information and felt the media provided it.

With time, that sentiment has begun to change. The percentage of Americans who think the press has done an "excellent" job covering the crisis has declined steadily, from 56 percent in September to 30 percent by mid-November, the last data to date.[3]

What accounts for the declining public approval? For years, surveys, focus groups, and other research sources have found consistent patterns in what people say they *don't* want from the press. For instance, people dislike anonymous sourcing. They want information more than interpretation. They resent journalists' offering what they think rather than what they know. They dislike hype and the sense that the media is manufacturing and sensationalizing stories.

As the war on terrorism progressed, the press began to rely more on the methods and habits disliked by the public. In the months ahead, as the war broadens beyond Afghanistan and becomes harder to see, the pressures on journalists to resort to these means of presentation are likely to only increase.

JUST THE FACTS

In the early days after September 11, critics praised the press for returning to a style of coverage that stuck more to reporting facts than interpreting them and for a notable caution about conveying rumor and speculation. "The word of the day is steady, steady," Dan Rather said out loud on CBS the day of the attacks. "We are going to try to separate the rumors from the facts."

To examine whether this impression was true, the study looked at every story pertaining to the war on terrorism during the nine days studied. Each statement or assertion was noted as one of the following: a fact, a piece of analysis that could be attributed to some kind of reporting, or an unattributed opinion or piece of speculation. Each paragraph was then categorized by which type of statement predominated.

In the early days of September, the coverage was strikingly straightforward. More than three quarters (75 percent) of all the coverage was factual—here is what happened—as opposed to analysis or opinion. Opinion and speculation accounted for just 11 percent of the reportage. Analysis made up 14 percent.

The coverage was also notably well documented. Nearly half of the coverage (45 percent) cited four or more sources. More than three quarters of all sources were named (76 percent).

The reporting was highly factual and well sourced in September across the more traditional news genres—evening news, morning news, and newspapers. Facts were not as dominate on the talk shows (54 percent) and during the prime time hours (52 percent).

By November, the coverage began to shift, becoming more analytical. Factual reporting dropped by 12 percentage points to 63 percent. Analysis rose by half, to 21 percent. The amount of punditry grew to 15 percent. In December, the numbers remained close to the November levels.

The level of documentation, however, shifted with time. By December, the percentage of stories citing four or more sources had dropped from more than 40 percent to just above a quarter (29 percent). The percentage of stories citing just one source had grown from 20 percent to 25 percent.

Why the change?

One reason may be that in the earliest days, as Americans were digging out of the shock and rubble, a premium was put on avoiding undue panic and speculation. As the situation stabilized and the war moved overseas, the temptation to analyze and speculate naturally increased.

Another factor may be access. In September, the story was largely a domestic one—and in the media's backyard in Washington and New York. Eyewitnesses and people with unique stories to tell were easier to find. The unrelenting financial cutbacks, particularly in television, were less of a factor when the events were occurring in the media's hometown.

As the war moved abroad, the Pentagon made access to soldiers and the battlefield more difficult than it has ever been. Websites with previously public information were suddenly removed. Sources quit talking. Reporters say they have never seen the Pentagon as intimidated about talking to the press as they are now. When facts are hard to come by, the press (as other studies have shown) tends to fill the vacuum with analysis, opinion, and speculation.

Even so, when the press was citing sources, a high percentage of them remained on the record, even if they were offering more analysis than strictly facts (76 percent in September and November, 73 percent in December).

SOME MEDIA ARE MORE FACT-ORIENTED THAN OTHERS

Newspapers stuck to the facts more than television. In September, 85 percent of what appeared in the papers was strictly factual. On television, it was 20 points

TABLE 12.2   Reporting in Newspapers

	Sept.	Nov.	Dec.	Total
Fact	85%	81%	73%	82%
Analysis	10%	13%	23%	13%
Punditry	5%	5%	4%	5%
Total	100%	100%	100%	100%

lower—64 percent. Over time, newspapers saw this level of strictly factual accounts decline, but even at its lowest, it was higher than it was in broadcast.

On television, the mix of fact versus opinion seemed to rise and fall according to the story being covered. During the collapse of the Taliban in November, for instance, factual reporting fell to less than half of all the coverage (to 46 percent, down from 64 percent in September) as journalists and experts speculated about whether the retreat was real, what would happen next, and whether al Qaeda would follow.

In December, during the hunt for bin Laden, factualness increased again (to 56 percent). Journalists and experts seemed more reluctant to guess about the terrorist leaders whereabouts, a matter that could easily be proved right or wrong.

THE CLINTON SCANDAL COMPARISON

If coverage of the war has become less straightforwardly factual with time, that fact contrasts to how the coverage evolved during the last great political upheaval the press contended with—the scandal involving Monica Lewinsky

TABLE 12.3   Reporting on Television

	Sept.	Nov.	Dec.	Total
Fact	64%	46%	56%	57%
Analysis	18%	28%	22%	22%
Punditry	17%	26%	22%	21%
Total	100%	100%	100%	100%

TABLE 12.4   Early Coverage: Clinton Scandal vs. War

	Clinton[1]	War[2]
Fact	59%	75%
Analysis	23%	14%
Punditry	18%	11%
Total	100%	100%

[1]Jan. 21–24, 1998
[2]Sept. 13–15, 2001

and Bill Clinton. During the Lewinsky scandal, the press was initially condemned for rushing to judgment, but over time, members became more factual and cautious. In the war on terrorism, the press was praised for caution at first, but it has become more interpretive since. By December, indeed, less of the press coverage of the war on terrorism was strictly factual (63 percent) than was true six weeks into the coverage of the Clinton–Lewinsky scandal (74 percent). In fact, the level of punditry in the later war coverage is actually higher than the amount later in the Lewinsky scandal.

The two stories differ in obvious ways. One was sordid and controversial. There were arguments about its importance and appropriateness. The other is an international crisis of undoubted significance. But the differences in the coverage say something about how the press works. The quick praise of the media's

TABLE 12.5   Later Coverage: Clinton Scandal vs. War

	Clinton[1]	War[2]
Fact	74%	63%
Analysis	18%	22%
Punditry	8%	14%
Total	100%	100%

[1]March 5–6, 1998
[2]Dec. 10–12, 2001

early work may have led some journalists to become less careful. The early criticism in the Lewinsky story may have caused more restraint later on.

The differences in the two events are likely a factor as well. The Lewinsky scandal occurred in media's home field. The war may have begun there, but it soon moved into mountains and caves in central Asia. Historians have long referred to the difficulty of getting accurate wartime information as "the fog of war." Nonetheless, one might expect a more factual tenor to coverage of war—a matter of life and death—than that of the ultimate media sport, a political scandal in Washington. In fact, some of the factual reporting in the Clinton scandal turned out to be inaccurate. While that is also often the case in wartime—for example, the precision bombing and Patriot missiles of the Gulf War proved far less effective than first reported—there is no basis at this point to suggest some misreporting of the war.

ARE YOU AMERICAN OR NOT?

From the start, the question of patriotism and perspective in the press coverage was an issue. Television journalists sparred over whether to wear flag lapel pins. Networks jousted over who would have the most notable flag in their logo. At least three network news presidents made news for their remarks over the question of perspective. ABC News President David Westin apologized for seeming too detached from patriotism in remarks made at Columbia Journalism School. CNN President Walter Issacson made news for a memo in which he said he did not want his network to appear to be "simply reporting for their (the Taliban) vantage or perspective."

Most combative was Fox News President Roger Ailes, a former Republican political consultant. Ailes suggested that Fox is more patriotic than other news organizations, singling out CNN, against which his network competes directly for advertising revenue.

Ailes suggested that CNN has generally been unfair to conservatives and has bent over backward to be fair to the enemies of the United States. "Suddenly, our competition has discovered 'fair and balanced,' but only when it's radical terrorism versus the United States," Ailes was quoted as saying in *The New York Times,* December 3.

At Fox, "We are not anti-the-United-States," Ailes said. "We just do not assume that America's wrong first."[4]

The study decided to find out to what extent the press culture was offering a mix of viewpoints on stories where the American point of view was an issue. This is a subset of all the stories studied. On many stories—such as those about

TABLE 12.6   Viewpoints in All Media (Relevant Stories)

	Sept.	Nov.	Dec.	Total
All Pro-U.S.	54%	39%	47%	49%
Mostly Pro-U.S.	17%	13%	3%	13%
Mixed	20%	38%	42%	30%
Mostly Dissenting	6%	4%	3%	5%
All Dissenting	2%	6%	4%	3%
Total	100%	100%	100%	100%

clean-up at Ground Zero, or the personal stories of victims and their families—the question of the propriety or political wisdom of the official American response was not at issue.

To measure viewpoint, the study examined all relevant stories and then tallied whether the statements and assertions in the story were entirely pro–official U.S. response (100 percent) or predominantly so (at least 74 percent), mixed (25 percent to 74 percent), predominantly anti–official U.S. response (less than 25 percent) or entirely anti–official U.S. response.

Overall, any suggestion that the media is by nature anti-administration or anti-American, or is somehow detached from being an American press, is simply not borne out by the numbers. The press coverage has been demonstrably pro-administration or pro–U.S. policy in the viewpoints it has reflected. Taking all the coverage combined, 49 percent of the applicable stories contained only viewpoints that favored U.S. policy. Another 13 percent contained predominantly pro–U.S. policy viewpoints. The percentage of stories that might be perceived as largely providing "the other side," or dissenting from the administration's point of view, never exceeded 10 percent.

Still there has been a growing balance of viewpoints over time. In September, just 20 percent provided a mix of perspectives. That, however, began to change in November. The percent of stories with a mix of views nearly doubled to 38 percent.

One reason may well have been events. The bombing in Afghanistan was continuing but was not yet decisive, and only a week or so before, it appeared to have perhaps stalled. It was not clear whether the Taliban were really collapsing or regrouping. The issue of federalizing airport security works was also under debate at the time, and it broke along highly partisan lines.

TABLE 12.7   Viewpoints in Newspapers (Relevant Stories)

	Sept.	Nov.	Dec.	Total
All Pro-U.S.	41%	23%	38%	35%
Mostly Pro-U.S.	19%	18%	2%	15%
Mixed	30%	46%	51%	39%
Mostly Dissenting	7%	7%	3%	6%
All Dissenting	3%	6%	7%	4%
Total	100%	100%	100%	100%

By December, as the U.S. military victory became more decisive, the lines of support had become clearer. Stories were either entirely pro–United States (47 percent), or they provided a balance of views (42 percent). Interestingly, the medium makes a difference. Television is more decidedly pro-administration (83 percent mostly or entirely in September, 62 percent in November, 74 percent in December).

Print, however, is more circumspect. By December, half of all relevant newspaper stories gave a mix of pro and dissenting views, an increase of 21 percentage points and the highest of any medium by far—in fact, 20 points higher than broadcast. Broadcast stories, by contrast, were twice as likely to be entirely pro-administration as to offer a mix of perspectives.

Within television, moreover, the genre of show makes some difference. Across time, talk shows carried a greater percent of stories with mixed and dis-

TABLE 12.8   Viewpoints on Television (Relevant Stories)

	Sept.	Nov.	Dec.	Total
All Pro-U.S.	68%	54%	59%	63%
Mostly Pro-U.S.	15%	8%	4%	11%
Mixed	10%	30%	31%	19%
Mostly Dissenting	5%	1%	4%	4%
All Dissenting	1%	7%	2%	3%
Total	100%	100%	100%	100%

senting views than morning or evening news, though they were still heavily pro-American. Almost two-thirds of the talk show assertions were mostly or entirely pro-administration in September, rising to better than three-quarters in November, and sliding down to less than six out of every ten in December.

The views were even more one-sided on morning television (82 percent mostly or entirely pro-administration in September, 61 percent in November, and 80 percent in December.)

On the traditional evening newscasts, the balance fluctuated as the story changed (93 percent mostly or entirely pro-United States in September, down to 45 percent in November, back to 83 percent in December).

CNN VERSUS FOX

For all Roger Ailes' talk of CNN's possible bias and Fox's patriotism, it isn't borne out in the numbers the study examined. With regard to the two signature evening newscasts of the two cable networks over nine days, no appreciable difference was noted.

In fact, with consideration to all three phases studied together, the sample is admittedly small. Most of the stories on these programs were not oriented to discussing the U.S. policy. Still, of the limited number of stories on CNN's *NewsNight* that did, 77 percent were entirely supportive of administration policy—with not even a hint of dissent. Just three stories related to U.S. policy over the nine days studied offered a mix of viewpoints, and only a single story focused on dissent.

On Fox's *Special Report with Brit Hume,* the numbers are also highly pro-U.S. policy. In the limited sample, 56 percent of the relevant stories were unequivocally supportive of the administration. Another 22 percent were mostly supportive, and 22 percent offered a mix of pro and dissenting viewpoints. No stories were primarily dissenting.

At least based on this snapshot, no meaningful difference exists between the two cable outlets' signature programs in presenting viewpoints. But together, both appear less likely to offer a mix of viewpoints than their over-the-air counterparts. Fox's motto is "We Report, You Decide," somehow suggesting less punditry. Is it true on the network's signature newscast? Across time, Fox's *Special Report* stayed at slightly over 50 percent fact, roughly 30 percent analysis, and 14 percent punditry. That is less straight-factual reporting and more punditry than we saw on any of the three evening broadcasts on ABC, CBS, or NBC. There, the level of factualness was closer to 65 percent. The level of punditry never rose above 7 percent. CNN's *NewsNight,* in contrast, varied widely, from 38 percent fact and 22 percent punditry in November, to 87 percent fact and 6 percent punditry in December.

When it came to naming sources, both CNN's and Fox's signature newscasts had comparatively high percentages of anonymity, as high as 57 percent on CNN in September and 44 percent on Fox in December, compared with a high of 27 percent for the media overall. What differs between the cable signature newscasts is tone. On Fox, for instance, Osama bin Laden's cave, in a Geraldo Rivera report December 10, is not a cave but a "rat's nest."

Not all of the tonal differences, however, are so blatant. On November 15, *Special Report* host Brit Hume suggested a more subtle disdain for anyone doubting the efficacy of U.S. military strategy with this segue: "We have to take a quick break for other headlines here, but when we return, find out what some of these military pessimists are saying now. . . ." Or listen to correspondent Brian Wilson describe the Republican economic plan: "There is some movement on an economic stimulus package that could put money in your pocket."

At CNN, while the people he interviews may offer the same range of perspectives, anchorman Aaron Brown is more vanilla—to a point where it is hard to disagree with him. "It's either been the longest three months in history or the shortest," Brown mused on December 11. "At times today to me, at least, it seemed like both." Or Brown trying to form a question for former general Wesley Clark: "All right, let's start ratcheting up the military option. Who do we bomb, where do we invade, who do we go after, how do we do it, where do we start? Where do we start?"

WHO'S YOUR SOURCE?

Another major issue facing the press culture in recent years has been sourcing. Cutbacks in newsrooms, the speed of the news cycle, and the scaling back of foreign coverage all have put pressure on the ability of journalists to have the time, resources, opportunity, and source lists to gather news carefully. All of these issues came into play during the Lewinsky scandal, for instance, when the Project found the use of single-sourced stories exceeded even the levels of punditry. Was the coverage of the war on terrorism showing signs of similar problems?

NAMED VERSUS UNNAMED SOURCES

For the most part, as noted previously, the sources were on the record, and they stayed that way. In both September and November, three-quarters (76 percent) of all sources were named.

TABLE 12.9 Sourcing in All Media

	Sept.	Nov.	Dec.	Total
Named Sources	76%	76%	73%	76%
Unnamed Sources	24%	24%	27%	24%
Total	100%	100%	100%	100%

That remained true across all media. The outlets with the lowest level of named sourcing, interestingly, were news magazines.

NUMBER OF SOURCES

Another sign of how solid a piece of reporting may be is how many sources it cites. Here, over time, the number fell considerably.

In September, nearly half of all stories (45 percent) cited four or more sources. By December, that had fallen to 29 percent. The number of stories with one source grew from 20 percent to 25 percent. The number of stories citing just two sources rose from 11 percent to 16 percent. This was true across the board. While print had the most sources, the number of stories with four sources or more dropped from 64 percent to 52 percent over the course of the study. In television, the number of stories with four or more sources fell from 27 percent to 18 percent.

This matters, in part, because as found in other studies, fewer sources translates into more opinion. Citizens might well expect the opposite: that only those journalists with the most sourcing and knowledge might venture into analysis

TABLE 12.10 Number of Sources

	Total			Newspapers			Television		
	Sept.	Nov.	Dec.	Sept.	Nov.	Dec.	Sept.	Nov.	Dec.
One-two	31%	37%	41%	18%	19%	24%	46%	53%	50%
Three	9%	10%	14%	8%	8%	11%	8%	11%	15%
Four+	45%	43%	29%	64%	62%	52%	27%	27%	18%

or opinion. But just the reverse is true. The accounts with the fewest sources seem to take up the slack by offering the most interpretation.

DIFFERENCES WITHIN NEWS GENRES
Newspapers

Newspapers remained the most factual, balanced, and widely sourced of any news outlets studied. They also changed character less as the crisis shifted in topic over time.

For the first two phases of the study, facts accounted for more than 80 percent of all the newspaper coverage, including the opinion pages (85 percent in September, 81 percent in November). By December, facts had begun to slide, though they still accounted for roughly three-quarters (73 percent) of the reporting. Opinion and speculation never rose above 5 percent.

One question of interest this study raised was, "Are there substantial differences among papers in general, or among large- and smaller-sized papers?" Generalizations are hard to draw from looking at four institutions, but the numbers do suggest that the answer is yes. Cleveland's *Plain Dealer* and *The Fresno Bee*, for instance, relied less on anonymous sources than either the *Post* or the *Times*. The smaller papers began with factual accounts making up more of their coverage. Both shifted more toward analysis and punditry over time. The reason was that they began to rely more on syndicated columnists for their coverage, a reflection of the high costs of covering the war with reporters. Interestingly, even from the start, both *The Plain Dealer* and the *Bee* relied little on wire service accounts. Instead, both leaned on staff writers to cover the crisis and often related the story back to events in their local communities.

In November, as the story moved to Afghanistan, the *Times* and *Post* began to show their muscle as news-gathering organizations with a broad reach of sources. *The Plain Dealer* and the *Bee*, by contrast, became even more local, increasing their reliance on community leaders as sources.

The New York Times was striking in that in December, it shifted more heavily toward interpretation. After more than 80 percent of its reporting constituted straightforward, factual accounts in September and November, that number dropped to 66 percent. The shift was toward analysis rather than outright opinion or speculation, which never rose above 5 percent.

Beyond that, what stands out between *The New York Times* coverage and *The Washington Post* coverage in the periods studied was how strikingly similar they were.

Time and Newsweek

When it came to coverage of the war in the three time periods studied, *Time* and *Newsweek* appeared to be very different animals.

Across all three time periods studied, *Time* stuck much more to the facts and was less concerned with analysis or opinion. In September, it was twice as likely as *Newsweek* to contain factual coverage (62 percent versus 34 percent). And *Time* was only about half as likely to publish pure punditry (13 percent for *Time* versus 22 percent of *Newsweek's*).

By November the factual nature of *Time* stood out even more. Fully 71 percent of *Time's* paragraphs were strictly factual. That is almost four times the percentage of *Newsweek's* factual paragraphs, which made up a mere 20 percent. *Newsweek* was also nearly four times as likely to offer opinion (19 percent versus 5 percent for *Time*). In addition, 60 percent of *Newsweek's* November coverage was analysis, compared with just a quarter of *Time's*.

In December, *Newsweek* became a little more factual, and *Time* offered slightly more opinion, though the gap between the two still remained solid. Factual reporting in *Newsweek* rose to just over a third (38 percent), while in *Time* it dropped slightly to two-thirds (65 percent). The percent of punditry in *Time* doubled to 11 percent, though there was still a greater percent in *Newsweek* (17 percent).

When it comes to sourcing, the two magazines had similar percentages of named versus unnamed sources (roughly 78 percent in September, and between 54 percent and 69 percent in November and December), but *Newsweek* tended to provide more sources per story. Part of the explanation is that *Time* was much more likely than *Newsweek* to run short factual sidebars and background boxes that offered no sourcing. In September and November, nearly a third of *Time's*

TABLE 12.11   Reporting in *Time* and *Newsweek*

	Sept.		Nov.		Dec.	
	Time	*Nwsk*	*Time*	*Nwsk*	*Time*	*Nswk*
Fact	62%	34%	71%	21%	65%	38%
Analysis	25%	44%	25%	60%	24%	45%
Punditry	13%	22%	5%	19%	11%	19%
Total	100%	100%	100%	100%	100%	100%

stories had no source, compared to less than one in ten for *Newsweek*. (The numbers evened out a bit in December: 12 percent unnamed sources for *Time*, 9 percent for *Newsweek*.)

Newsweek, on the other hand, consistently offered more sources for its coverage, though these sources may have been offering their opinion rather than facts—in every time period studied.

The two magazines differed in whom they chose as sources. Across all three time periods, *Newsweek* looked more to community leaders than did *Time*. *Newsweek*'s reliance on these leaders continued to rise across time, rising to 19 percent in December, while *Time*'s use of community leaders never rose above 7 percent.

By November, however, *Time* became much more focused on what international officials had to say—three times more likely as *Newsweek*, and in December four times more likely. *Newsweek*, in contrast, focused more on what U.S. officials had to say.

Morning Shows

In the first days following the attack, the network morning shows provided some of the most serious reporting around. It was full of facts and well sourced. Within the various broadcast genres studied, these shows had the greatest percent of factual reporting (74 percent) with only 12 percent opinion and speculation. In addition, it was clear where those facts were coming from. Fully 92 percent of the morning show sources were named, again higher than any other broadcast genre studied.

The morning shows also gave viewers more information from members of the public. On-scene sources, community leaders, families, friends, coworkers, and "people in the street" accounted for roughly half, 49 percent, of their

TABLE 12.12 Reporting in Morning News				
	Sept.	**Nov.**	**Dec.**	**Total**
Fact	74%	46%	55%	64%
Analysis	14%	28%	22%	19%
Punditry	12%	26%	22%	18%
Total	100%	100%	100%	100%

sourcing in early days. But if viewers in November were still relying primarily on morning shows for their news of the war, they were getting something quite different. Factual reporting dropped to less than half of the coverage, 46 percent. Analysis doubled to 26 percent, and punditry, too, more than doubled. And instead of offering the highest percentage of sources on the record in television, morning news offered the lowest.

Good Morning America

ABC's *Good Morning America (GMA)* stood out among the early shows for its seriousness and adherence to fact. In every period studied, *GMA*'s factualness outweighed that of the other morning shows. In December, the gap in factualness between *GMA* and CBS's *Early Show* reached 21 points (65 percent versus 44 percent).

These findings reaffirm an earlier study of October coverage by the Project, which found *GMA*'s story topics to be much more serious than the other network morning shows.[5] Here, the broad list of topics looks quite similar. The seriousness emerged in how the story line was developed.

The Early Show

CBS, on the other hand, is notable for its greater tendency toward punditry. Even in September, opinion mongering accounted for 18 percent of the coverage compared with 6 percent on *GMA* and 12 percent on *Today*. By November, punditry had risen to roughly a third of all *The Early Show* coverage (32 percent) and remained at that level in December.

While *The Early Show* had more talk than other networks, its coverage was more likely to include views that dissented from the administration. Of all the stories dealing with an administration view, 17 percent contained a mix of views and another 13 percent mostly dissented. In short, one in three contained dissenting voices compared to 19 percent on *GMA* and 17 percent on *Today*.

The *Today* Show

The *Today* show on NBC once again emerged as something of a hybrid between the more serious style of *Good Morning America* and the looser style of *The Early Show*. It was not as factual as *GMA*, for instance, but it was more so than CBS. It had more opinion mongering than ABC, but less than CBS.

One place where *Today* did stand out was that it had more sources per story—in all three time periods studied. In September, for instance, a quarter of its stories had at least four sources, compared with roughly one in ten stories on both *GMA* (13 percent) and *The Early Show* (10 percent).

The reasons for this discrepancy are hard to know. But it might be worth studying to see if it has anything to do with the synergy NBC has with its cable cousins, CNBC and MSNBC. Do correspondents who know that their stories may be broadcast multiple times across three networks have more time for more voices when they put those packages together?

Network Evening News

What about those who still turn to the four traditional network evening newscasts each night—ABC, CBS, NBC, and *The NewsHour with Jim Lehrer*? Overall, these shows were less given to punditry, but more likely to use anonymous sources, than other television newscasts. Their commitment to the story also changed less over time than was true on morning television, which moved away from the story by November, then returned to it somewhat more in the December period.

If one wanted to keep up with the war on terrorism on television, evening news was the most consistent source of information. In general, about two thirds of the evening newscast coverage was factual reporting, and one quarter was analysis. Unlike morning television, that level of factual reporting remained consistent in every month studied.

Evening news also had the fewest sources on the record of all broadcast genres (just 60 percent in September and December, though it spiked to nearly 80 percent in November). Much of the anonymity came from those programs' reliance on U.S. officials for information. Roughly half of the U.S. officials cited on the evening news were unnamed. Another reason may be the fact that stories on the nightly newscasts tend to be shorter than elsewhere.

Jennings, Brokaw, and Rather

The numbers for individual programs in this study are limited. Still in this snapshot, the three commercial network evening broadcasts looked strikingly similar in their coverage of this crisis so far: they were all highly factual; they all had similarly low levels of punditry; and they all had similarly high numbers of sources in each story. Perhaps, after nearly forty years of close competition, they have so assimilated each other's virtues that they have become indistinguishable in the way they are put together.

One of the few areas of difference (though the numbers of relevant stories over nine broadcasts are admittedly small) came in how likely each program was to offer viewpoints that did not necessarily support U.S. policy. CBS was the most likely to air stories that contained no dissent whatsoever, doing so 64 percent of the time when the subject of U.S. policy came up. NBC fell in the middle at 54 percent. ABC was the least likely to do so, 45 percent.

The *NewsHour*

The one program that stood out was PBS's *NewsHour with Jim Lehrer*, perhaps the most consistent broadcast program studied. *NewsHour* represents a striking mix. It has about the same level of straightforward factual accounts as the other networks. But the program seemed to avoid analysis, in which conclusions are attributed to facts and evidence, and it instead moved more into outright punditry. Roughly 17 percent of the program during the time periods studied was punditry, more than double that of other network evening newscasts. This tendency is almost certainly due to the show's format, which comprises packages followed by interview segments. It is interesting, however, that these interviews involve less analysis and more opinion. The Lehrer show also stood out for its use of named sources. In the three periods studied, 81 percent, 85 percent, and 97 percent of its sources were on the record.

Although the number of relevant stories was small, *NewsHour* was the evening news broadcast most likely to entirely support the administration's stance. Overall, more than three-quarters (77 percent) of its applicable stories entirely supported U.S. policy, the same as CNN's *NewsNight*.

So much for the supposed liberal slant of PBS—at least in the periods covered by this study.

Talk Shows

Talk shows comprise an increasingly large part of the television news landscape. In an effort to reduce its cost-per-minute of news time, even CNN, which once made its worldwide bureaus its hallmark, has fired scores of journalists and added more hours of talk to its broadcast day. While many talk shows generate relatively small audiences by broadcast standards, the genre cumulatively makes up a key part of the prime-time lineup of most cable networks.

For this study, we examined two types of talk programs, the Sunday show lineup on ABC, CBS, NBC, and CNN and a sample of weekday talk shows (*Larry King Live* on CNN, *Hardball with Chris Matthews* on MSNBC, and *The Charlie Rose Show* on PBS). Some journalists have speculated that one reason public approval of early press coverage of the crisis was so high was that even the talk shows seemed more factual than before. "I think even the cable shows themselves are somewhat more information focused," *The New York Times* Washington Bureau Chief Jill Abramson suggested at a Brookings Institution forum. "It isn't just a partisan or ideological debate about the war. That debate really isn't happening. . . . I don't sense as much that tone on shows like Larry King."[6]

Was this really true? For a short time, the answer was a relative yes. In September, just over half the statements on the talk shows (54 percent) were guest's offering factual information. The level of outright opinion and speculation was 30 percent. Even so, the talk shows in September were nearly four times more likely than the evening news and three times more likely than morning news to engage in opinion mongering. But by November, the talk shows abandoned even this measure of factuality. Factual accounts dropped to just 32 percent of what was on the talk shows; punditry surged to 40 percent; and analysis nearly doubled to 28 percent. In December, the talk shows were basically a three-way split between punditry, fact, and analysis.

At times, the speculation was as wild as ever. Consider the reaction on CNN's *Capital Gang* to the idea that the November crash of American Airlines Flight 587 in Queens might actually be an accident: "If it's an accident, there's never been an accident quite like it," columnist Robert Novak theorized.

"Within thirty minutes of the crash, before anybody really knew anything much, the government was asserting there's no evidence of sabotage, because they are so anxious for it not to be," agreed *National Review* editor Kate O'Beirne.

It was curious, *The Wall Street Journal* columnist Al Hunt added, "that just within a matter of weeks or months after this, that suddenly we have an unprecedented crash of this sort." With universal agreement on the conspiracy, even Connecticut Senator Joseph Lieberman conceded, that, yes, there had been similar air crashes, "but nothing exactly like it."

As for balance, as noted previously, the talk shows were slightly more likely than other broadcasts to provide some dissent about administration policies, though not nearly as much as in print. But the dissent existed only within a limited range. Of the viewpoints on the talk shows, 60 to 75 percent were predominantly or entirely pro-administration, depending on the time period. Outright criticism of U.S. policy never rose on the talk shows above 7 percent.

Sunday Shows

There were, despite the basic format of journalists' interviewing officials, clear differences among the four Sunday interview shows studied—ABC's *This Week,* CBS's *Face the Nation,* NBC's *Meet the Press,* and CNN's *Capital Gang.*

CNN's *Capital Gang* had the most outright punditry. Even in September, there was as much opinion mongering as fact on the program, 38 percent—the only show to do so soon. By November, punditry outweighed facts, accounting for more than 40 percent of the program in November and December. The supposedly staid *Face the Nation* was close behind. The CBS show saw a steady rise in punditry from 24 percent in September to 41 percent in November, and finally 43 percent in December. On *This Week* and *Meet the Press,* punditry fluctuated over time but only once (*Meet the Press* in November) did it exceed 30 percent.

Weeknight Talk

As a rule, talk shows on weeknights (*Larry King Live, Hardball with Chris Matthews,* and *The Charlie Rose Show*) were even less factual and more engaged in punditry than the Sunday talk shows—except for *Capital Gang.* Larry King started out the most factual of the bunch (more than two-thirds fact in September compared to 49 percent on *Hardball* and 30 percent on *Charlie Rose.*)

By November facts took a beating even from Larry King, falling to less than half (49 percent) of what was originally broadcast on his shows, though that was still more than twice that of *Hardball* (20 percent) and four times that of *Charlie Rose* (12 percent). In December, the three shows had flip-flopped. *Hardball* was the most factual (47 percent), followed by *Charlie Rose* (31 percent), with Larry King bringing up the rear (23 percent).

Apparently, it's all about the guest.

Nightline

ABC's *Nightline* stands out among media outlets, especially on television, for bucking the trend. As the press grew more interpretive, less factual, and not as heavily sourced with time, *Nightline* moved in the other direction. The program's reports became more factual. The level of punditry declined. More of its reporting was on the record, and the number of stories with multiple sources increased.

Nightline also stood out for being far more likely than any other television broadcast to provide views that dissented from the administration's—levels equal with print.

TABLE 12.13 *Reporting on Nightline*			
	Sept.	Nov.	Dec.
Facts	49%	74%	71%
Analysis	31%	15%	26%
Punditry	21%	11%	3%
Total	100%	100%	100%

Nightline also gave viewers an international view of the war that others on television did not. In November, nearly a third of its sources were international officials, well ahead of any other type of broadcast news show and more than twice that of the talk shows. By December, these foreign voices accounted for more than half (56 percent) of *Nightline* sources, compared with 20 percent on the evening news and 15 percent on the talk shows.

Prime-Time News Magazines

On prime-time magazines, such as *Dateline, 20/20,* and *60 Minutes II,* we can see the arc of the crisis and the return to media normalcy most clearly. In September, news in prime time became highly serious and dedicated exclusively to the crisis. By November, the war on terrorism was losing its place on these shows, and what did air tended to focus on emotional stories about heroes (Rudy Giuliani's exit interview as New York's mayor, with Barbara Walters and a firefighter who donated bone marrow) or victims (in this case, con artists prey-ing on survivors of the World Trade Center attacks). One researcher—having noted a habit of the shows to assemble everyday survivors in such stories for in-studio, group interviews—called these stories "victims on risers."

NOTES

1. Overall totals for the study, however, do not include Fox's *Special Report with Brit Hume*. See "Project Methodology," chapter 1.13.

2. Pew Research Center for the People and the Press, "Terror Coverage Boosts News Media's Image," November 28, 2001.

3. Despite this, the percentage of Americans who rate the coverage "good" or "excellent" remains comparatively high, above 70 percent.

4. Public survey work on the question has proved nuanced on the question of what Americans prefer. A Pew Research Center for the People and the Press study in November found that while 53 percent of people said they thought it more important that the government be safe than that the press have access, at the same time 73 percent thought it was more important for the press to tell all sides than to be pro-American.

5. Project for Excellence in Journalism, "Before and After, How the War on Terrorism Has Changed the News Agenda, Network Television, June to October, 2001," November 19, 2001.

6. Brookings/Harvard Forum, "The Role of the Press in the Anti-Terrorism Campaign: What the Public Thinks of News Coverage since September 11," November 28, 2001; available online at brookings.org/gs/research/press/112801.htm.

Project Methodology
Selection/Inclusion of Broadcasts and Publications
Project for Excellence in Journalism

Newspapers, news magazines, and broadcast news shows were chosen on an ad hoc basis to provide a snapshot of nationally influential media, as well as regional outlets. Diversity within the sample regarding audience, ownership, and editorial outlook was also a factor in selection.

Newspaper and network news stories were reviewed for three series of days: September 13–15, 2001; November 13–15, 2001; and December 10–12, 2001. Within each phase, the closest broadcast date of weekend talk shows and closest newsstand appearance of news magazines determined selection.

During the September 13–15 time frame, events dictated schedule revisions for network and cable news. However, these findings reflect the broadcasts that appeared during the regularly scheduled time periods (7:00 A.M. to 9:00 A.M., eastern time for weekday morning shows; 6:30 P.M. to 7:00 P.M., eastern time for evening news; and so on). Because network prime-time magazine shows were not presented in a uniform way during this period, a substitution was made. The hour of programming broadcast at 9:00 P.M., eastern time on Friday, September 14, on ABC, CBS, and NBC constitutes the prime-time magazine component for the initial phase of the study.

SOURCES AND SEARCH TERMS

Newspaper and news magazine stories were downloaded from the NEXIS database. To cast the widest possible net, broad language was employed. The original search term from September was appended as appropriate in November, and again in December, as dictated by changing story lines. The following reflects the final comprehensive statement as utilized for December stories:

> (Bin Laden) or (World Trade Center) or (WTC) or (Pentagon) or (airline!) or (terror!) or (anthrax) or (Afghan!) or (Taliban) or (Pakistan) or (Kabul) or (Northern Alliance) or (Al Qaeda) or (U.S. military) or (U.S. forces) or (tribunal)

Researchers screened newspaper stories and eliminated those that appeared in the business, sports, entertainment, or lifestyle sections. For both newspapers and news magazines, letters to the editor were eliminated. (Note: when the NEXIS database provided nearly identical stories from different editions of one newspaper, the longer of the two stories was coded.) Broadcast news show transcripts were downloaded in their entirety from the NEXIS database when available. In limited cases, professional transcript services or network websites served as sources for show transcripts.

Note: Fox transcripts were not made available until after all other coding was complete; as such, they are to be used for comparison purposes only. Results reported for particular time periods, genres, or project totals do not reflect Fox broadcasts.

SCREENING AND INCLUSION

A one-fifth rule was established for inclusion across all media. Only stories where one-fifth (20 percent) or more of the article was specific to the events of September 11, ensuing U.S. action or events, or background regarding terrorism, terrorists, and the like were included.

CODING

Researchers analyzed each news story in its entirety, working through the sequential variables. Project rules for coders were established prior to that process and were applied during all phases of coding.

INTERCODER RELIABILITY

Intercoder reliability measures the rate at which two coders, operating independently of one another, code the same material in the same way. Throughout the project, a researcher working off-site served as the control coder for print stories, while a senior project director worked as the control coder for broadcast stories. Intercoder testing occurred throughout the coding process, and no significant systematic errors were identified.

TABLE 13.1 Post-Terrorism Content Analysis: Selected Results, September through December 2001

1. Source	Total (#)				Newspapers (#)				Broadcast (#)				News Magazines (#)			
	Sept.	Nov.	Dec.	Total	Sept.	Nov.	Dec.	Total	Sept.	Nov.	Dec.	Total	Sept.	Nov.	Dec.	Total
Print																
Newspapers	627	315	228	1170												
New York Times	577	273	201	1051	577	273	201	1051								
Washington Post	259	127	107	493	259	127	107	493								
Cleve. Plain Dealer	202	120	70	392	202	120	70	392								
Fresno Bee	72	15	18	105	72	15	18	105								
	44	11	6	61	44	11	6	61								
News Magazines	50	42	27	119									50	42	27	119
Newsweek	22	16	11	49									22	16	11	49
Time	28	26	16	70									28	26	16	70
• Broadcast	569	343	414	1326					569	343	414	1326				
ABC	167	85	91	343					167	85	91	343				
G.M. America	82	36	39	157					82	36	39	157				
Wrld. Nws. Tonight	25	21	20	66					25	21	20	66				
Nightline	16	15	13	44					16	15	13	44				
20/20	17	2	5	24					17	2	5	24				
This Week	27	11	14	52					27	11	14	52				

1. Source	Total (#)				Newspapers (#)				Broadcast (#)				News Magazines (#)			
	Sept.	Nov.	Dec.	Total	Sept.	Nov.	Dec.	Total	Sept.	Nov.	Dec.	Total	Sept.	Nov.	Dec.	Total
CBS	149	66	84	299					149	66	84	299				
Morning Show	89	30	45	164					89	30	45	164				
Evening News	33	27	26	86					33	27	26	86				
60 Minutes II	13	4	6	23					13	4	6	23				
Face the Nation	14	5	7	26					14	5	7	26				
CNN	69	64	87	220					69	64	87	220				
Newsnight/A.Brown	19	26	37	82					19	26	37	82				
Larry King	40	31	45	116					40	31	45	116				
Capital Gang	10	7	5	22					10	7	5	22				
NBC	157	94	115	366					157	94	115	366				
Today	76	35	41	152					76	35	41	152				
Nightly News	41	17	19	77					41	17	19	77				
Dateline	18	1	–	19					18	1	–	19				
Meet the Press	8	6	10	24					8	6	10	24				
Hardball (MSNBC)	14	35	45	94					14	35	45	94				
PBS	27	34	37	98					27	34	37	98				
NewsHour	15	29	21	65					15	29	21	65				
Charlie Rose	12	5	16	33					12	5	16	33				

(Continued)

TABLE 13.1 Continued

2. Placement/Category	Total (%)			Newspapers (%)			Broadcast (%)			News Magazines (%)		
	Sept.	Nov.	Dec.	Sept.	Nov.	Dec.	Sept.	Nov.	Dec.	Sept.	Nov.	Dec.
Newspaper Stories Only												
Page one				38	11	16						
National/International				34	25	27						
Editorial				4	4	4						
Op-ed				7	9	9						
Metro/Local/Regional				8	26	15						
Special section/Incident-specific				40	23	28						
Other				–	1	*						
Don't know/Can't tell				–	–	–						
Newspaper (Total)				100	100	100						
Broadcast Stories Only												
Anchor—read only							6	10	16			
Anchor read, some video or audio							4	4	7			
Anchor lead-in/produced piece w/reporter							34	40	29			
Anchor(s) back and forth w/reporter; no editing							19	13	13			
Anchor(s)/reporters interview w/source; no editing							31	31	27			
Anchors/interview with network expert, unedited							–	–	1			
Anchors back/forth, no other participants; unedited							–	–	6			
Group discussion (anchors and others)							5	2	–			
Television (Total)							100	100	100			

2. Placement/Category

2. Placement/Category	Total (%)			Newspapers (%)			Broadcast (%)			News Magazines (%)		
	Sept.	Nov.	Dec.	Sept.	Nov.	Dec.	Sept.	Nov.	Dec.	Sept.	Nov.	Dec.
News Magazines												
Predominant cover story										84	93	81
Cover mention/flag										–	–	–
No cover appearance										–	–	–
Cover-related/Column										16	7	19
News magazines (Total)										100	100	100

3. Story Length

3. Story Length	Total (%)			Newspapers (%)			Broadcast (%)			News Magazines (%)		
	Sept.	Nov.	Dec.	Sept.	Nov.	Dec.	Sept.	Nov.	Dec.	Sept.	Nov.	Dec.
Less than 100 words	2	6	8	1	5	5	2	8	9	–	2	4
100–500 words	33	35	46	26	16	24	41	50	57	16	40	44
501–1000 words	42	37	31	46	50	39	39	28	27	38	31	26
1001–1500 words	16	14	10	19	21	21	11	9	4	20	14	7
More than 1500 words	8	7	6	8	8	10	7	6	2	26	12	19
	100	100	100	100	100	100	100	100	100	100	100	100

(Continued)

TABLE 13.1 Continued

4. Wire Service

	Total (%)			Newspapers (%)			Broadcast (%)			News Magazines (%)		
	Sept.	Nov.	Dec.	Sept.	Nov.	Dec.	Sept.	Nov.	Dec.	Sept.	Nov.	Dec.
Staff reporters	96	93	97	92	88	92	100	97	100	100	95	89
AP	2	1	*	3	2	1	–	–	–	–	–	–
Reuters	*	1	*	1	2	*	–	–	–	–	–	–
Other wire service	*	2	*	*	*	2	–	3	–	–	–	4
Combo: Staff and wires	1	2	2	2	4	*	–	–	–	–	5	4
Op-ed, nonstaff	1	1	1	2	3	4	–	–	–	–	–	4
	100	100	100	100	100	100	100	100	100	100	100	100

5. Dateline

	Total (%)			Newspapers (%)			Broadcast (%)			News Magazines (%)		
	Sept.	Nov.	Dec.	Sept.	Nov.	Dec.	Sept.	Nov.	Dec.	Sept.	Nov.	Dec.
International	5	19	20	9	17	19	2	20	20	2	7	7
Afghanistan	*	11	16	1	5	12	–	16	19	2	7	7
Iran	–	–	*	–	–	*	–	–	–	–	–	–
Iraq	*	–	–	*	–	–	–	–	–	–	–	–
Israel	1	*	*	2	*	*	–	–	–	–	–	–
Russia	*	–	–	*	–	–	–	–	–	–	–	–
Saudi Arabia	–	–	*	–	–	*	1	–	*	–	–	–
U.K.	1	1	1	1	1	1	1	–	*	–	–	–
All other non-U.S. datelines	3	7	3	5	11	6	1	4	1	–	–	–

5. Dateline

	Total (%)			Newspapers (%)			Broadcast (%)			News Magazines (%)		
	Sept.	Nov.	Dec.	Sept.	Nov.	Dec.	Sept.	Nov.	Dec.	Sept.	Nov.	Dec.
U.S. datelines	95	78	80	91	81	59	98	80	77	98	93	93
New York area	45	42	36	31	28	28	54	47	36	–	–	89
Washington area	32	31	37	37	43	31	29	30	41	–	–	4
All other U.S. datelines	18	5	7	23	10	18	15	3	2	–	–	–
	100	100	100	100	100	100	100	100	100	100	100	100

6. Topic

	Total (%)			Newspapers (%)			Broadcast (%)			News Magazines (%)		
	Sept.	Nov.	Dec.	Sept.	Nov.	Dec.	Sept.	Nov.	Dec.	Sept.	Nov.	Dec.
The attacks	8	1	*	8	1	–	9	*	1	4	–	–
Rescue efforts	12	*	1	7	*	*	18	1	1	2	–	–
Personal connections	19	3	4	25	3	4	13	3	5	22	2	4
Negative outcomes	3	1	1	4	2	1	1	1	*	2	–	–
Citizen response	8	3	8	10	3	10	6	4	8	6	2	–
Community response	5	3	3	6	5	3	5	2	3	4	7	4
Municipal/ state government response	1	1	1	3	3	2	*	*	1	–	–	–
Investigation	8	2	7	5	3	6	12	1	6	2	2	11
War on terrorism	23	16	12	17	16	19	28	15	8	26	21	11
U.S. action in Afghanistan	–	35	49	–	25	33	–	43	58	–	36	37
International response	4	10	5	7	8	8	2	13	2	2	7	7
Anthrax	–	5	2	–	8	5	–	3	*	–	10	7

(Continued)

TABLE 13.1 Continued

6. Topic

	Total (%)			Newspapers (%)			Broadcast (%)			News Magazines (%)		
	Sept.	Nov.	Dec.	Sept.	Nov.	Dec.	Sept.	Nov.	Dec.	Sept.	Nov.	Dec.
AA Flight 587	–	11	*	–	13	–	–	11	*	–	–	–
Terrorism/terrorists	2	4	3	1	3	1	3	3	3	12	7	11
Other indicators	1	1	2	2	1	1	1	1	3	2	2	–
Economic implications	4	3	2	5	5	3	3	1	*	10	2	4
Other	*	–	*	*	–	–	*	–	*	6	–	4
	100	100	100	100	100	100	100	100	100	100	100	100

7. Sourcing

	Total (%)			Newspapers (%)			Broadcast (%)			News Magazines (%)		
	Sept.	Nov.	Dec.	Sept.	Nov.	Dec.	Sept.	Nov.	Dec.	Sept.	Nov.	Dec.
All attributed	76	76	73	77	78	72	75	77	75	79	62	62
All unattributed	24	24	27	23	22	28	25	23	25	21	38	38
	100	100	100	100	100	100	100	100	100	100	100	100

8. Source Quantity

	Total (%)			Newspapers (%)			Broadcast (%)			News Magazines (%)		
	Sept.	Nov.	Dec.	Sept.	Nov.	Dec.	Sept.	Nov.	Dec.	Sept.	Nov.	Dec.
None	15	10	16	10	11	11	20	9	18	22	17	11
One	20	23	25	10	10	15	32	34	30	10	12	22
Two	11	14	16	8	9	9	14	19	20	6	12	19

8. Source Quantity

	Total (%)			Newspapers (%)			Broadcast (%)			News Magazines (%)		
	Sept.	Nov.	Dec.	Sept.	Nov.	Dec.	Sept.	Nov.	Dec.	Sept.	Nov.	Dec.
Three	9	10	14	8	8	11	8	11	15	22	12	11
Four	8	9	7	8	9	9	9	10	6	6	5	15
Five or more	37	34	22	56	53	43	18	17	12	34	43	22
	100	100	100	100	100	100	100	100	100	100	100	100

9. Balance of Viewpoints

	Total (%)			Newspapers (%)			Broadcast (%)			News Magazines (%)		
	Sept.	Nov.	Dec.	Sept.	Nov.	Dec.	Sept.	Nov.	Dec.	Sept.	Nov.	Dec.
Entirely supports U.S./admin. viewpoint	54	39	47	41	23	38	68	54	59	22	42	33
Predominantly supports U.S./admin.	17	13	3	19	18	2	15	8	4	22	17	33
Mixed: Supports and dissents U.S./admin.	20	38	42	30	46	51	10	30	31	44	42	33
Predominantly dissents from U.S./admin.	6	4	3	7	7	3	5	1	4	11	–	–
Entirely dissents from U.S./admin.	2	6	4	3	6	7	1	7	2	–	–	–
	100	100	100	100	100	100	100	100	100	100	100	100

(Continued)

TABLE 13.1 Continued

10. News Story Elements	Total (%)			Newspapers (%)			Broadcast (%)			News Magazines (%)		
	Sept.	Nov.	Dec.	Sept.	Nov.	Dec.	Sept.	Nov.	Dec.	Sept.	Nov.	Dec.
Factual reporting	75	63	63	85	81	73	64	46	56	50	21	52
Analysis	14	21	22	10	13	23	18	28	22	33	60	34
Opinion/judgment	9	11	10	4	4	3	14	19	15	14	12	13
Speculation	2	4	4	1	1	1	3	7	7	3	4	1
	100	100	100	100	100	100	100	100	100	100	100	100

*Based on applicable stories: September total, n = 309; November total, n = 159; December total, n = 118.

**Note: Totals may not equal 100 due to rounding.

The War on Terrorism
The Not-So-New Television News Landscape
Project for Excellence in Journalism

MAY 23, 2002

W as journalism, or at least that of network television, changed by the events of September 11?

Despite the war on terrorism and the conflict in the Middle East, the news Americans see on network television has softened considerably since last fall, to the point that it now looks more like it did before the terrorist attacks than immediately after, according to a new study.

Celebrity and lifestyle coverage, which last fall had all but vanished from evening news and was subordinated even in morning news, has returned to levels close to those of last summer, according to the study by the Project for Excellence in Journalism. Traditional hard news, meanwhile, has shrunk, reestablishing a trend toward the softening of network news, evident since the late 1970s. At night, stories about national and international affairs have fallen by 35 percent since October to half of all stories. Lifestyle coverage, which had disappeared almost entirely, again makes up 20 percent of the evening newscasts. Evening news, in other words, now looks much as it did before September 11.

The return to form of morning news is less complete. Lifestyle and celebrity coverage again dominate—up threefold since October. Hard news has fallen by more than half. Still, viewers now can get a diet of some hard news in the mornings, something that was not true last summer, the study found.

The findings seem to refute the idea that television journalism was somehow scared straight or fundamentally changed by the attack on America and the war on terrorism. Rather, the data suggest that traditional broadcast networks have established levels—perhaps a formula—of how much hard news a show will broadcast, and the networks will stray from that formula temporarily only when major news is breaking. Research from media analyst Andrew Tyndall suggests that this deviation from the formula generally happens in just 5 to 10 percent of the network evening broadcasts each year. Whether this either–or mentality actually reflects the tastes of American citizens, the cost of covering hard news, or simply the habits and tendencies of news executives, is more difficult to discern.

This work is the third report of war coverage by the Project, which is affiliated with the Columbia University Graduate School of Journalism and funded by the Pew Charitable Trusts. The study examined story counts, rather than minutes, for the first thirteen weeks of weekday network news programming from January 1, 2002, through April 5. It was executed and coded by the Project in collaboration with media researcher Andrew Tyndall.

The earlier studies indicated that the war did engender a colossal shift in emphasis in network news. For a time last fall, television journalism took on a seriousness even beyond that of the 1970s. Eight out of every ten evening news stories concerned government, national, or international affairs, up 76 percent from a few months earlier. On morning shows, coverage of such matters was up sevenfold. The findings defied historical trends, which had seen the quotient of such hard news on television steadily drop across three decades. An earlier study by the Project had found that traditional hard news about government, the military, and national and international affairs had fallen from close to 70 percent of the nightly news in 1977, to about 60 percent in 1987, down to 40 percent in 1997.[1]

Separate research addressing the same issue by Andrew Tyndall also indicates that the ratio of hard news to features has shrunk. Since 1988, as the networks have sold more advertising and shrunk their newshole, the time spent on features has remained steady, and the lost minutes have been subtracted from hard news instead.

The reversal of this trend after the attack led many observers to speculate that the country and news media were both entering a new phase. One reason for the speculation was that the sudden change in the news agenda last fall was coupled with changes in attitudes toward journalists. Public opinion polls

TABLE 14.1 Evening News Topics over Time[1]			
All Networks	1977	1987	1997
Hard news	67.3	58.3	41.3
Celebrity news	2.0	3.3	7.7
Crime/law/courts	8.0	6.8	13.0
Business/economy	5.5	11.1	7.4
Science and technology	3.5	4.5	5.8
Lifestyle features	13.5	16.2	24.8
Total	100	100	100

[1]Based on overall percentage.

showed that Americans thought favorably of the more serious coverage. Even more significant, pollsters found the first upturn in approval of journalists' morality, intentions, and impact on society in fifteen years.[2]

As people thought better of journalists and their coverage, more people started watching television news, reading newspapers, and using news websites, again in contrast with long-term trends. Between late September and mid-November last fall, all three evening newscasts enjoyed sizable increases in viewership over the year before, in contrast with long-term declines. Morning news shows were seeing a smaller but still real increase.[3]

This year, the number of total viewers is still up in the first quarter over the year before, though not as much as last fall. According to figures from Nielsen Media Research, ABC's *World News Tonight* is up 6 percent, NBC's *Nightly News* is up 2 percent, and CBS's *Evening News* is up 1 percent.

The morning shows, which saw more subtle increases last fall, have actually done a better job of holding on to some of that audience. ABC's *Good Morning America,* which was up 8 percent last fall in total viewership, is now up 11 percent compared to the same period last year while NBC's *Today* is up 5 percent. Total viewership for the CBS *Early Show,* however, has fallen by 1 percent.

THE FACE OF EVENING NEWS

The new findings do not mean the evening news programs are identical to before September 11.

While the amount of hard news contained in the programs is roughly the same as before September, the makeup of that hard news has shifted. Coverage of military and foreign affairs, for instance, has supplanted many domestic issues. Military stories are up threefold since last summer, to 15 percent of all stories. Coverage of domestic issues, such as concerns of an energy crisis or the HMO bill of rights, is down by almost half since summer, from 18 percent of stories in June to 10 percent this year. And if homeland security stories are removed, coverage of domestic affairs this year drops further, to just 6 percent of the nightly news.

The number of homeland security stories on the evening news (4 percent) may strike some people as surprisingly low. The bulk of these stories came in January, suggesting that on the network news at least, that topic was considered somewhat played out by early this year.

This decline in domestic affairs coverage, including the low level of homeland security stories, seems significant. It suggests that in the face of major news events, the networks are less inclined to shift from feature coverage than they are to stop covering certain areas of hard news—exchanging one area of hard news for another. It is "like an on-off switch," according to Tyndall. "Ultra heavy news days are maximum hard news. All other days (even marginally heavy news days) are half-and-half."

"What was remarkable about the September 11 crisis (and before that the Florida recount, the Lewinsky impeachment and the Gulf War, for example)," he adds, "was the protracted sequence of successive days on which that rule was violated."

TABLE 14.2 Hard News in the Evenings[1]		
	June 2001	**Early 2002**
Government	5.2	4.0
Military	5.6	15.4
Domestic affairs	17.8	10.3
Homeland security	n/a	4.1
Foreign affairs	16.9	22.0
Total	49.5	51.7
[1]Based on overall percentage.		

Traditionally, religion and business don't rise to front-page coverage; they are considered something in between hard news and softer feature stories. Religion stories are often more about spirituality and morality, and business more about financial figures and Wall Street interests. This year, however, saw two significant news events that fell under these topics: the sex scandals in the Catholic Church and the collapse of Enron. Adding these three stories to the traditional hard news would bring that category just slightly higher to 58 percent. Still, one in five stories was a traditional lifestyle feature, such as male nannies gaining acceptance as caregivers (on NBC), the fattest cities in America (on ABC), or predictions for next winter's El Nino (on CBS).

Why is this?

One possible explanation is that this tendency is audience-driven—that Americans will watch only a certain amount of serious news before they need the program leavened by something else. Audience demand is usually hard to pin down in television. The fact is, audiences have shriveled as network news has gotten softer over the years. But the last six months have seen an upturn in audience as the broadcasts, at least initially, carried a greater percentage of hard news.

There are other explanations to consider as well.

The first is that the dramatic and sustained cutbacks in resources and staffing at the networks have made it enormously difficult for network television journalism to cover world events, especially over any sustained period of time. The networks, in effect, were staffed for a pre–September 11 world and basically remain so. When it comes to foreign coverage, for instance, Tyndall's numbers show that "the consequence of mid-90s cutbacks in foreign coverage has never been that major overseas stories suffer." Often, however, the networks jump from crisis to crisis, parachuting in reporters, producers, and photographers. What gets cut, Tyndall finds, are the medium-sized, more sustained stories, like the financial collapse of Argentina this year.

The second factor is that even if the networks' staffs could be stretched, the cost of doing so—or adding the staff to do so—is no longer considered acceptable. Instead, the nightly network newscasts have redefined news as breaking or feature. With this definition, they are capable of doing a superb job of covering hard news that is fast-breaking—temporarily throwing their limited resources all in one direction. But as these breaking stories slow down, whether they are the war on terrorism, the implications of Enron, or the crisis in the Catholic Church, the networks return to more familiar formulae, even if the stories themselves remain unresolved.

Sustained coverage of the incremental has largely been lost. It is the kind of journalism that advances stories perhaps more slowly through what used to be a normal practice—beat reporting. Assigning a journalist to cover a particular topic, region, or issue day-in and day-out was for the most part lost as budgets shrank. Yet this may be precisely the kind of journalism that builds an informed audience over time. Because of the reach of network news, even now, the absence of this kind of sustained coverage influences the news agenda of all other journalism.

The third explanation is that the executives, after over twenty years of lightening the diet of network news, have come to program their newscasts a certain way. They have developed certain assumptions, beats, and sources, and they have shed themselves of hard-news reporters in favor of feature reporters who can service their magazine programs. Again, Tyndall finds this formula of half-hard/half-soft in roughly 90 to 95 percent of evening broadcasts each year.

Some combination of all these factors is probably at play. But it suggests that the idea of network television news substantially changing is far more complicated, and unlikely, than some observers had hoped last fall. In foreign news, for example, the Arab–Israeli conflict, the bulk of it coming since March 15, accounted for nearly half (45 percent) of all the foreign affairs coverage on the nightly news this year. The kidnapping and subsequent death of reporter Daniel Pearl comprised another 10 percent, a sign of television journalism's capacity to be captivated by stories focused around one individual.

All other foreign stories paled. Afghanistan, for instance, made up just 5 percent of all foreign coverage. Tensions between India and Pakistan came next, accounting for 3 percent. The Yemen terror crackdown made up 3 percent, with President Bush's trip to Asia, and various stories involving Iraq each making up 2 percent of the foreign coverage.

Why the big jump in serious news again in March with the Israeli-Palestinian flare-up, after months of getting softer? The news itself doesn't fully explain it. Al Qaeda and Taliban troops remain in Afghanistan to this day. The heaviest fighting with American and allied troops, indeed, occurred in 2002, with the battle during Operation Anaconda in March. The second heaviest fighting may be occurring now, with Operation Condor. The stories of the search for Osama bin Laden and the struggle for stable democracy in Afghanistan could easily have become major stories.

One reason may be that Israel remains a place where the networks, even with their cutbacks in resources, still maintain bureaus. Other topics that can be treated as either serious or soft shifted between this year and last. Crime coverage, which some researchers argue has been rising in recent years, dropped to almost nothing (4 percent of stories) last fall. It is up again, but not all the way, to 8 percent of stories (versus 12 percent last summer).

THE FACE OF MORNING NEWS

While morning news has softened, it does not strictly resemble its image from last summer.

What were largely lifestyle and celebrity programs last June—and became serious sources of information of overnight events last fall—have now become something of a hybrid. Americans can now see some level of serious news each morning on the networks. Roughly a quarter of what appears on morning news shows could be categorized as traditional hard news about national and international affairs. That is triple the amount from last June, when fewer than one in ten stories (7 percent) fit that description.

On the other hand, it is still significantly less than the nearly six out of every ten stories (58 percent) that hard news comprised of morning news in our sample period in October. And make no mistake, these morning shows are still dominated by stories about gardening, recipes, celebrity chatter, and product promotion. The lifestyle and celebrity fare this year has made up roughly three-fifths (58 percent) of all morning stories, after dropping to just 24 percent last fall. That, however, is somewhat lower than last summer, when celebrity and lifestyle stories made up nearly 75 percent of the morning shows.

Indeed, most of the increase in hard news comes at the expense of lifestyle feature stories. Those stories are down 9 percentage points since June (38 percent

TABLE 14.3   Topics on the Morning News over Time[1]

All Networks	June 2001	Oct. 2001	Early 2002
Hard news	6.9%	58.1%	22.5%
Homeland security	n/a	n/a	3.6%
Celebrity/entertainment	25.3%	12.2%	20%
Crime/law/courts	11.5%	1.7%	13.4%
Business/economy	4.3%	2.6%	3.3%
Science/technology	5.1%	13.5%	1.7%
Lifestyle	46.7%	12%	38.3%
Religion	0.2	0%	0.8
Total	100%	100%	100%

[1]Based on percent of total stories.

now versus 47 percent in June). The quotient of interviews with stars of the latest movies and news of celebrity weddings has declined only slightly, from 25 percent of the stories in June to 23 percent this year.

If someone were turning to morning programs for news of the day about a subject such as a bombing in the Middle East, one would also find the style of reporting could shift from day to day or hour to hour. Tyndall finds that morning shows are regularly divided into two components—the first half hour and the final 90 minutes (*Today*'s final hour has been disregarded for this study). The first half hour, he says, is a balance between hard news, business and economic news, and crime stories including true crime, such as the Andrea Yates case. The next ninety minutes are filled with celebrity and lifestyle features. "The massive impact that post–September 11 stories had on the morning programs was in their final 90 minutes where celebrity/lifestyle features were temporarily supplanted," Tyndall remarks, adding, "The same displacement occurred in November 2000 during the Florida General Election recount."

At times, the coverage consists of live, on-scene reports of the sort seen from Ground Zero following the attacks and Pakistan in the early days of the war in Afghanistan. The *Today* show, for example, featured Tom Brokaw reporting live from Tel Aviv about a bombing that took place overnight. Or there might be interviews with some of the principal newsmakers, such as *The Early Show*'s interview with the mayor of Netanya, where one of the bombings occurred.

Those harder stories, though, are scattered amid a largely human-interest approach to the news. At one point, a morning show might give a detailed news report. Another time, this same news might come in quick anchor-reads to make room for any number of features: *Good Morning America*'s piece about how children of a war zone live a normal life, an interview on *The Early Show* with a man who had near misses at both the World Trade Center and the bombing in Jaffe, or correspondent Martin Fletcher's reflection for the *Today* show on what it is like to live in the Middle East.

MONTH BY MONTH

Were it not for the Israeli–Palestinian crisis, the story of network television this year would likely have been the trend toward its becoming even softer than before September 11.

In January, less than half of the evening news, and less than a quarter of the morning shows, could be considered traditional hard news.

TABLE 14.4   2002 Evening News Topics by Month[1]

	Jan.	Feb.	Mar.	Apr.[2]
Total Hard News	48	45	59	68
Government	4	4	4	1
Military	19	12	17	11
Domestic affairs	10	9	13	6
Foreign affairs	15	20	25	50
Celebrity news	2	1	2	0
Crime/law/courts	10	10	6	5
Business/economy	20	14	11	12
Science/technology	2	2	2	2
Lifestyle features	17	26	16	8
Religion	1	2	4	5
Total	100	100	100	100

[1]Based on overall percentage.

[2]One week only.

By February, during the Olympics and a lull in war activities, that number had fallen further to 45 percent on the evening news. That is as low as the summer of 2001, when Gary Condit dominated the news and some critics were bemoaning that journalism had fallen to a new modern low of sensationalism and questionable priorities. Lifestyle coverage, especially involving the Olympics, surged to a quarter of all evening news stories.

Mornings in February had become even more focused away from the war. Hard news had fallen to 15 percent of stories. Lifestyle pieces now made up more than half (55 percent) and celebrity coverage another 15 percent. It was a thorough return to the pre–September 11 summer formula. The decline in serious news continued into March, well after the Olympics had ended. But when the Middle East conflict erupted in the middle of that month, there was a notable shift back to seriousness. On the evening news, there was a 14-percentage-point increase in hard news over February, and a 10-percentage-point decline in lifestyle coverage. In the mornings, there was a 9-percentage-point increase in hard news and a drop of 27 percentage points in lifestyle stories. That hard news

TABLE 14.5   2002 Morning News Topics by Month[1]

	Jan.	Feb.	Mar.	Apr.
Total Hard News	23.4%	15.1%	23.9%	41.3%
Government	4.1%	1.2%	1.5%	0.5%
Military	4.9%	1.9%	8.3%	1.0%
Domestic affairs	10.4%	5.6%	9.4%	4.4%
Foreign affairs	4.0%	6.4%	4.7%	35.4%
Celebrity news	18.4%	15.4%	27.3%	15.5%
Crime/law/courts	15.4%	10.6%	15.7%	6.8%
Business/economy	6.3%	1.8%	2.1%	1.0%
Science/technology	2.3%	1.3%	1.5%	1.5%
Lifestyle features	34.0%	54.5%*	28.3%	34.0%
Religion	0.2%	1.3%	1.2%	0.0%
Total	100%	100%	100%	100%

[1]Based on overall percentage.

[2]Increase partly explained by Olympics, which aired on NBC and was also covered extensively by ABC.

focus continued into April. In the first week of the month, hard news, primarily that of the Middle East conflict, accounted for nearly seven out of every ten evening news stories. Foreign affairs made up half the stories on the evening news. In the mornings, 41 percent of stories were hard news, and lifestyle and celebrity stories made up half the news.

The Enron scandal also stood out, particularly in the evening news. Though, perhaps to the surprise of many, it did not dominate, accounting for just 6 percent of the stories on the nightly news in the first thirteen weeks of the year. Mostly—by a factor of about four-to-one—it was covered as strictly a business story. Only twenty-five stories in all focused on the regulatory, investigative, or political aspects of the Enron case. And in all, only two stories focused on Enron as a crime piece. Most of the Enron coverage, too, was concentrated in January. In the mornings, Enron was a story, but not a huge one, accounting for less than 3 percent of all stories. Interestingly, morning news was twice as likely to push the political or regulatory focus of the Enron story as the nightly news was.

By comparison, the Andrea Yates case (about the Houston woman who drowned her children) was actually a bigger story on morning television than Enron. The child molestation scandal in the Catholic Church was also a notable story on television, though smaller than Enron. It made up 2 percent of all stories in the evening news and 1 percent of stories in the mornings.

In morning news, indeed, the scandal in the church was only as big a story as Valentine's Day, and it was outstripped by the trial of the "Hockey Dad," the San Francisco dog mauling, and Andrea Yates.

NETWORK BY NETWORK

With regard to the three networks separately, the most significant finding is that the aftermath of September 11 may have brought them all a little closer together. Many of the differences evident in June and even in October have either lessened or vanished altogether.

Among the evening programs, CBS led in June as the network most committed to hard news (53 percent, compared with 44 percent at ABC and 39 percent at NBC), and it remained that way in October. So far in 2002, the hard news

TABLE 14.6 2002 Evening News Topics by Network[1]			
Weekdays, January–April			
	ABC	**CBS**	**NBC**
Hard news	54.1%	53%	47%
Celebrity news	1.5%	1.2%	2.6%
Crime / law / courts	8.5%	9.1%	7.1%
Business / economy	11.3%	16.5%	18.6%
Science / technology	2.2%	2.6%	1.4%
Lifestyle features	19.7%	15.4%	21.5%
Religion	2.7%	2.2%	1.8%
Total	100%	100%	100%
[1]Based on overall percentage.			

TABLE 14.7 2002 Morning News Topics by Network[1]
Weekdays, January–April

	ABC	CBS	NBC
Hard news	24.2%	22.2%	21.5%
Celebrity news	16.8%	20.8%	22.6%
Crime/law/courts	18.4%	11.2%	10.2%
Business/economy	3.4%	4.1%	2.1%
Science/technology	1.4%	2.6%	0.9%
Lifestyle features	35%	38.6%	41.6%
Religion	0.9%	0.5%	1.1%
Total	100%	100%	100%

[1]Based on overall percentage.

quotient at CBS has remained at 53 percent while ABC's and NBC's have both risen by nearly 10 percentage points since last June. The change has left CBS and ABC roughly equal and NBC not far behind.

CBS also had significantly less celebrity and lifestyle feature news last June. Again, even with the Olympics (hosted by NBC), those differences have lessened considerably so far this year, leaving ABC and NBC more in line with the other. Among the three morning news programs, the measurable differences apparent in both June and October of last year have largely vanished as well. The hard news levels are now within two percentage points of each other, and celebrity and lifestyle stories both fall on a small, uphill curve across networks, with ABC at the bottom and NBC at the top.

WAR COVERAGE

Overall, little more than a quarter of all the stories on the nightly news (28 percent) were about America's war on terrorism, whether those were stories about activities overseas, feature stories about how people were coping, a celebrity benefit concert, the possible impact on the stock market, or news about presidential action. In mornings, it was half that, at 14 percent.

In both the evenings and mornings, NBC was slightly less likely to air these stories than either of the other two networks.

TABLE 14.8 War Related Coverage[1]

	Evening	Morning
All Networks	28%	14%
ABC	29%	15%
CBS	30%	14%
NBC	25%	13%

[1]Based on percent of newscast.

What kinds of war stories did television carry? The majority in both the evening and morning was a part of the program's hard news. In evening news, half of the stories were military pieces, about, for example, casualties and military conditions in the battle of Gardez. One in every five stories concerned domestic affairs, such as airport security, and another 20 percent were foreign affair stories, such as the kidnapping of Daniel Pearl or the terror crackdown in Yemen. A smaller percentage of the war stories were related to crime and legal prosecutions, such as the charge of treason against John Walker Lindh (the California Muslim who fought with the Taliban) and the Zacarias Moussaoui trial.

Among the morning shows, hard news was still, by far, the most common source for war stories (87 percent), but the breakdown is a little different. Morning news was less likely to run stories about the military (30 percent) or foreign affairs (15 percent) and more likely to cover domestic issues relating to the war (40 percent). In addition, the morning shows did manage to inject in a handful of entertainment stories related to the war—pieces such as how the World Trade Center disaster inspired comic book writers, as well as PBS's intention to have Sesame Street address the attacks, and charity concerts to benefit victims. Such features accounted for 2 percent of their war stories.

METHODOLOGY

The study examined the three network evening news programs and three network morning news shows weekdays from January 1, 2002, to April 5, 2002. The specific programs studied were ABC's *World News Tonight*, CBS's *Evening News*, NBC's *Nightly News*, ABC's *Good Morning America*, CBS's *The Early Show*, and NBC's *Today*. (Note: Only the first two hours of *Today* were coded to match the other morning show time periods.) All topic breakdowns were based

TABLE 14.9   Breakdown of War Related Stories[1]

	Evening	Morning
Total Hard News	90.5%	86.6%
Government	*0.8%*	*2.2%*
Military	*49.2%*	*29.5%*
Domestic affairs	*19.9%*	*39.9%*
Foreign affairs	*20.6%*	*15%*
Celebrity / entertainment	0%	1.9%
Crime / law / courts	7.8%	9.3%
Business / economy	0.3%	0%
Science / technology	0.3%	0%
Lifestyle	1%	1.6%
Religion	0.1%	0.6%
Total	100%	100%

[1]Based on overall percentage.

on data compiled by media researcher Andrew Tyndall for the Tyndall Report. For the evening news programs, Tyndall monitors all news segments in which the reporting involves more than an anchor read. For the morning show, Tyndall monitors all packaged segments outside the local and national newsbreaks. The Project adapted Tyndall's research to the topic breakdowns it has used in earlier studies.

NOTES

1. Project for Excellence in Journalism, "Changing Definitions of News: A Look at the Mainstream Press over 20 Years," March 6, 1998.

2. The Pew Research Center for the People and the Press, "Terror Coverage Boosts News Media's Image," November 28, 2001.

3. In evening news, during the four-week period between September 24 and November 11 of last year, ABC was up 15 percent over the same period a year earlier, CBS was up 9 percent, and NBC was up 7 percent, according to Nielsen Media Research. In the morning, in the four-week period following September 11, the biggest winner was ABC's *Good Morning America,* up 8 percent in total viewers.

TABLE 14.10 Evening News Topics

January 1–April 5, 2002 (Weekdays)

	ABC	CBS	NBC	Total	Total(%)
Hard News					
Government	39	48	34	121	4.0
Military	172	185	111	468	15.4
Domestic affairs	135	93	87	315	10.4
Homeland security	*59*	*36*	*30*	*125*	*4.1*
Domestic affairs feature	0.0	0.0	0.0	0.0	0.0
Foreign affairs	276	225	169	670	22.0
Total	622	551	401	1,574	51.7%
Percentage of newscasts	54.1%	53%	47%		
Celebrity News					
Entertainment/celebs	15	11	19	45	
Celebrity crime/scandal	2	1	3	6	
Total	17	12	22	51	1.7%
Percentage of newscasts	1.5%	1.2%	2.6%		
Crime/law/courts	98	95	61	254	8.3%
Percentage of newscasts	8.5%	9.1%	7.1%		
Business/economy	130	172	159	461	15.2%
Percentage of newscasts	11.3%	16.5%	18.6%		
Science and Technology					
Science	21	22	9	52	
Technology	4	5	3	12	
Percentage of newscasts	25	27	12	64	2.1%
	2.2 %	2.6%	1.4%		
Religion	31	23	15		
Percentage of newscasts	2.7%	2.2%	1.8%		2.3%
Lifestyle Features					
Fashion/lifestyle	2	1	3	6	
Personal health	69	43	46	158	
High arts/culture	2	1	0	3	
Sports	45	14	57	116	
Weather/natural disaster	50	46	33	129	
Sci-Fi/supernatural	0	0	0	0	
Other	25	19	17	61	
Family/parenting	6	4	6	16	
Cooking/food	0	0	0	0	
Travel	14	16	5	35	
Oddball news	6	5	4	15	
Consumer/product	7	11	13	31	
Total	226	160	184	570	
Percentage of newscasts	19.7%	15.4%	21.5%	18.7%	
Total	1,149	1,040	854	3,043	100%

TABLE 14.11 Morning News Topics:

January 1–April 5, 2002 (weekdays)

	ABC	CBS	NBC	Total	Total(%)
Hard News					
Government	20	25	12	57	2.1
Military	43	43	39	125	4.7
Domestic affairs	71	75	70	216	8.2
Homeland security	*37*	*31*	*28*	*96*	*3.6*
Domestic feature	2	0	2	4	.1
Foreign affairs	82	62	51	195	7.4
Total	219	205	174	597	22.5%
Percentage of newscasts	24.2%	22.2%	21.5%		
Celebrity News					
Entertainment/celebs	141	189	176	506	
Celebrity crime/scandal	11	3	7	21	
Total	152	192	183	527	20.0%
Percentage of newscasts	16.8%	20.8%	22.6%		
Crime/law/courts	167	103	83	353	13.4%
Percentage of newscasts	18.4%	11.2%	10.2%		
Business/economy	31	38	17	86	3.3%
Percentage of newscasts	3.4%	4.1%	2.1%		
Science and Technology					
Science	7	11	2	20	
Technology	6	13	5	24	
Total	13	24	7	44	1.7%
Percentage of newscasts	1.4%	2.6%	.9%		
Religion	8	5	9	22	.8%
Percentage of newscasts	.9%	.5%	1.1%		
Lifestyle Features					
Fashion/lifestyle	35	29	24	88	
Personal health	72	81	50	203	
High arts/culture	10	13	14	37	
Sports	52	60	162	274	
Weather/natural disaster	7	7	6	20	
Sci-Fi/supernatural	3	2	0	5	
Other	15	39	15	69	
Family/parenting	50	40	17	107	
Cooking/food	17	31	14	62	
Travel	15	10	9	34	
Oddball news	13	14	8	35	
Consumer/product	28	30	18	76	
Total	317	356	337	1,010	38.3%
Percentage of newscasts	35.0%	38.6%	41.6%		
Total	906	923	810	2,639	

TABLE 14.12   Evening News Topics

All Networks

	June	October	Change
Hard News			
Government	11	15	4
Military	12	58	46
Domestic affairs	35	62	27
Domestic affairs feature	3	6	3
Foreign affairs	36	21	-15
Total	97	162	65
Percentage of newscasts	45.5%	80.2%	
Celebrity News			
Entertainment/celebs	9	0	-9
Celebrity crime/scandal	1	0	-1
Total	10	0	-10
Percentage of newscasts	4.7%	0.0%	
Crime/law/courts	25	7	-18
Percentage of newscasts	11.7%	3.5%	
Business/economy	30	9	-21
Percentage of newscasts	14.1%	4.5%	
Science and Technology			
Science	5	21	16
Technology	4	1	-3
Total	9	22	13
Percentage of newscasts	4.2%	10.9%	
Lifestyle Features			
Fashion/lifestyle	1	0	-1
Personal health	11	2	-9
High arts/culture	0	0	0
Religion	3	0	-3
Sports	2	0	-2
Weather/natural disaster	9	0	-9
Sci-Fi/supernatural	0	0	0
Other	6	0	-6
Family/parenting	1	0	-1
Cooking/food	0	0	0
Travel	6	0	-6
Oddball news	1	0	-1
Consumer/product	2	0	-2
Total	42	2	-40
Percentage of newscasts	19.7%	1.0%	
Total	213	202	-11

TABLE 14.13   Evening News Topics June 2001 versus October 2001

All Networks

	June	October	Change
Hard News			
Government	11	15	4
Military	12	58	46
Domestic affairs	35	62	27
Domestic affairs feature	3	6	3
Foreign affairs	36	21	-15
Total	97	162	65
Percentage of newscasts	45.5%	80.2 %	
Celebrity News			
Entertainment/celebs	9	0	-9
Celebrity crime/scandal	1	0	-1
Total	10	0	-10
Percentage of newscasts	4.7%	0.0 %	
Crime/law/courts	25	7	-18
Percentage of newscasts	11.7%	3.5 %	
Business/economy	30	9	-21
Percentage of newscasts	14.1%	4.5 %	
Science and Technology			
Science	5	21	16
Technology	4	1	-3
Total	9	22	13
Percentage of newscasts	4.2%	10.9 %	
Lifestyle Features			
Fashion/lifestyle	1	0	-1
Personal health	11	2	-9
High arts/culture	0	0	0
Religion	3	0	-3
Sports	2	0	-2
Weather/natural disaster	9	0	-9
Sci-Fi/supernatural	0	0	0
Other	6	0	-6
Family/parenting	1	0	-1
Cooking/food	0	0	0
Travel	6	0	-6
Oddball news	1	0	-1
Consumer/product	2	0	-2
Total	42	2	-40
Percentage of newscasts	19.7%	1.0 %	
Total	213	202	-11

TABLE 14.14 Evening News Topics, June 2001 versus October 2001

Network-by-Network Breakdown

	ABC			CBS			NBC		
	June	Oct.	Change	June	Oct.	Change	June	Oct.	Change
Hard News									
Government	3	5	2	5	4	-1	3	6	3
Military	5	16	11	3	22	19	4	20	16
Domestic affairs	9	26	17	15	19	4	11	17	6
Domest. aff. feature	1	2	1	1	3	2	1	1	0
Foreign affairs	14	4	-10	13	9	-4	9	8	-1
Total	32	53	21	37	57	20	28	52	24
Percentage of newscasts	44.4%	75.7%		52.9%	86.4%		39.4%	78.8%	
Celebrity News									
Entertainment/celebs	5	0	-5	1	0	-1	3	0	-3
Celebrity crime/scandal	0	0	0	0	0	0	1	0	-1
Total	5	0	-5	1	0	-1	4	0	-4
Percentage of newscasts	6.9%	0.0%		1.4%	0.0%		5.6%	0.0%	
Crime/law/courts	10	4	-6	9	0	-9	6	3	-3
Percentage of newscasts	13.9%	5.7%		12.9%	0.0%		8.5%	4.5%	
Business/economy	7	5	-2	12	2	-10	11	2	-9
Percentage of newscasts	9.7%	7.1%		17.1%	3.0%		15.5%	3.0%	
Science and Technology									
Science	2	7	5	0	6	6	3	8	5
Technology	2	0	-2	1	0	-1	1	1	0
Total	4	7	3	1	6	5	4	9	5
Percentage of newscasts	5.6%	10.0%		1.4%	9.1%		5.6%	13.6%	
Lifestyle Features									
Fashion/lifestyle	1	0	-1	0	0	0	0	0	0
Personal health	4	1	-3	1	1	0	6	0	-6
High arts/culture	0	0	0	0	0	0	0	0	0
Religion	2	0	-2	1	0	-1	0	0	0
Sports	1	0	-1	1	0	-1	0	0	0
Weather/natural disaster	4	0	-4	3	0	-3	2	0	-2
Sci-Fi/supernatural	0	0	0	0	0	0	0	0	0
Other	2	0	-2	1	0	-1	3	0	-3
Family/parenting	0	0	0	1	0	-1	0	0	0
Cooking/food	0	0	0	0	0	0	0	0	0
Travel	0	0	0	1	0	-1	5	0	-5
Oddball news	0	0	0	0	0	0	1	0	-1
Consumer/product	0	0	0	1	0	-1	1	0	-1
Total	14	1	-13	10	1	-9	18	0	-18
Percentage of newscasts	19.4%	1.4%		14.3%	1.5%		25.4%	0.0%	
Total	72	70	-2	70	66	-4	71	66	-5

TABLE 14.15   Morning News Topics June 2001 versus October 2001

	ABC		CBS		NBC		All Nets	
	June	Oct.	June	Oct.	June	Oct.	June	Oct.
Hard News								
Government	0	8	1	7	2	8	3	23
Military	0	29	0	23	1	20	1	72
Domestic affairs	4	44	4	40	1	44	9	128
Domestic feature	1	2	1	3	0	3	2	8
Foreign affairs	4	18	2	10	5	13	11	41
Total	9	101	8	83	9	88	26	272
Percentage of newscasts	7.6%	62.7%	5.9%	52.9%	7.4%	58.7%	6.9%	58.1%
Celebrity News								
Entertainment/celebs	15	11	31	22	31	22	77	55
Celebrity crime/scandal	7	2	5	0	6	0	18	2
Total	22	13	36	22	37	22	95	57
Percentage of newscasts	18.6%	8.1%	26.7%	14.0%	30.3%	14.7%	25.3%	12.2%
Crime/law/courts	16	4	7	3	20	1	43	8
Percentage of newscasts	13.6%	2.5%	5.2%	1.9%	16.4%	0.7%	11.5%	1.7%
Business/economy	4	4	6	3	6	5	16	12
Percentage of newscasts	3.4%	2.5%	4.4%	1.9%	4.9%	3.3%	4.3%	2.6%
Science and Technology								
Science	2	23	4	19	2	18	8	60
Technology	4	1	3	2	4	0	11	3
Total	6	24	7	21	6	18	19	63
Percentage of newscasts	5.1%	14.9%	5.2%	13.4%	4.9%	12.0%	5.1%	13.5%
Lifestyle Features								
Fashion/lifestyle	11	0	8	2	5	1	24	3
Personal health	10	1	16	2	9	1	35	4
High arts/culture	0	2	1	1	2	1	3	4
Religion	0	0	1	0	0	0	1	0
Sports	2	4	7	3	4	3	13	10
Weather/disaster	4	0	2	0	2	3	8	3
Sci-Fi/supernatural	0	0	0	0	0	0	0	0
Other	20	3	16	5	16	1	52	9
Family/parenting	10	4	6	4	4	1	20	9
Cooking/food	2	0	7	5	1	0	10	5
Travel	1	0	5	1	1	3	7	4
Oddball news	0	0	1	0	0	0	1	0
Consumer/product	1	1	1	2	0	2	2	5
Total	61	15	71	25	44	16	176	56
Percentage of newscasts	51.7%	9.3%	52.6%	15.9%	36.1%	10.7%	46.9%	12.0%
Total	118	161	135	157	122	150	375	468

An Indian Perspective on Media Coverage

Sutanu Guru, New Delhi
Senior Journalist and Lecturer at
Makhanlal Chaturvedi University

The Press seems to be stricken with war hysteria, as evidenced by almost the full space being allotted in each and every newspaper in the country to the post–September 11 events. No doubt that this information-overload represents a desire on the part of the Press to "participate" in history, but in giving such excessive coverage, it often seems that the Press is tending to get overtly sensational, rather than being sensitive. The war has provided the Press with grist for the news mill to which it has responded more in the form of sensationalism and getting carried away.

The social responsibility function of the Press has been largely forgotten, as evidenced in the media hype over terrorism and its repercussions. Biowarfare, anthrax cases, reports of anti-America sloganeering are making greater news in the Press reports, thus obscuring issues that appeal to public reasoning. The moderate voices that condemn the use of religion for spreading unrest are relegated to back pages while the statements of extremist leaders and networks grab the front pages of newspapers. An editorial in a leading daily notes that "the characterization of Islam as a religion that breeds terror has gathered greater momentum as media networks have begun to project the Islamic world as a uniform entity."

The post-September media stereotype is this: "Islam equals fundamentalism equals terrorism equals war." Some of the glaring news headlines on biowarfare only spread fear psychosis rather than assuaging panic. The focus is never on remedial measures or precautions to be taken in the wake of the anthrax spread. Such reporting on the part of the media is cause for grave concern, and it is time that the media redefined its news priorities in the highly volatile situation arising from the American response to the September 11 holocaust.

As far as the Western Press is concerned, it has come in for criticism for lacking in credibility in reporting the day-to-day developments. The Inter-American Press Association has criticized the U.S. media coverage of the war; it has lashed out at them for not projecting anything anti-American and restricting the reportage of the standpoint of the Taliban. Other criticisms levied against the Western Press on the present war coverage condemn the lack of explanations on the events that led to the terrorist assault on America. A recent article by a leading Western journalist rightly points out that hyping the threat of terrorism tears at the very fabric of a democratic society. It promotes hatred, suspicion, and racism. It leads to repressive domestic measures that trample civil liberties, and it makes citizens support a violent and reactionary foreign policy. The Indian Press has been largely dependent on the Western media because of the latter's penetrative reach to the scenes of action. The reports put out by the Arab media have received far less attention.

The Indian Press is also tending to toe the line of the Western Press, barring the reportage of the Pakistani angle in the current theatre of war. At sensitive times like these, it is important that the Indian media throw light on the government's perspective rather than adopt a critical posture. In a country like ours, where communal tensions and strife are a common occurrence, it is important for the media to exercise self-restraint in their reports and give more coverage to moderate voices, rather than blow out of proportion the voices of war actors and extremists. Some of the leading Indian dailies can also be blamed for trivializing the war by having cartoon series caricaturing the key actors of the war. One of the Indian dailies even speculated about whether the Americans were from outer space.

All this goes to substantiate the Agenda Setting Theory, propounded by mass communication theorists who rightly point out that the media ultimately determines what the public thinks about. In determining the subjects we think about, the media sets our agendas and ultimately shapes our decision making on political and social issues. By drawing attention only to certain kinds of news, they make the people think only about certain topics brought to their attention. Built within this structure is the bias that the media tends to have on certain subjects that they automatically pass on to the readers by reordering news according to what they (the media) think of as significant. The media decides what is worthy to be released to the audience. In doing so, they investigate, among all possible elements of reality, the more useful ones for attracting their audience. The media as gatekeepers show only their versions of "reality" and thereby manipulate the readers' minds.

It would be interesting at this point to draw parallels between media reportage of the Gulf War and the present U.S. attacks on Afghanistan. The media drew flak for its one-sided presentation of the Gulf War. Public opinion surveys indicated that the American media's coverage of the Gulf War produced substantial agenda setting, priming, and framing effects, notwithstanding censorship, fillers, and subjective coverage. Research studies on media reporting during the Gulf War noted that in extreme cases such as wartime, objectivity (although present) was reduced to a ritual ornament of media discourse, at the expense of the informative function.

War is at all times evil, and it results in extreme hardships to the common people and destruction of civilian assets—and thus not merely damage to the enemy. It can only be hoped that the war in Afghanistan will end soon and be replaced by political confabulations among all parties concerned. Meanwhile, the media owes it to its readership to shift the emphasis from one of sensationalism to one of strong advocacy of peace and moderation.

MEDIA CREATES PARANOIA

A few issues raised by the terror attacks of September 11 and its hysterical aftermath will be brought up once the media frenzy dies down, as it inevitably will. Analysts in India have already started dissecting the media coverage of the carnage and America's cowboy-style quest for revenge in the garb of "justice." But their efforts have been scattered. In any case, they have made no difference to the manner in which global and Indian mass media have been bringing the crisis to our doorsteps and living rooms.

At the risk of offending the sultans of the so-called fourth estate, let us dispassionately try to zero in on what could be safely called the four maladies evident in the mass media's coverage of the slugfest between a "patriotic, freedom-loving, and determined" Texan George Bush and an "evil, barbaric, and fanatic" Arab Osama bin Laden. The four maladies are as follows: hysteria, paranoia, amnesia, and myopia—and there have been many honorable exceptions.

But by and large, one can safely conclude that hysteria, paranoia, myopia, and amnesia mark the ongoing coverage of the crisis.

First, hysteria has been evident in television images and words right since September 11 when the second plane hit the World Trade Center in New York. For days on end, television screens around the world relentlessly telecast the gruesome images of those huge jets crashing into the towers. In fact, the signature tune of practically all news bulletins (American as well as Indian) started and ended with visuals of a jetliner crashing into the 110-story building. In some cases, this was reduced to the theater of the absurd: The Hindi news channel Aaj Tak had so seamlessly merged the signature tune, the headlines, and the content of its news bulletins with visuals of terror and of sponsor's ads that one got a feeling that the images of death and destruction were "brought to you" by biscuits, pens, shirts, and sundry other consumer goods.

CNN, Fox News, and NBC kept telecasting reports that a car bomb had attacked the Congress, that the president was advised not to come to Washington, that more hijacked planes were hurtling across American airspace, and that Los Angeles, San Francisco, and other cities were the "next" targets . . . and so on. In hindsight, none of these stories had been "verified" or confirmed. But their impact on American (and even global) audiences was clearly traumatic. This kind of hysteria has extracted a heavy social and economic cost. In the immediate aftermath, all civilian flights in the United States were grounded. Ban orders were issued on all international flights entering the United States. As a result, thousands of people were literally stranded all over the world. Global airlines lost billions of dollars in revenue. More than a hundred thousand employees were sacked by the airlines. And the damage continues. Images of aircraft as carriers of fiery death have become so deeply embedded that there has been a 50 percent drop in airline passenger traffic in the United States. Can mass media justifiably claim that it has absolutely no role to play in triggering this mass hysteria and its attendant costs?

While the bombardment through audiovisual images has provoked trauma, words in the print medium have only reinforced the images. Day in and day out, newspapers and magazines have used words and sentences like "Armageddon," "disaster," "Americans can never feel safe again," "you could be next on the hit list," "third world war," "bio-terrorism," "nuclear attacks on cities." A recent study by the Center for Media Studies indicates how even the Indian mass media got caught up in the hysterical coverage. About one-third of editorial space was dedicated by the major newspapers to cover the Kargil war. In the case of attacks on New York and Washington, Indian newspapers devoted more than two-thirds of editorial space for more than a fortnight. Was there no other important news coming out of India, or other parts of the world? Or was Kargil a lesser story than the September 11 attacks for Indians?

The hysteric coverage almost inevitably led to paranoia among large sections of mass media, provoking attacks on "Arab-looking" or "Muslim-looking" minorities in the United States, Australia, Canada, and many other "democracies." More than 200 attacks have been reported on Sikhs in the United States alone. Who provoked an apparently harmless citizen in Arizona into gunning down a person who "resembled" bin Laden? How did the American associate a harmless, hardworking Sikh with Osama bin Laden? It is easy to blame ignorance and prejudice for these outrageous acts. But didn't mass media initially fan this paranoia by linking all terror with "bearded, Arab-looking" people? And what about headlines in leading American newspapers: "Shoot those bastards," "nuke them," "send them back to the hellholes they came from," and "bomb them into basketball courts." The bitter irony of this was revealed when Rahul Gandhi, who has lost his father and grandmother to terrorism, was detained temporarily by security personnel at an American airport for the crime of "looking" like a suspected terrorist.

This paranoia has been fed further by major sections of mass media's projecting the whole thing as a clash between civilizations—between a democratic, tolerant Christianity and a feudal, intolerant Islam. No matter what leaders say about the fight against terrorism not being one against Islam, mass media has ensured that the average viewer and reader have fallen hook, line, and sinker for the dubious hypothesis of Samuel Huntington. Even in India, some publications have gone on to scream "Islamic Terror," though India suffers from what you may call "Hindu" (ULFA, LTTE), "Christian" (Mizoram, Nagaland), as well as Islamic terrorism. Saddled with paranoia, it has become a blithe task for mass media to label communities "Hindu fundamentalist BJP," "Islamic Terrorist Taliban," and so on. Do these labels and images reduce ignorance or fuel more hatred?

That brings us to the third affliction haunting mass media—that of myopia, or the inability to see beyond a narrow horizon. As India and the Vajpayee government have been realizing bitterly over the last month, the global mass media (dominated primarily by American networks) is simply unable to see the existence of terror and its victims beyond the backyard of the United States. CNN had barely thirty seconds for the suicide bombing of the assembly in Kashmir. Most newspapers there barely mentioned it in passing, devoting more space and time to how American forces were planning to capture bin Laden, "dead or alive." The narrow focus of mass media on "national interests" or "allied interests" have also led to downright hypocritical contradictions in the manner in which issues are portrayed: For mass media in the United States, there are no gray areas when it comes to portraying bin Laden; he is simply an evil terrorist, who needs to be wiped off the face of the earth. For a majority of mass media there, Azhar Masood is not even a known name, while in Indian mass media, Masood is the evil terrorist, who needs to be wiped off the face of the earth. And for a majority of mass-circulated Urdu papers in Pakistan, Masood and even bin Laden are simply jehadis responding to cries of oppressed Muslims.

These hypocritical and self-serving practices lead global mass media to premises such as the following: It is "morally right" for the U.S. president to publicly call for the killing of bin Laden, while Russian forces are given lectures on human rights violations when they remorselessly hunt Chechen "rebels" for bombing apartments in Russia; it is morally justified for the United Kingdom to send warships and troops thousands of miles to "recapture" the Falklands by fighting a war with Argentina's military, but wiser for Palestinians to "negotiate" with the invading Israeli army; "the call of freedom" demands that Saddam Hussein be thrown out and democracy brought to Iraq, while "culture and circumstances" demand that dictatorships flourish in Saudi Arabia and Kuwait. The list of such contradictions is endless. And they have been highlighted even more harshly after the September 11 terrorist attack. Can mass media really claim to be "objective and fair"?

And what about amnesia? How is it that words like "militants," "guerrillas," "rebels," "separatists," "freedom fighters" seem to have vanished from the lexicon of mass media? How is it that selective definitions of terrorism have given way to the evocative term "global terror" in mass media? Some analysts in India have praised the mass media in the United States for solidly backing the government there and exercising the patriotic duty of not lambasting intelligence failures. In contrast, Indian media has been portrayed as irresponsible when it comes to national crises. Does that mean that mass media is a mere extension of the "state"?

"Terrorism" Is a Term That Requires Consistency

Newspaper and Its Critics Both Show a Double Standard on "Terror"

Media Advisory: FAIR—Fairness and Accuracy in Reporting

APRIL 8, 2002

A group called Minnesotans Against Terrorism (MAT)—which includes Governor Jesse Ventura, Senator Paul Wellstone (before his death in 2002), and other prominent political figures—has condemned the *Minneapolis Star Tribune* for what it calls a "double standard" on the use of the word "terrorism." But in fact, neither the newspaper nor the organization applies the term "terrorism" in a consistent way—a problem that is widespread throughout U.S. media.

The organization's grievance against the *Star Tribune* is that the paper says it avoids using the term "terrorist" in its reports on the Mideast conflict. As the paper's assistant managing editor, Roger Buoen, explained in a comment to the paper's ombudsman (February 3, 2002):

> Our practice is to stay away from characterizing the subjects of news articles but instead describe their actions, background and identity as fully as possible, allowing readers to come to their own judgments about individuals and organizations.
>
> In the case of the term "terrorist," other words—"gunman," "separatist" and "rebel, " for example—may be more precise and less likely to be viewed as judgmental. Because of that we often prefer these more specific words.
>
> We also take extra care to avoid the term "terrorist" in articles about the Israeli-Palestinian conflict because of the emotional and heated nature of that dispute.

This policy of avoiding the term "terrorism" in favor of more specific descriptions is a defensible policy—so long as it is applied consistently. But Buoen went on to acknowledge that the paper does make exceptions: "However, in some circumstances in which nongovernmental groups carry out attacks on civilians, the term is permitted. For example, al Qaeda is frequently referred to by the *Star Tribune* and other news organizations as a 'terrorist network,' in part because its members have been convicted of terrorist acts and because it has been identified by the United States and other countries as a terrorist organization."

Here the paper is making distinctions that are not defensible. First, to limit "terrorism" to "nongovernmental groups" is an illogical restriction. Does a plane being blown up stop being terrorism if it turns out that some nation's intelligence agency secretly ordered its destruction? To make such an arbitrary distinction over the use of a word with such powerful connotations certainly doesn't sound like "allowing readers to come to their own judgments." (The *Star Tribune*'s ombudsman noted that the Associated Press also reserves the word "terrorist" for nongovernmental groups.)

Similarly, to decide that it is all right to label al Qaeda as a "terrorist network," not because its specific actions fit a definition of terrorism, but because the U.S. government has used that label in public statements or in legal actions, is not allowing readers to make up their minds but letting the state make up their minds for them.

Furthermore, the September 11 attacks are certainly an "emotional and heated" subject—probably more so than the Israeli-Palestinian conflict for most of the *Star Tribune*'s readers. Since the reasons the paper cites for calling al Qaeda "terrorist" also apply to the Palestinian organization Hamas, one can't help but wonder if the *Star Tribune*'s different treatment of these groups has to do with the greater degree of outrage its readers would feel if the paper declined to use the term in al Qaeda's case.

So MAT has a point when it charges the paper with a double standard. But the organization itself has a similar double standard when it comes to its definition of terrorism. "Calling the targeted killing of innocent civilians anything but terrorism is completely unconscionable," says Marc Grossfield, the group's cofounder, in a press release (April 2, 2002). But do they really mean it?

FAIR asked Grossfield if his organization would refer to the bombing of Hiroshima as a terrorist act. "No, we would not," he responded. Yet it would seem to fit MAT's definition precisely: Hiroshima was targeted precisely because the city, lacking significant military targets, had escaped previous bombing damage, so its destruction by a single bomb would send the starkest possible message to Japan about the price the nation would pay if it refused to surrender. So why isn't that targeting of civilians, who died on a scale undreamed of by any suicide bomber, considered to be terrorism?

"The use of weapons of mass destruction in World War II against an evil force who had engaged in genocide is not something that this organization is willing to judge," was MAT's official response.

So targeting civilians stops being "terrorism" when it's done to combat an "evil force." Of course, you would be hard pressed to find anyone who targeted civilians anywhere who did not consider the force they were fighting to be "evil." This is a definition of terrorism that hinges on whether or not one agrees with the reasons for killing civilians.

In fact, the only consistent definition of terrorism is based on the deliberate killing of civilians to achieve political goals—not on whether the killers are backed by a state or not, and certainly not on the methods they choose to use to kill their victims. A consistent definition, however, is one that virtually no news organization would be willing to use.

They would have to refer to the "terrorist" bombings of Hiroshima and Nagasaki, to U.S. support for "terrorist" governments in Central America that killed hundreds of thousands of civilians, to the United States "terrorist" attacks on civilian infrastructure in Iraq and Yugoslavia. (The attacks on water treatment facilities in Iraq alone have certainly—and deliberately—killed more civilians than any Palestinian group; see the *Progressive*, September 2001.)

And they would have to use the word "terrorism" to describe actions by both sides in the Israeli–Palestinian conflict. Consider a May 1996 report from Human Rights Watch on Israel's tactics in Lebanon earlier that year:

In significant areas in southern Lebanon whole populations—indeed anyone who failed to flee by a certain time—were targeted as if they were combatants. . . . The intention of the warnings that were broadcast and subsequent shelling is likely to have been to cause terror among the civilian population. . . . The IDF [Israeli Defense Forces] also executed what appear to have been calculated direct attacks on purely civilian targets. . . . The IDF at times hindered and even attacked ambulances and vehicles of relief organizations, and carried out a number of attacks on persons attempting to flee the area.

If news organizations are prepared to describe such tactics as terrorism, then they should consistently apply the same term to nongovernmental groups that target civilians. If media are unwilling or unable to be consistent, then they should indeed avoid the use of the word "terrorism," instead describing specific activities and letting readers make up their own minds what they should be called.

The Government and the Press: War–Media Connection

Now that Operation Infinite Justice is underway, am I the only one wondering who coined that phrase? Apparently, the name of the U.S. military buildup has now been changed to Operation Enduring Freedom to avoid offending Muslims. It reminds me of the name change that a small radio company called Hemisphere Broadcasting underwent some years back when it renamed itself Infinity Broadcasting, a term emblematic of its ambition. Infinity was later bought by CBS, which was, in turn, acquired by Viacom.

On September 7, four days before the hell we are now coping with erupted, Infinity's Mel Karmazin and company were deep into what might be called "Operation Infinite Just-us." Their lawyers and counterparts in other media companies were battling in a Washington, D.C., appeals court to overturn rules limiting how many television stations they can own. For ten years now, regulations on broadcasters have been relaxed to their benefit. Now, the Viacomese and their allies want to scuttle the rest, demanding an end to Federal Communications Commission (FCC) rules that limit any one company from reaching more than 35 percent of the country or from owning a television station in an area where they own a cable company.

COMPETITION THROUGH CONSOLIDATION

In a cleverly worded brief, this preemptive strike for more media consolidation is wrapped in language defending diversity and free competition. According to experts cited by the *Los Angeles Times,* if the media moguls get what they want, only a dozen or so companies will own most U.S. stations, giving them even more control over the marketplace of ideas than they already have.

As judges wrestled with these issues in one part of the capital, the FCC across town was launching a second front in a stealth effort to transfer more media power to a relative few. Under the chairmanship of Michael Powell, son of Secretary of State Colin Powell, the FCC scheduled a "proceeding" to weaken the rules if the courts did not choose to throw them out. Policy wonks know about this, but most of the public does not because big media rarely cover issues in which their own financial interests are at stake.

And then the day that changed the world forever arrived. When the Twin Towers fell and the Pentagon was hit, Washington was paralyzed, with only the White House, State Department, and "Defense" establishment in motion. Oh, and one other key development was not suspended: the FCC's determination to serve the industry it is supposed to oversee.

Like a Broadway producer, Michael Powell decided that "the show must go on," and he moved full speed ahead with a planned "comment period" to solicit reaction to proposed changes. Imagine, in the middle of a national emergency, at the outset of a war, when the country is totally shocked and distracted, he expects public comments on key regulatory proposals. His stated reasons were wrapped in patriotism: "Our reaction must be to defy these dastardly acts and not cower or be deterred from our duties: to our families, to our friends, and to our coun-

> "Limiting access, limiting information to cover the backsides of those who are in charge of the war, is extremely dangerous and cannot and should not be accepted. And I am sorry to say that, up to and including the moment of this interview, that overwhelmingly it has been accepted by the American people. And the current administration revels in that, they relish that, and they take refuge in that."
>
> — CBS News Anchor
> DAN RATHER on BBC
> *NewsNight,* May 16, 2002

trymen. The flame of the American ideal may flicker, but it will never be extinguished. So we are here today. We will do our small part and press on with our business—solemnly, but resolutely." Sound the trumpets! (The "comment period" was later extended.)

Jeff Chester of the Center for Digital Democracy explains why this issue is so important:

> The ownership rules on the FCC chopping block have been developed over the last fifty years. They have been an important safeguard ensuring the public's basic first amendment rights. The rationale for these policies is that they help provide for a diverse media marketplace of ideas, essential for a democracy. They have not been perfect. But the rules have helped constrain the power of the corporate media giants.

WHAT'S THE CONNECTION?

Although the media usually likes to speculate about government intent, this official comment period on cross-ownership has gone largely uncommented upon on television or in the press, perhaps because many newspapers also own television stations.

It reminded me of a similarly unexplored story ten years ago, when George W.'s dad was gearing up for the Gulf War. The media at that time reported on a public debate that included many peace sentiments, much to the displeasure of many in the administration. The vote in Congress to authorize the war was very close (in what were clearly different circumstances).

At that time, the broadcast industry was lobbying the FCC hard for a change in financial syndication rules that would enormously bolster its bottom line. They ultimately won those changes and much, much more when the Telecommunications Reform Act passed in 1996. Those changes promised big money, as do the rule changes proposed today.

When the Gulf War erupted, some aggressive questions were raised by journalists at Pentagon briefings, especially because of the restrictions imposed on media coverage in the Gulf. Network bureau chiefs in Washington, D.C., had originally agreed to those restraints but later, after the war was over, complained that they'd been had and denounced the Pentagon's largely successful efforts at censorship.

This spectacle of the press doing its job in 1991 infuriated some in the FCC, especially commissioner James Quello, who was seen as the television industry's voice on the commission. Quello gave a high-profile speech to the Indiana Broadcasting Association, questioning the patriotism of television journalists for demanding hard information about the war. Here was a veteran in the television business turning on the very people who report news. His speech sent a worrying signal to the suites of media power. Later, CBS anchor Dan Rather would characterize television journalism during the war as playing the role of "lap dogs, not watchdogs." Most television coverage soon was marching in lockstep with government policy. The networks, and especially CNN, enjoyed high ratings and profits when they turned the Gulf War into a television newsathon. (I tell this story in more detail in my 2001 book, *News Dissector: Passions, Pieces and Polemics, 1960–2000*, from Akashic Books.)

After the war, I spoke to Quello, who was pleased as punch at the networks' performance. I later spoke to a respected producer at CBS's news magazine *60 Minutes,* who insisted on anonymity. He told me he had wanted their coverage to feature more debates. Higher-ups asked him to propose a plan to do it. He did, but, to his surprise, he never received a response. I quoted what he said happened in a piece I wrote for *Spin,* namely that a "prominent network fixer" was in the White House regularly during that period, lobbying for the FCC rule change, and that there was no way the administration could be confronted when the networks had such an important economic agenda under consideration in Washington. There is no way to confirm this story, but other journalists I've told it to say it sounds plausible.

WHAT'S HAPPENING NOW?

Fast-forward to the present. The FCC is, in effect, holding out the possibility of freeing the networks from restrictions on buying up more stations. At a time when the industry is hurting financially, big bucks are once again being dangled in front of media moguls. Who among them would challenge the government now on the current war effort? I think it is safe to predict the media will be chilling, in a time of more killing.

There is no way of knowing how this FCC initiative will influence news reporting in "the first war of the twenty-first century." Already an executive (who I know and respect) at NBC has counseled journalists there to be wary of reporting anything that can help the enemy. This is the same network news division that fired freelancer Jon Alpert when he brought back pictures showing the pain of Iraqi civilians in the aftermath of Desert Storm. NBC refused to show them.

We have experienced waves of media mergers, amidst a merger of newsbiz and showbiz. Is a military–media merger in the offing because of economic and political forces that seem invisible to many in the media, or is it in place already? It is not naïve to fear the emergence of a new media–military industrial complex taking shape as Americans enter this next round in our quest for "Infinite Justice."

At first glance, the relationship between media concentration and "America's New War" (as CNN puts it) seems tenuous. But is it? The cutbacks in coverage of the world that left so many Americans uninformed and unprepared for what is happening took place amidst this greatest wave of media consolidation in history. It has already had an effect. Will it get worse?

Warning—Media Management Now in Effect: From the News Dissector's Weblog

November 14

I am not sure when the Bush administration realized it had a media problem. The White House was humming along with a well-oiled media management machine. The president was riding high in the polls. He clearly had the country behind him. And yet, something wasn't working on the world stage, even after savvy handlers turned a politician denigrated as a bumbler to a more self-assured and even inspiring leader. Their media makeover was as meticulous as the makeup applied to movie stars playing monsters.

The turning point had come early on with Dubya's well-crafted speech to the U.S. Congress, which plainly had been designed with applause lines in mind and stirring but measured phrases. He had mastered the teleprompter and was well practiced in his delivery. It worked: One day he was laughed at as a global village idiot; the next he was hailed by the same pundits, on the strength of one performance piece, as a statesman par excellence.

Hungry for a leader, the American people rallied behind his call for unity, alertness, and patriotic patience. There were some murmurs about the mixed message that on the one hand counseled vigilance, and on the other, encouraged shopping as usual. Overseas, some eyebrows went up when phrases like "crusade" and "smoking out the evil ones" were dropped from his rhetorical lexicon.

But a serious communications problem remained because of a more objective problem: Many realists, especially in other countries, weren't clear that bombing and bombast could bring terrorists to heel. Those issues began to be raised by skeptics and even comics.

Three Steps

In response to the growing criticism and skepticism, the White House seems to have taken three steps.

First, keep critics off the air (and not just videos of bin Laden or Al-Jazeera, which "coincidentally" had its Kabul office bombed). It soon became clear that the media was allocating little space for domestic critics, much less harder-line opponents, of the policy. While administration officials condemned the ideological fundamentalism of the Taliban, a certain ideological intolerance began to be practiced in the homeland media. Fairness and Accuracy in Reporting (FAIR), noted on November 2 that forty-four columns in *The Washington Post* and *The New York Times* stressed a military response, with only two that suggested diplomatic and international law approaches.

The second step was to bring the press on board. The American media empires soon seemed to be marching in lockstep with the government. Despite a tightening of information policies and the total exclusion of reporters from most battlefields, nary a critical word was heard from many of those who have been the loudest in defense of freedom of the press. Even a champion of freedom of the press like Walter Cronkite said he was willing to countenance a censorship board of some kind, if camera crews were allowed in. (They weren't, and his proposal went nowhere.)

The media is going along to get along. Will government media managers soon boast about what a great job they did, as they did ten years ago in the aftermath of Desert Storm? Then, Michael Deaver, President Reagan's public relations honcho, was ecstatic, contending, "If you were to hire a public relations firm to do the media relations for an international event, it couldn't be done any better than this is being done." Hodding Carter, President Jimmy Carter's former chief flack, seconded the emotion. "If I were the government, I'd be paying the press for the coverage it's getting," he said.

Yet the press—and this was a television story above all else—did not have to be paid. Pete Williams, the man who "handled" media for the Pentagon during the Gulf War and was rewarded with a job on NBC news, boasted: "The reporting has been largely a recitation of what administration people have said, or an extension of it." Is this true today? Not totally. Happily, there are still some exceptions, like Seymour Hersh, who still catches the Pentagon in blatant lies, as happened recently in conflicting stories about casualties U.S. troops suffered on the ground.

The third and final step the government took was to get the West Coast studios to jump in. On the day this column was written, media moguls and movie studio heads strategized with White House aide Karl Rove on how they can do even more than they already have to boost the war effort. Tom Cruise, star of *Mission: Impossible* and the sequel, is just one star who has met with the CIA, and according to MSNBC.com, "He was emphatic about presenting the CIA in as positive a light as possible."

The military is quietly infiltrating Hollywood. The little-known Institute for Creative Studies at the University of Southern California brings top Hollywood talent into secret contact with top military officials. The think tank received funding of $45 million from the U.S. Army in 1999. According to the *Sunday Herald,* "One of the few members named publicly, by the Hollywood newspaper *Daily Variety,* is Steven de Souza, co-writer of the hit 1988 action movie *Die Hard.*" Michael Macedonia—of the U.S. Army's Simulation, Training, and Instrumentation Command said: "You're talking about screenwriters and producers. These are very brilliant, creative people. They can come up with fascinating insights very quickly."

While movieland is key because of its global reach, the cooperation of the television networks is vital for the engineering of consent on the domestic front. The networks have their own reasons to cooperate. Remember that while war unleashes devastation and death on people, it delivers ratings and brings life to television. War is often the "big story" (when sex isn't) and a defining moment for many journalists. It's the story that permits news departments to mobilize their "troops"—that's what ABC called employees when I worked there—and show off their high-tech deployments. Many reporters who make it to the top do so because of war reporting. Ask Peter Arnett, Christiane Amanpour, or even Peter Jennings—no disrespect intended—if being under fire helped or hurt their careers. The answer is obvious. Less obvious is the relationship between our bloated defense budget and war coverage. The Pentagon uses and manipulates television's military boosterism to hype adventures, secure appropriations, and sell weaponry.

Worldviews

The problem in an age of globalization is that harnessing domestic media is no longer enough. The fact is that coverage outside the United States seeps back in, and despite the government's media strategists, it is growing more critical by the day. Growing skepticism in influential media outlets overseas is worrying to policy makers here. On November 11, the front page of *The New York Times* carried a long piece on "the battle to shape opinion," reporting on the Bush administration's latest strategies. The article acknowledges that the administration has enforced "policies ensuring that journalists have little or no access to independent information about military strategies, successes and failures."

But it also notes that public opinion worldwide, led in part by the press, increasingly opposes U.S. policies. The Arab press is hostile; the Asian media, unconvinced. Over 60 percent of the people in Tony Blair's Britain—the only real partner the United States has in its leaky coalition—say they want a bombing pause. Half of Italy agrees; most of the German press is critical. I know because many media outlets in that country have interviewed me.

Reports the *Times,* with understated candor way at the bottom of a story that consumed an acre of print, "European journalists have also become suspicious that the American news media have been co-opted by the government or at least swept up by patriotism." One German calls this a "Post Vietnam Patriotic Syndrome." To massage this problem, the Bush administration has hired public relations firms and created a task force for coordinating U.S. and U.K. communications directors with daily conference calls between the White House, London, and Islamabad.

So far, there is no evidence that this public relations offensive is working internationally. In fact, a growing number of Americans are looking for news and information elsewhere, from the very sources that alarm Bush media strategists. NPR reports that Americans are flocking to foreign websites while England's BBC and Canada's CBC report a big spike in viewing by Americans. Our own Globalvision News Network is generating considerable traffic by offering articles and analysis from other countries. Clearly, other viewpoints are there for those willing to look for them. I was delighted to find *Vanity Fair* this month quoting me on this very issue (p. 182).

In the Soviet Union, most of its citizens didn't trust the state-managed press, fully aware of its propaganda function. In the United States, most people tend to trust the press, unaware of its role in what Noam Chomsky and Ed Herman call "manufacturing consent." I heard Max Robins of *TV Guide* report that news viewing is way up. True enough, but skepticism is also rising on both the right and the left, and it is likely to erupt in the mainstream sooner rather than later.

I hope that it is not too late for the U.S. media establishment to get the message, distance themselves from "official sources" and "coded" propaganda, and seek out more diverse sources of information.

Information Warriors: From the News Dissector's Weblog

January 23, 2002

A n acronym we haven't seen too much in the flow of reporting from every media pore over the course of our "holy war" on terror is IO. But "I" and "O" are two letters that have great importance among those charged with steering and massaging media coverage to ensure that it puts the military in the best possible light.

"IO," short for Information Operations, is the Pentagon's Ministry of Truth in the best *1984* sense of the term. Now it is time for us to focus in, and "eye-o," open our eyes to how this increasingly sophisticated military science works and why it has been so effective in shaping our images and ideas about a faraway war on many fronts.

There is an excellent exposé about this by former Associated Press correspondent Maud S. Beelman, director of the International Consortium of Investigative Journalists, a project of the Center of Public Integrity, in a provocative new issue of *Nieman Reports*, the journal of Harvard's Nieman Fellows in Journalism.

"IO groups together information functions ranging from public affairs to military deception and psychological operations or PSYOP," she writes. "What this means is that people whose job traditionally has been to talk to the media and divulge truthfully what they are able to tell, now work hand-in-glove with those whose job it is to support battlefield operations with information, not all of which may be truthful."

An August 1996 U.S. Army field manual, *100-6,* puts it point-blank: "Information is the currency of victory." To help decode this, let us turn to Major Gary Pounder, the chief of intelligence plans and presentations at the College of Aerospace Doctrine Research and Education at Maxwell Air Force Base. (That's a mouthful. Somehow I doubt this college of high-tech, war-fighting study deploys a cheerleading squad!) "IO practitioners," he explains, "must recognize that much of the information war will be waged in the public media." The military thus needs public affairs specialists, "to become full partners in the IO planning and execution process developing the skills and expertise required to win the media war."

Fighting On Three Fronts

There you have it. The Pentagon has set out to win at least three wars: the one on the battlefield of the moment, the so-called war for hearts and minds in the countries under attack, and "the media war." To translate further, we rely on blunt diplobully Richard Holbrooke, a Balkans negotiator and former U.N. ambassador, who, true to form, doesn't mince words. "Call it public diplomacy or public affairs, or psychological warfare or," he pauses, to cut through this fog, "if you really want to be blunt—propaganda."

So let's be blunt: IO is a way of obscuring and sanitizing that negative-sounding term "propaganda" so that our "information warriors" can do their thing with a minimum of public attention as they seek to engineer friendly write-ups and cumulative impact. They achieve this objective by pursuing the following strategies.

1. Overloading the Media

IO operates in some conflicts by providing too much information. During the Kosovo War, briefers at NATO's headquarters in Belgium boasted that this was the key to information control. "They would gorge the media with information," Beelman writes, quoting one as saying, "'When you make the media happy, the media will not look for the rest of the story.'" How's that for being blunt?

2. Ideological Appeals

We saw an appeal to patriotism and safeguarding the national interest in the fall when Condoleezza Rice and other Bush administration officials persuaded the networks to nix bin Laden videos and other Al-Jazeera work. This is nothing new. All administrations try to seduce and co-opt the media. Back in 1950, President Harry S. Truman appealed to top newspaper editors to back the Cold War with a "campaign for truth" in which "our great public information channels," as Secretary of State Dean Acheson referred to the media, would enlist. Nancy Berhard, author of *U.S. Television News and Cold War Propaganda, 1947–1960* (1999, Cambridge University Press), says "none of the assembled newsmen blanched" at Truman's "enlistment to propagandize."

It is this ideological conformity and worldview that makes it relatively easy for a well-oiled and sophisticated IO propaganda machine to keep the U.S. media in line. The Pentagon enjoys the avid cooperation of the corporate sector, which owns and controls most media outlets. Some of those companies, such as NBC parent General Electric, have long been a core component of that nexus of shared interests that President Eisenhower called the military–industrial complex. As Noam Chomsky and others have argued, that complex has expanded into a military, industrial, and *media* complex, in which IO is but one refinement.

3. Spinning Information

Spinning has become an art form. We see this every day at Pentagon briefings where what's really happening is, at best, secondary. For example, the weekly *Washington Post* edition of January 14–20 tells how reporters who scoured the bombed-out ruins of the town of Qalai Niazi in Afghanistan found an estimated eighty civilians dead, yet little or no evidence of Taliban or al Qaeda forces. The villagers they interviewed insisted, "there was nothing of the Taliban here." Yet most of the media minimized their own findings and instead relied on pronouncements by Pentagon officials who insisted that they were right to bomb the village to smithereens. In Washington, Secretary of Defense Rumsfeld gave the story what struck me as an IO spin: "There were multiple intelligence sources that qualified the target," he insisted. No reporter challenged him to produce evidence. Rumsfeld's words were enough, apparently because he is so personable, in an aw-shucks kind of way. In the end, newspapers like the *Post* always seem to conclude that what their reporters saw is insufficient. "There is much that is not known—and maybe never will be—about what happened on that December night," concludes Edward Cody, who filed the dispatch. Translation: No one is to blame, especially not the United States

4. Withholding Information

"Sorry, I am not at liberty to explain. But do I really have to?" says Ted Gup, who teaches journalism at Case Western Reserve University in Cleveland and writes about the secret lives of CIA operatives: "It is easy operating behind the curtain of secrecy to conceal setbacks and pronounce progress." Underline that word "easy."

Another disclosure appears in the *New Yorker,* where Seymour Hersh reveals that Pakistan, with U.S. permission, airlifted out its own military officers from Konduz on the eve of a battle. His version of these events contradicts the impression we had that the U.S. military explicitly prohibited any negotiations or escapes by forces under attack. Clearly, an exception had been made for our Pakistani "allies" who were still advising Taliban forces. This information was suppressed at the time in line with a policy of selective disclosure.

5. Co-Option and Collusion

But why do we in the media go along with this approach time and again? We are not stupid. We are not robots. Too many of us have *died* trying to get this story (and other stories). Journalists will tell you that no one tells them what to write or what to do. Yet there is a homogenized flavor and Pentagon echo to much coverage of this war that shames our profession. Why? Is it because reporters buy into the ideology of the mission? Is it because there are few visible war critics to provide dissenting takes? Or is it because information management has been so effective as to disallow any other legitimate approach? An uncritical stance is part of the problem. Disseminating misinformation often adds up to an inaccurate picture of where we are in this war.

Stratfor.com, a global intelligence consulting website, says the media has been reporting the war as a great victory, while the Pentagon itself is saying that the war in Afghanistan is just the first battle and that they are planning for six more years, with consequences unknown. Here is Stratfor.com's take: "Coverage of the 'war on terrorism' has reversed the traditional role between the press and the military. Abandoning the hypercritical coverage of the past, the media have become cheerleaders—allowing the conflict in Afghanistan to become synonymous with the war at large and portraying that war as an unalloyed success. The reversal of roles between media and military creates public expectations that can affect the prosecution of the war."

Pentagon–Media Rules

After the Gulf War, the bureau chiefs of the networks sat down with the Pentagon to work out guidelines that would permit independent access and end the pool system used during Desert Storm by the military to manage the press so successfully. The negotiations took eight months of haggling within the media, and between media and Pentagon representatives. Nine general principles were agreed on. The key one was this: "Open and independent reporting will be the principal means of coverage of U.S. military operations."

Once the "war on terror" began, the Pentagon reaffirmed its commitment to these principles and then promptly forgot about them, applying an IO strategy of appearing to be open while defining the terms and framing the story themselves whenever possible. Did the media chiefs yell bloody murder? Hell no. They acquiesced and seemed to forget that independence should govern the relationship between Washington and those that write about its machinations.

I will give the last word to Stanley Cloud, who ran *Time* magazine's Vietnam reporting, and was one of the post–Gulf War media negotiators: "No government can be depended upon to tell the truth, the whole truth, and nothing but the truth—especially not when that government makes mistakes or misjudgments in war time. The natural inclination then is to cover up, to hide, and the press's role, in war even more than in peace, is to act as a watchdog and truth seeker."

If the press is not playing this role, it may be because the media is no match for IO specialists who have learned all too well how to massage, manipulate, and manage news coverage.

Is the Media Ready for a New War?

Who wants to think about war on Valentine's Day? I am part of the "make love not war" generation, yet it was on the eve of the day for roses and romance that the Bush administration started ratcheting up the next major front in its war on terror. The saber-rattling over Iraq began with threats by Colin Powell and with reports in *The Washington Post* and the *Guardian* of a shadowy "principals committee" orchestrating covert teams and psychological operations aimed not just at Baghdad but at the American people, who are being readied for a conflict that may involve as many as 200,000 U.S. soldiers.

As the Humvees hum into gear, as the B-52s are refueled, and as another Gulf War (and possible syndrome) looms on the horizon, media organizations need to start lobbying to make sure they will have access. As we know all too well from the last time out in the Gulf, coverage was contained by the Pentagon, with few exceptions.

In Afghanistan, the media have once again, for the most part, been odd man out, scrambling to survive killers and marauders on the road while being targeted by death threats by our "allies."

We still don't know all that much of what was won and at what cost. The number of civilian casualties was downplayed. Few journalists were close to the action, except perhaps Fox's Geraldo Rivera, who can always be counted on to create some of his own action. Think of the blur of the images—caves being bombed, breathless accounts of Osama bin Laden's suspected whereabouts, images of heroic liberators who turned out in many cases to be gangsters, opium growers, and despots. The Taliban was toppled, but Shari'ah law—strict Islamic edicts backed up by harsh punishments—survives.

And for several weeks, more reporters died than soldiers. As I write, the fate of *The Wall Street Journal's* Daniel Pearl is unknown. His captors are (so far) unpersuaded by appeals from the newspaper of business or even a parade of Muslim Americans, including Louis Farrakhan, leader of the Nation of Islam. [Publisher's note: Daniel Pearl was later found to have been slain by terrorists in Pakistan. A Pakistani court has since found his murderers, four Islamic militants, guilty of murder, kidnapping, conspiracy to kidnap, and tampering with evidence.] Journalists appear to be fair game, perhaps in part because of the belief—which, in some instances (unfortunately), is all too true—that they (we) are one-sided transmission belts for their governments.

A column in the *Dallas Morning News* by Carolyn Barta points out that war correspondents have become an endangered species:

> "American journalists are no longer considered noncombatants. At one time they were considered like the Red Cross," said Stephen Hess, a Brookings Institution scholar and author of the book *International News and Foreign Correspondents.* . . . A few years ago, extremists might have kidnapped an American corporate executive or bombed a diplomat. Now they go after a journalist. "It's part of the anti-American feeling in the world and [the feeling that] journalists are not objective professionals who are *above country,*" Mr. Hess said.

The question that American news outlets have to ask is what it means to be "above country." Media companies that have their anchors wearing American flags and plaster their programs with patriotic imagery are taking sides—especially when they give little or no airtime to critics and dissenters. Surely, one can express pride of country and practice its tradition of supporting the right to dissent at the same time. The most current example is the red, white, and blue Olympics, where dissenters are forced to demonstrate in penned areas miles from the crowds, virtually uncovered on television.

THE NEW MEDIA WAR

The Afghan war is being stage-managed, not from a tent in some outback or cave but from the central command's military base in Tampa, Florida. When the war started, the enemy was projected—as was the "crack" Iraqi Republican

Guard a decade earlier—as 10,000 strong, fearsome, and ferocious. In a matter of weeks, enough bombs moved enough rocks, and killed enough jihad junkies, to facilitate a quick victory. Meanwhile "O & O," Osama and Omar, the evil twins of terror, managed to disappear. With that, the public, which had been primed to believe that the posse would bring them back dead or alive, began to lose interest as network coverage began to shrink. There was no pound of flesh, and most Americans never heard the reports that more Afghan civilians died as a result of U.S. bombing than those killed at the World Trade Center, as reported by professor Marc W. Herold at the University of New Hampshire.

What was also new was that Washington-based Pentagon reporters became the media's front line. Television news showed canned video of weapons systems while the "Rumsfield Follies"—the Secretary of Defense's press conferences—updated the old "Five O'clock Follies" from Vietnam, where the line was always that the light is at the end of the tunnel. At least in those days, some reporters in the tunnel could see that there was no light. Today, there is not even a tunnel. In all too many cases, reporting has turned into stenography, without context or analysis.

WHAT'S NEXT?

The Washington Post's Bob Woodward reports that CIA operations may be underway in as many as eighty nations. Reports suggest that a string of assassinations of opposition leaders in Indonesia, the Philippines, and Nigeria may be linked. Intelligence bureaucracies have ballooned. They now have legal authority and the resources to do pretty much whatever they want. Whether they can succeed is another matter.

Do we have any grasp of how massive and well-funded this web of military power is? Are we being alerted to the risks and dangers? I was startled to hear South Africa's Bishop Tutu (whom I always considered a pragmatist, not a paranoid) raise a fear many find unthinkable. "Can you imagine any scenario," he asked at a session of the recent World Economic Forum, "in which America would suspend its democracy?" The room quieted down. Some heads began to nod. No one challenged him. The growing fear: It could happen here.

To prevent that, *now* is the time for media institutions, journalists' organizations, and citizens' groups to seize the initiative and demand that a free press must have the right to cover wars the way they need to be covered. If the people have a right to know, if that often-cited fog of war is to be lifted, then media institutions have to speak up—loudly. And the public has to press for them to do it.

WHAT WE NEED TO KNOW

We need to know more than what the government is saying. We need hard facts about what it is doing. And not just the government. What about the industrial side of the military–industrial complex? What are the oil companies really up to in the Middle East and Central Asia? Tell us about interests as well as issues.

Also, how about some attention to alternatives to war and to the principles of peace journalism that offers a promising new way of covering conflict, going beyond the role of cheerleader?

Wanting the truth is not enough. It is like waiting for Godot. We have to press for it.

Israeli journalist and peace activist Uri Avnery writes this week about the way public opinion in his country is beginning to shift against uncritical support for hard-line policies, even as Israelis confront attacks from terrorists:

> It always starts with a small group of committed people. They raise their feeble voice. The media ignore them, the politicians laugh at them ("a tiny, marginal and vociferous group"). The respectable parties and the established old organizations crinkle their noses and distance themselves from their "radical slogans." But slowly they start to have an impact. "Important" journalists, serving as weathercocks, smell the change and adapt themselves in time to the new winds.
>
> The famous anthropologist Margaret Mead said about this: "Never doubt that a small group of thoughtful, committed citizens can change the world. Indeed, it's the only thing that ever has." And German philosopher Arthur Schopenhauer said, "All truth passes through three stages. First, it is ridiculed. Second, it is violently opposed. Third, it is accepted as self-evident."

Let us hope that in the case of this most recent war, and in any wars to come, these three stages will kick in, at least insofar as media coverage goes. We need more skepticism of official claims, more independent investigations and, of course, more truth.

Media War: The Cultural Dimension

FREEDOM OF SPEECH VS. FREEDOM OF THE PRESS: HOW MEDIA THREATENS CIVIL LIBERTIES

Civil liberties are really about exercising the liberty to be civil, which is to participate in the discourse in civil society. The first amendment that proscribed Congress from making no laws against freedom of speech also implies support for the right to speak, perhaps even the democratic duty to do so.

Most debates about civil liberties focus on governmental abuses and Big Brother laws that intrude on our privacy and censor what we can read, see, or hear. But what happens to these issues as power shifts from the public to private and, in an era of globalization, from national governments to less accountable international bodies and multinational corporations who operate beyond the reach of U.S. law and tradition?

Just as these forces and new global realities have reframed many political debates and options, they are restructuring the civil liberties challenge, even though many of its advocates continue to act as if nothing has changed in the way we have to think about the threats to free expression.

A recent NATION Institute forum on the subject illustrated the problem. Prominent journalists, advocates, and even the president of the American Civil Liberties Union spoke articulately about the new threats to civil liberties in the post–September 11 environment. Critiques were offered of the draconian terms of the U.S. Patriot Act, and the growing suspension of legal protections of immigrants, especially of Arab descent in the name of fighting terrorism.

But:

Most Americans don't fully appreciate these dangers, in large part because they are not being told about them. They are also not being told about them by the one power center in American life that, in my view, currently poses the greatest threat to the exercise of our civil liberties.

Our media.

On the face of it, this conclusion may sound preposterous in a country that boasts of the freest media in the world. How can it be that freedom of speech is being menaced by freedom of the press? Has the traditional conflict between the First Amendment and government abuses given way to a deeper but often invisible intra–First Amendment conflict between the right, needs, and interests of the public to have its say and the power and priorities of our communications system that continues to muzzle and restrain its voice?

Oddly enough, I had to raise the question of the media role from the floor, after the civil liberties panel (which, ironically, was moderated by the media maven Phil Donahue). The audience applauded, and at least two people took up my line of questioning. Yet the civil liberties traditionalists didn't even have this aspect of the issue on the agenda. Once it was raised, they all jumped in with personal testimonies to its importance.

In the aftermath of the attacks of September 11, it was common to hear journalists and pundits alike say we were at a turning point, as in "the world will never be the same." But, since then, not only has our commercial-dominated media system remained largely the same, but it has steadily narrowed and limited a national conversation about the parameters, logic, and effect of the U.S.-sponsored global "war on terrorism" that followed.

THE WAR IN THE MEDIA

In the extensive coverage in the aftermath of September 11, institutional and systemic flaws began to appear for the discerning analyst. It is not really the amount of coverage that determines its comprehensiveness, but its thoroughness and ability to ask questions from a multiplicity of perspectives. And this did not materialize in the coverage.

Americans who worried about the impacts on our civil liberties, or who protested hate crimes and roundups of suspects on ethnic grounds, found themselves largely shut out of the discourse, marginalized and unable to have much of an impact on public opinion. Institutional trends within the media have been to downgrade serious news and global coverage. Promoted in its place has been a fusion of newsbiz and showbiz known as "infotainment," which had been underway for years with the consequence of depoliticizing politics itself.

With the emergence of "terror-tainment" came the blurring of the lines between jingoism and journalism, punditry and commentary laced with patriotism while all other viewpoints moved out of sight. As a period of "patriotic correctness" began, self-censorship and corporate censorship snapped into place. There was a flurry of incidents—editorial writers fired for raising the wrong questions, editorial cartoonists dropped, and advertisers pulling out a comedy show whose host had made a remark that offended a conservative talk show big mouth, who mounted a campaign to drive the program off the air.

The signal had been sent. Soon, the media began marching in lockstep with the government with dissenters hard to find. A hypercompetitive and fast-consolidating media system has time and again put its bottom-line, free-market concerns ahead of its responsibility to protect and vitalize the marketplace of ideas. The problem was not just the government's largely successful attempts to limit information but the media's unwillingness to challenge or flout them.

We live in a "mediaocracy," where the media is no longer a separate fourth estate functioning as an independent watchdog, but, rather, it is an active participant in the policy debate and electoral process. Government and media tend to synergize and interact with shared assumptions and common messages, especially on national security steps.

Within this background, as government media strategies are put in effect and as they quietly manage media practices, the space for the exercise of free speech narrows. Crude censorship is not the problem today. The media are.

My question is this: what will it take for the civil liberties movement to recognize that it has a common interest with the growing media reform movement? When will it begin educating its members and constituencies that freedom of the press must not be interpreted as freedom only for the press lords and their monopolistic uber-merged companies?

Criticizing media practices is not censorship. It is the work of saving democracy.

Cultural Responses—Music As Media: From the News Dissector's Weblog

October 10, 2001: "Before The Deluge"

It was September 23, 1979. Battery Park City was a pit of sand then, not from fallen towers as it is today, but because that corner of lower Manhattan, next door to the World Trade Center, was still a landfill site on which a city within a city would soon rise.

Two decades ago, 250,000 people converged in the shadow of the Twin Towers for a giant "No Nukes" rally headlined by Jackson Browne and other musical superstars. That rally was the culmination of five days of the MUSE (Musicians United for Safe Energy) Concerts for a Non-Nuclear Future at a packed Madison Square Garden.

Jackson Browne sang his big hit that Sunday afternoon alongside the majestic Hudson River. It was prophetically called "Before the Deluge" and contained the line: "And let the buildings keep our children dry." He and his counterparts had come to sing against the dangers of an energy policy built around nuclear plants. Many others had come to hear the stars sing, to sing along, to stand with them against a corporate threat that seemed to promise only destruction. In those years, there was a strong intersection between popular culture and movements for change. I helped anchor coverage for a national string of commercial FM rock stations, coverage a political rally would never get today.

Back then, years before we'd heard the term *globalization,* the World Trade Center was considered a symbol of world greed. "Do you lie down and let those corporations roll over you?" Browne asked. "Can you leave your life in the hands of those people?"

That 1979 event and events like it slowed (and some think stopped) the momentum of nuclear plant construction. The nuclear industry was put on the defensive and lost billions in the following years after some of the problems critics warned against surfaced in places like Three Mile Island and Chernobyl.

Oil's Role

None of us then could have foreseen the events of September 11, 2001, or how the politics of energy and oil would become the backdrop for conflicts and wars to come. Many of us still don't recognize that the "new war" most Americans support as a just campaign to wipe out a band of evil terrorists may morph quickly into a war to control the oil fields dominated by Iraq and the Saudis, whose society produced bin Ladin and funds Islamic extremism as a counterweight against political radicalism and democratic change. As the world economy shrinks and corporate profits decline, there will be pressures for more intervention in other lands in a fight over resources.

For many in the desperately poor and developing world, the America they hate or call the great Satan is experienced through the presence of the oil and energy industries. Many of their opposition movements are aware of the power and influence of multinational corporations as the wedge of U.S. influence, even if they aren't much investigated or reported either abroad or here. I have so far seen only one thoroughgoing analysis, for example, about the oil aspect of this conflict in an American newspaper, a report by Frank Viviano in the *San Franscisco Chronicle*. "The hidden stakes in the war against terrorism can be summed up in a single word: oil," he writes. "Rather than a simple confrontation between Islam and the West, [these energy sources] will be the primary flash point of global conflict for decades to come."

Most Americans are not exposed to much coverage of the interests that shape our policies or the problems they exacerbate. At the same time, the people who rally against our country overseas are not terribly well informed about the "Other America." Their media are rarely objective and do not feature the views of American critics and dissenters. This is a shame because it is important to know that the interests of the majority of working people are often at odds with the interest of oil companies. How many readers and viewers in other countries know that an attack on a symbol of financial power also took the lives of 1,000 members of trade unions? Unhappily, the media in many countries keep their cultures in a bubble of insularity and ignorance.

As Benjamin R. Barber makes clear in his thoughtful study, *Jihad vs. McWorld*, much of the world is locked in a battle between two fundamentalisms that are equally at odds with the spirit and demands of democracy. Islamic fundamentalism and global market capitalism share more in outlook than is commonly recognized, he says. Both want to silence the voices of ordinary people and impose forms of control from above; both use media shamelessly and all too effectively to promote their ideological mission and values.

Flashing Forward

Today, Jackson Browne is still at it, this time joining as many as 200 other artists, athletes, and others in recording another musical anthem, "We Are Family," a song that originally came out in the year of the "No Nukes" rally at the World Trade Center. "We Are Family" has been remade by one of its original producers, Nile Rodgers, as an anthem of our common humanity, a song to help promote a sense that we are all part of a global family that has to stand up against the intolerance and hate crimes that have crawled out of the rubble of September 11. I documented the ten-day production and recording sessions for a "making of and meaning of" film. Spike Lee is producing the music video.

Other artists have been quite visible in this crisis. A telethon broadcast on thirty-five U.S. networks and in 156 countries featured top musicians singing powerful songs of social concern (and raised $150 million for disaster relief). A long-scheduled John Lennon tribute was also turned into a fund-raiser. Both events featured renditions of Lennon's anthem "Imagine," which was on the list of songs that Clear Channel communications seemed to want to censor from the radio. Music still has the power to do what journalism does so rarely: reinforce empathy, caring, and a sense of a world with other possibilities.

Ten years ago, on the eve of the Gulf War, I produced a documentary on the making of another message song, a remake of "Give Peace a Chance" by John Lennon's son Sean, and Lenny Kravitz, with thirty-seven other artists from every musical genre. That song was powerfully done but totally suppressed by the media at the start of the Gulf War. No outlets would play a peace song then. It was considered traitorous. Today, Yoko Ono has posted a billboard with the words "Give Peace a Chance" on a billboard affixed to an office building in Times Square. It is not signed or identified in any way.

Today, as what CNN calls "America's New War" cranks up, as the flags fly in the news and on the sets of newscasts, will the loving vibe of "We Are Family" get a proper hearing? Let's hope so, even as we seem to be in for a new period of censorship, self-censorship, and the muzzling of dissent. It is a message we need more than ever as bombs and missiles crash down on their targets.

Media, Celebrity, and Family

ost media critics have the luxury of holding forth via the safety and security of academe. Or they lob their jeremiads at the media thanks to a staff job on some media outlet permitting the luxury of biting the hand that feeds. In the indy media world, sustainability is a goal to aim for while "multiple revenue streams" (i.e., hustling on all fronts) is the order of the day. This News Dissector is also a media maker, working as a filmmaker by day and critical voice by night. For most of us in the world of documentaries, hopes for a big payday spring eternal, but the reality is that one lives close to the edge, roller-coasting between short if sweet moments of recognition and harsher financial realities.

That is why it is such a breakthrough when a documentary you make breaks out of the ghetto of good intentions and actually gets some attention. Most people don't write about the process while living through it—many fear a jinx of words that will come back to bite them—but some of my recent experiences may be instructive on the challenges and obstacles along the way, especially when you work on a project with celebrities in a country that adores them while also trashing them.

The story has more than a few points of interest and drama. A terrorist attack. A response by well-known artists, actors, and athletes. The antics of a big-mouthed diva. The difficulties of having an independent cultural statement not backed by big media companies taken seriously.

SEPTEMBER 11 SETS THE STAGE

This one started with the Twin Towers' crashing down on September 11, with the whole news business scrambling to cover the biggest story of this new century, and with our company sidelined with no network to feed or outlet to supply. Like many indies, we had the means of production, but not distribution.

Like everyone in New York, we were shaken, but we wanted to offer journalism of substance, to do or contribute something to our public understanding. The big news machine was in high gear, but alas, there didn't seem to be much of a role for independent journalists to play.

Then a call came in from Tom Silverman of Tommy Boy Records with the opportunity to document an effort by artists to respond to the events by remaking the song "We Are Family." Director Spike Lee had signed on to direct a music video featuring more than 200 artists, actors, and athletes, and we were being asked to produce the documentary. Unlike many of the straight-out fundraising efforts then underway, such as a telethon, this project (sparked by producer Nile Rodgers) was about raising awareness and infusing the unity that so many of us felt with the spirit of tolerance, condemnation of hate crimes, and a sense of global humanity. The idea of family was projected as a counterpoint to the jingoistic focus on nation and retaliation, which was then in vogue.

THE STARS TURN OUT

We leapt at a chance to get involved, even though we didn't know what to expect. I feared it might turn into another feel-good, celebrity-ego session. After all, here in one room, were Diana Ross, Patti LaBelle, Dionne Warwick, and a whole list of greats. But I was wrong. The singing and sense of solidarity one felt was transcendent; it renewed me spiritually in much the same way it did many of the participants, who spoke of how a collective effort like this was a chance to be at once positive and to celebrate America's values of multicultural expression. The money they hoped to raise was to benefit organizations promoting tolerance and defending our freedoms. Not enough attention was being paid to this, especially in the media.

The hope was that having so many high-profile people would give these issues more momentum. The stars get attention; hence, we would be able to help the culture heal. Yet it never quite works out that way because our cynical media has a love–hate relationship with the celebrity world. All too often, media outlets that devote acres of print to detailing their most trivial pursuits turn into attack dogs when some aspire to take a stand or transcend the acting or singing roles they are confined in.

The New York Times reported on March 10 that magazines that once manu-factured celebrities now just want to use them for their own purposes. But when celebrities have their own ideas—or any ideas at all—they often get put down as if they know nothing about issues. Bono told me recently that his motives were called into question when he started campaigning for debt relief. It was only after he met with the Pope that he began to be treated as someone who knew what he was talking about.

Much of the press prefer celebrities as one-dimensional court jesters and entertainers, not as people with concerns and as citizens who also want to play a role in our cultural and political life. This is especially true of people who do not have the imprimatur of a current hit record or a big media brand behind them with bucks to buy ads in their publications. Don't ever think that quid pro quos don't exist between the entertainment industry and the media outlets they own and control. At the same time, however, not all celebrities check their egos or agendas at the door.

EGO WARS

And so it might have been predicted that something would go awry. And it did on the very first day, when comedienne Joan Rivers, who had agreed to take part, reversed herself and went on the radio and to the press with exaggerated charges that she had been duped because the list of original beneficiaries the organizers initially hoped to support had been diversified. Known for a big mouth and punchy one-liners, Rivers attacked the project and in doing so, freaked out the people who had worked so hard to organize it. As a result of her aggressive and visible stance, other stars dropped out, wanting to avoid getting tarnished. Her verbal assault turned a gesture of compassion into the kind of controversy the tabloids love—a food fight among celebrities. Fortunately, the show went on, but Rivers reaped as much publicity as the project did. She under-stood just how to orchestrate media attention her way. When pressed by one of the organizers (Bryan Bantry) to reconsider, she reportedly told him, with his aide listening in on the conference call, "Fuck world peace." Later Nile Rodgers would say, "If we had world peace, September 11 wouldn't have happened."

Dealing with outsized egos like this is one of the drawbacks of relying on big names, who can often be mercurial, self-promoting, insincere, and so used to being coddled and sucked up to that they can't function without "their peo-ple" present. Their personalities also tend to draw more attention than the causes they promote. I raise this only because this tempest in a teapot was nevertheless part of the story that I documented. There was no time to include the episode in a shortened version of the film that played at the Sundance Film Festival, but as a journalist, I thought it had to be part of the feature-length film. I was more interested in how the people running the project handled a defection in their ranks than in the actual content of the inanities she supposedly uttered.

THE FILM PREMIERES IN NEW YORK

On March 4, we showed the film for the first time. The story of Rivers' refusal to take part, the epithets she used, and Nile Rodgers' response was included. (Rodgers was more disappointed than angry and said that Rivers was "entitled to own her own feelings.") After the event, Fox's Roger Friedman ran into Rivers at Elaine's, an East Side watering hole patronized by celebrities. He would later write a positive review of the film, but he also reported that Rivers was furious to hear that she is in the film and vehemently denied having ever said "Fuck world peace," even though two publicists on the project heard her. Those are not words you forget. Anyway, Friedman asked her what she did remember saying. She now says that she said, "Fuck the Muslims" and "Fuck the terrorists." In reporting on this, Friedman used "expletive" rather than "fuck." We later confirmed with him that his account was accurate, but then, just to make sure, we called Rivers to see what she would say.

Instead of responding to our questions, Ms. Rivers called in the attack dogs by contacting her lawyer, who sent Nile Rodgers a letter threatening legal action, claiming the depiction was false, "disparaging, defamatory, and put Ms. Rivers in a bad light." Here she is, a public figure who used her access to the media and celebrity to disparage and undermine "We Are Family," now demanding an apology and using a big law firm with offices in eight cities to bully, intimidate, and try to get us to self-censor the film. We decided to apologize by noting what she now claims she did say, the bit about Muslims, but we would not buckle to what struck us as a demand to censor our views. "We Are Family," by the way, is a call for tolerance and speaks out against the hate crimes that irresponsible hotheads who say "Fuck the Muslims" intentionally or unintentionally inspire.

Her threats provoked a debate in our own ranks because we believe that even though the claims she makes are baseless and would be thrown out of court, according to the president of the American Civil Liberties Union whom I consulted, she is rich enough and possibly annoyed enough to sue. That's my opinion anyway. A lawsuit would also force us to spend money we don't have defending ourselves. This is the scary part. We were then faced with the question of how much risk we could afford to absorb to stand up for our rights and artistic vision. At the same time, we know that the more this issue becomes about what Joan Rivers did or did not say, we will end up unintentionally promoting her status and help her pander to the lowest common denominator, which has often been her stock and trade. She may be a funny woman, but the joke would be on us.

Many of my colleagues felt the hassle was not worth it and that her stance, which distracted public support once, threatened to do so again. The sad truth is we could not get errors and omissions insurance to defend the film if we were sued. When an insurer suspects that there is problem, they decline to get involved. So we were left with the choice of putting our company at risk by doing what we felt was fair and accurate. The result, to my shame and displeasure as a documentarian, was that we cut her out altogether. The pragmatists won the day. But at least I have this outlet to tell the story that the film will not because of these pressures. She may be able to use her showbiz clout against the film, but as far as I know, a columnist still has a right to express an opinion and dissect a controversy. Not everyone has this type of an outlet, so incidents like this, which happen every day, are rarely brought to light.

REVIEWING THE REVIEWERS

This issue turned out to be not that central to anyone but Rivers and me as the journalist. More upsetting were some of the reviews. We couldn't afford to hold press screenings, so we sent out cassettes, which I am told never get the same attention from critics because they are not watching the film with an audience or necessarily in a quiet space. Since the movie is about music and a message, it tends to fall in the cracks between film buffs oriented toward dramas or traditional documentaries, and music critics who don't focus on the quality of the film or its message. More important, here in New York, we have had an overload of September 11 coverage, and this film falls outside the usual treatment the issue receives, which focuses more on what happened than what it means for our culture.

Many entertainers had raised money for the established causes, but this project goes beyond that. It captures the effect of the attacks but in a far more personal way, and it calls for tolerance, not a theme widely echoed in the media. I know it is always bad form to respond to reviewers, but as a media writer, I am very conscious of how stories get misrepresented. Now that it has happened to me, I can't just shut up without talking back and letting the chips fall where they may. The truth is that, whatever one's taste or sensibility, accuracy is at least a standard everyone would agree on. What surprised me was that three critics didn't seem to know what the film was about, and they instead vented their negative feelings toward the motives of the artists. *The New York Times* sent a music critic who panned the artists more than the movie. The *Daily News* falsely pictured it as a film about Spike Lee's movie, which it clearly is not. *The Village Voice* praised it with a faint damn.

And Murdoch's *Post*—which amplified Joan Rivers' original denunciation of "We Are Family" because it made good copy back in September in its ongoing culture war against all progressive ideas—compared the artists (I love this) to the Manson Family. I guess that is what happens when you deviate from the script on how we all were supposed to understand what happened on September 11 and how to feel about it. Now that "patriotic correctness" is in, the solidarity of "We Are Family" is apparently off message.

Curiously, Fox reviewer Roger Friedman, working for the one outlet I would have expected to be hostile (and that's my stereotype at work) was supportive. "The film . . . is wonderful. It is a must-see experience for everyone interested in the effects of September 11. Go see it, and if it's not playing in your town soon, ask your local small movie house to get it." Go figure!

At the same time, the real goal of "We Are Family" remains unrealized at this writing—to get it shown on television and seen widely. If you live in the New York area, you can see it at the Screening Room on Varick Street, the closest movie house to Ground Zero. This is a big breakthrough because so few documentaries ever get theatrical runs. We hope you go to support the cause and charities the film champions, as well as to get a taste of the infectious spirit and musical energy that inspired me to make it. A music video version for children featuring Sesame Street characters, Barney, and other faves of the under-five set received extensive airplay.

But if you should buy a ticket just as a way to say (expletive) Joan Rivers, I am sure the theater won't throw you out. By the way, I do know that her behavior is a symptom of a deeper cultural insensitivity, not just an act of self-interested personal neurosis. In the end, I give her the benefit of the doubt even as she doubts our benefit.

(The Trio Channel, a part of USA networks run by Barry Diller, bought "We Are Family" for airing on September 11, 2002.)

Independent Film and Media Coverage
The Independent Film Channel, 2002

R ory O'Connor, cofounder of Globalvision and producer of the documentary *The Meaning and Making of "We Are Family"*, talks to the Independent
Film Channel about the reformed media and the need for information in a
democracy.

JANUARY 2002

Rory O'Connor, President and CEO of Globalvision, served as executive producer of *The Meaning and Making of "We Are Family"* and was also in the studio
shooting footage during the two-day recording session. A veteran journalist who
has worked as a writer, director, producer, and broadcaster, Rory talked to
IFCTV.com about how the documentary marries entertainment and information, and about the responsibility of the media in a democracy.

> *IFCTV.com:* Since the attacks, the media publicly discussed how it will shift
> its focus from fluff to hard news. Do you think they have been suc
> cessful? How long do you think that effort will last?

Rory O'Connor (RO): Well that seems to be the operative question. Is this a permanent change, or a temporary change? My stock answer to that is, Will you ever get on an airplane again and feel the same way as you did before September 11? Will you ever open your mail again and not think of anthrax? I think you know the answer to that, and the answer is no. So, when people say to me, is this a change in people's immediate desires or interests? I say I think it's a permanent change. Americans no longer have the luxury of thinking that we're this island that can't be touched by the rest of the world—we are separated by these oceans, and bad things happen, but they happen out there, and we don't want to know about it, and we don't need to know about it.

Of course, this is the $64,000 question but, looking back, doesn't it seem incredibly silly to all of us now that the entire country and all of its media was obsessed with one missing person for six months? What are the top stories before the attacks? Shark attacks in Florida and Chandra Levy. By the way, if Chandra Levy were the most important story in the world, which you would think from the coverage, what happened? Did they find her, and nobody told me? How could it be the most important story one day, and drop off the media screens permanently the next day? That tells you a lot about the silliness and the lack of focus in the mainstream media in America. Now these people say we are giving the audience what the audience wants, but we've had a company for fifteen years that we think has been testing that supposition and proving it wrong. What we've found in doing hard news, as opposed to soft news, and international news, as opposed to American, is that when we can get to the audience, the audience is interested.

The real problem is the gatekeepers between the people with the information and the audience. There's a supply of meaningful information around the world, and there's a demand from the audience to get it; but the gatekeepers, the distributors and the networks, are standing in between the supply and the demand. At least they were prior to September 11. The ones that get it, that stop being an obstacle and matching that supply of information with the demand for information, are going to be the big winners. And the ones that don't are going to become dinosaurs and go away.

IFCTV.com: A part of your mission is to cover stories that aren't being covered, from angles that aren't being taken. Are you experiencing a more open environment for those stories?

RO: We've already experienced a big change. First of all, on one of our websites, the Media Channel (Mediachannel.org), traffic doubled. Secondly, in terms of press reaction—and these things are cyclical—but all of a sudden, we are being written about a lot more sympathetically. Before, people would ignore us; but to the extent that people would write about us at all, they would take this, "Oh, these poor earnest serious minded guys who really don't get it" angle. Again, that permanent change in terms of the media has obviously had a bit of a trickle down affect on us.

IFCTV.com: One of the attacks on the media that is coming is that there was a lot going on in Afghanistan before any of this happened.

RO: There is a whole big, wide world out there. I left CBS news, and Danny [Schechter] left ABC news not because we didn't want to reach millions of people, but that we didn't want to reach them with meaningless content. This was pre-O.J., pre-Elian, and pre-Chandra, and already the handwriting was on the wall. So, we wanted to take those skills of reaching large audiences, and match them with some meaningful content; and that's what we've been doing for the past fifteen years. Sometimes we're hot, and sometimes we're not. Right now, we're hot. And I have to say, emotionally, I feel conflicted about that, because the bad news has been good news for us in a sense, and there's a certain amount of guilt that comes along with that.

IFCTV.com: How do you feel *The Meaning and Making of "We Are Family"* documentary fits into the overall mission of the company?

RO: Well, *We Are Family,* in a sense, is the perfect Globalvision project, because it marries information and entertainment value. That's something that we always try to do. I was a rock critic before I became a film director; Danny was the news director of the number one rock and roll station in New England. So, we come from a pop cultural place where we always felt we could communicate a lot of the information and the meaning in an entertaining way.

I'll give you an example. For three years, we did a weekly series about South Africa when it was under apartheid. It was a news magazine and a serious concept, but every half hour show had a culture component. We often would lead with that component, whether it was Mzwakhe Mbuli, who was the people's poet of South Africa, or whether it was Bruce Springsteen and the Human Rights Now tour. If millions of people are buying Bruce Springsteen's album, and we have Bruce Springsteen footage, don't you think we're going to use it, and we're going to lead with it? But, we're not just going to put it up because it's a song; we're going to put it up because it's going to take you somewhere and it's going to be meaningful.

So, with *We Are Family,* you have the elements of a film that could really do it all. It's got celebrity, its got entertainment value, it's got information, and it's got meaning and every time I watch it, I cry. Because of the events of September 11, you can't help but cry. It touches you deeply. Also, you laugh. There's a lot of joy in there, and there's a lot of entertainment in there. There are some incredible singers in there: Patti LaBelle, Luther Vandross, the Pointer Sisters, Roberta Flack. There are some very meaningful moments with people—Matthew Modine, for example, who I find quite moving in many of the things that he says. I'm executive producer of the film, as you know, but I also was shooting in New York, and it was an incredible day when 150 people came together in this tiny little recording studio; and the vibe was fantastic. Everyone from firefighters, to police officers, to actors, to athletes, to musicians, and for some reason it all fit together, and it all worked. It doesn't sound like it would. Going into it, I was thinking this seems like a big mish-mosh; but the vibe and the spirit of the song, and the day really carried it through. I hope that we captured that, and it's something that comes across when people see the film.

IFCTV.com: What do you feel is the responsibility of people in your position, or people in television who are covering this?

RO: Thomas Jefferson said information is the currency of democracy. Not only have I often quoted that, but also I felt that in the last twenty years—not to be too highfalutin, but I feel like our democracy was in peril by a lack of information. Mainstream media, particularly the mainstream broadcast media, turned its back on the rest of the world for reasons that I would argue are directly related to profit and the market, and only that. They did a real disservice to the country and to their audience. The audience is not just consumers, they are citizens. Don't forget that the television airwaves are public airwaves that are only licensed to television networks. In cable, they insisted they put in something called public access. There is a public space and a public need, and one of the real dilemmas in the media that has gotten shaken and stood on its head that needs to be reexamined now as a result of September 11, is that relationship between private media and public need.

For example, we just decided there is a public need to have security in airports. So, we're going to take that out of private hands, and we're going to make it public. Twenty-eight thousand people are going to become public employees to make sure when we get on an airplane, it's safe. I'm not advocating making public all the private media; I think the private media needs to take responsibility for what it has done in the past, and maybe change its ways. They need to recognize that the market and the private space is not the only imperative here. It's part of the equation, but I would say that part of the equation is also the public need to know, and the responsibility on the part of the media to provide that information to the public, so our democracy can truly function. Again, that sounds highfalutin, but I think that when everybody saw those airplanes fly into the towers, they understood a lot of things. We came out of a deep sleep.

Cultural Responses: Humor
Frankfurter Allgemeine Sonntagszeitung

Missing in the Media

One of the first casualties in crises is the sense of humor, especially political satire—although you do hear jokes about how if we don't laugh (or shop), "the terrorists have won."

Humor, of course, targets the nerve concealing what we really think, as effectively as those "smart" bombs we keep reading about. The *Onion*—a satirical publication that calls itself "America's Finest News Source," because it openly makes up the news while real news sources take themselves so seriously (even when they are wrong or miss key stories)—ran this news brief over the holidays:

Report—U.S. Must Reduce Dependence on Foreign Turmoil: The United States has become overly dependent on foreign turmoil for its conversations and media coverage. "The American people consume as much as 60 million barrels of crude speculation every day using it for everything from driving discussions to heating up political debates," the report stated.

I laughed, but what isn't funny is that this "joke" is half-right when it comes to mainstream media coverage. Speculation, alarmism, rumors, conspiracy theories, jingoism, agenda-driven punditry, and endless spores of government managed half-information contaminate the news agenda just as dangerously as the anthrax we lived in dread of.

There were many underreported stories that weren't pursued at all in the nonstop, twenty-four/seven news flow. Some rocketed around the Internet without finding airtime or ink. I don't have space to elaborate, but I have been pointing to them daily in my weblog on Mediachannel.org. Here are ten:

1. Intelligence failures: What did government agencies know before September 11, and when did they stop knowing it?
2. Was the attack on Afghanistan planned before September 11?
3. What role, if any, does oil play in U.S. strategy?
4. Why was Afghanistan bombed when most of the hijackers came from Saudi Arabia?
5. Why have the Saudis received so little media focus while Iraq, with no link to the terrorists, receives so much?
6. What is the full tally of civilian casualties—from all sources, including our allies and those dead from war-related food delays?
7. Has "terrorism" replaced communism, as Washington's needed "enemy" to justify a permanent war economy?
8. What economic interests are behind the "Star Wars" program?
9. What construction failures contributed to the collapse of the World Trade Center?
10. Why has so much of the media fallen in uncritical lock-step with government policies?

Getting at the reality of hidden truths takes journalistic enterprise and investigative reporting, not hyped up formats and stenography. The former is in short supply; the latter is not.

End of story.

Israel–Palestine

WHAT'S A JOURNALIST TO DO WHEN THE POLITICAL GETS PERSONAL?

When you write about the world or report on what's happening "over there," the issues can seem far away enough to permit disengagement. The distance encourages detachment and objectification.

When warring peoples are labeled and treated like competing sports teams, coverage can easily desensitize us as well as inform us. The world can then look like a chessboard, as it appears to many policy makers and television pundits, who move toy soldiers in their minds across maps of their imaginations. A writer named Tom White from Odessa, Texas, was commenting about this tendency that one sees in journalism all the time. He raised the issue in reference to the way that an "expert" was quoted in Nicholas Lemann's brilliant policy dissection of "The Next World Order" in *The New Yorker.* White explains,

> What caught my eye more than anything else in the piece was Lemann's rendering of an interview with Ken Pollack, who was, he said, the National Security Council's staff expert on Iraq during the last years of the Clinton administration. Here are Lemann's prize lines on Pollack: "When I went to see him at his office in Washington, with a little encouragement he got out from behind his desk and walked over to his office wall, where three maps of the Middle East were hanging.

"'The only way to do it is a full-scale invasion,' he said, using a pen as a pointer. 'We're talking about two grand corps, two to three hundred thousand people altogether. The population is here, in the Tigris-Euphrates valley.' He pointed to the area between Baghdad and Basra. 'Ideally, you'd have the Saudis on board.' He pointed to the Prince Sultan Air Base, near Riyadh. 'You could make Kuwait the base, but it's much easier in Saudi. You need to take western Iraq and southern Iraq'—pointing again—'because otherwise they'll fire Scuds at Israel and at Saudi oil fields. You probably want to prevent Iraq from blowing up its own oil fields, so troops have to occupy them. And you need troops to defend the Kurds in northern Iraq.' Point, point. 'You go in as hard as you can, as fast as you can.' He slapped his hand on the top of his desk. 'You get the enemy to divide his forces, by threatening him in two places at once.' His hand hit the desk again, hard. 'Then you crush him.'"

White then comments: "Nice, vivid writing you will agree. Grown men used to play with painted lead soldiers reenacting the Civil War or the campaigns of Napoleon. Clearly the fun has not gone out of that kind of thing for men like Pollack. You'd hardly think he was talking of human beings. Indeed he'll *smash* the Iraqis. He and his army of two or three hundred thousand people, two grand corps, whatever."

THE POWER OF PERSONAL OBSERVATION

But, hey, wait a minute, what about the people who are in the way when those marines come *smashing* through? Journalists like England's John Pilger are worried about them. The reason: He's met them, and he feels an empathetic connection that often gets lost in media coverage.

Listen:

I have seen the appalling state of the children of Iraq. I have sat next to an Iraqi doctor in a modern hospital while she has turned away parents with children suffering from cancers that are part of what they call a "Hiroshima epidemic"—caused, according to several studies, by the depleted uranium that was used by the United States and Britain in the Gulf War and is now carried in the dust of the desert. Not only is Iraq denied equipment to clean up its contaminated battlefields, but also cancer drugs and hospital equipment.

His report goes on, but the point I am making is that Pilger's personal presence there gave him a vantage point that few of the many Iraq-bashers have. Incidentally, I know that other journalists who have been to Iraq, such as Maurice Murad, contradict the "500,000 dead Iraqi children due to UN sanctions" story that has circulated for years. In an essay in *Into the Buzzsaw* (Prometheus Books), Murad writes that he visited many hospitals and saw few sick children, and he says that it is in Saddam's interest to let people think this. Without revisiting the details, I do think that personal investigations are important, and what journalists see and choose to report often reflect their values and political outlook. Sadly, it is far too easy for them to disconnect from the human realities of this conflict, perhaps because of the difficulties of gaining access. That is why, for instance, that reporters who covered Vietnam are far more skeptical than many of the gee-whiz crowd in Afghanistan, including the "exclusive" CNN crew who are allowed to tag along to show American soldiers picking their way through the caves on Operation Mountain Lion.

TWO JEWS, SIX OPINIONS

As a Jewish American who has been enmeshed in the debate over Israel for years, I feel a responsibility and a connection to what's going on in the Mideast because Israel's leaders generally claim to be acting not just in their national interest but in the interests of Jews everywhere. I am constantly being exposed to and involved in emotional arguments on these issues, and I feel them directly, not just intellectually. I have been exposed to them since I was a child.

The editor of my weblog comes from a family of Holocaust survivors. She lives in a complex emotional universe of fear and militant pro-Israeli conviction. We share many values. We quarrel constantly, but I know how vexed she is about Sharon and at the same time, the hate directed at Jews all over the world. I can feel her pain, as well as the feelings of families who have lost children in terror attacks and suicide bombings. We must not be callous about these losses.

At the same time, this pain mustn't blind us to the history of the conflict. For years, Noam Chomsky has compared Israeli policy to colonialism and was criticized for exaggeration. Now centrists like former *New York Times* columnist Anthony Lewis and former National Security advisor Zbigniew Brzezinski are using similar language. The Israeli occupation of the West Bank and Gaza has been justified for all these years as necessary for Israel's security. I do believe

Israel has the right to exist and like many, think that its future will only be secured after a settlement that also secures the rights of Palestinians.

THE TRASHING OF A TELEVISION STATION

As I write, I am reading about an educational television station in Ramallah that was just trashed by the Israeli army. A few years ago, the journalists and educators who launched the channel as a democratic counterpoint to the authoritarianism of the Palestinian Authority *and* the fanaticism of Islamic fundamentalists, visited our offices to seek help for their plans to create an independent media voice. We had a lot in common. I was pleased to follow and report for Internews (a California-based organization that trains journalists and disseminates information from conflict zones) about their progress as well as their conflicts with and criticisms of Yasir Arafat's government. Today, Al Quds television is in ruins.

Two days earlier, a friend gave an independent filmmaker, another Palestinian, my phone number. She called from Bethlehem, hoping we could help her get the news out about what was happening in her hometown. Suddenly, a conflict I was watching on television was in my ear. Literally, in the form of a real person. Her house was surrounded by tanks, she told me. "What did we, the ordinary people here, do to deserve this?" she asked. Click. The phone was soon cut off, as was her electricity and water.

And then I started thinking about an exchange I witnessed between two young teenagers, one Israeli and one Palestinian, who had become fast friends in the Seeds of Peace camp. The program was organized by John Wallach, a journalist who, after years of covering the conflict, was moved to do something about it by creating an oasis of conflict resolution, hope, and dialogue.

One day in the camp, as I was filming a documentary for Globalvision, the Israeli youth explained that he would soon be drafted into the army. And the Palestinian, who was hanging on his arm, said, "Yeah and if he invades my neighborhood, he will shoot me." He laughed, but the Israeli boy did not.

I wonder where they are today?

And I wonder, as well, where my colleagues in the news business are. Why aren't more speaking out against well-documented attacks on journalists who are covering the crisis? I have heard from a friend at a television station here in New York City that their newsroom has been charged with internal wrangling over the need for more even-handed coverage, even as most of the city's editorial columnists and politicians are supportive of Israel.

Years ago, activists used to say that the personal is the political. Today, for me, this news is very personal, leading to debates with friends and family members, who I feel, in some instances, react more as knee-jerk members of a tribe than as citizens in a global community committed to compassion and human rights for all. As a Jew, I identify with an appeal for a cessation of hostilities now making the rounds in Scandinavia. Our alternative to Sharon should be based in the Jewish tradition of humanism and faith in the future, the statement says. When challenged by a stranger to sum up Jewish principles, the great Rabbi Hillel replied simply, "That which you find hateful to yourself, do not do unto others. That is all of the law. The rest is commentary. Go and study."

Israel on Receiving End of Media's Image of Terror
MEDIA TENOR

International television news show very little other news. News coverage of Israel offers a rare paradox in the field of international news reporting. Though Israel is one of the top countries in the world regularly being reported on, it will most likely be the one that television audiences will get to know the least about, as most of the news coverage deals only with one topic, namely violence.

As MEDIA TENOR research shows, "bad news is still very much good news," as far as television coverage of Israel on television news channels in four countries for the period September 2000 to August 2001 goes. Israel features high on the international news list of main television news channels in the United States, the United Kingdom, Germany, and South Africa. Among all countries, Israel is reported most on in the United States and rates second on television news channels in the United Kingdom. In Germany it is sixth and in South Africa, fifth. More than 60 percent of the news coverage in these four countries deals with the conflict situation in Israel and Palestine. Of the coverage that is of a violent nature, Germany rates almost 50 percent; in the United Kingdom and South Africa, more than 66 percent; and in the United States, about 90 percent. This is exacerbated by the fact that two out of every three spokespersons in television news are shown in, or in connection with, conflict situations in Israel. Of the television coverage in the four countries, the news channels in Germany offer the largest variety of news. Television channels in South Africa are much in line with those in the United Kingdom and the United States, focusing on terror and war, and conflict in politics and internal affairs, rather than on issues such as the economy, culture, religion, and science development. News reports on these issues were swept from the world's television screens by news on conflict. In terms of the two protagonists, Israel and Palestine, the conflict news itself is also off-balance. While South African television gives 65 percent coverage to the Israeli side of the conflict and 35 percent to Palestine, U.K. channels give 8 percent coverage to Palestine.

Media and the Middle East

THE DANGERS OF TELEVISION'S TUNNEL VISION

Those of us outside the war zones are all bystanders, television witnesses of the tragedy as it is unfolding. We are watching the deadly game of tit-for-tat slowly ratcheting up the crisis in the Middle East. It has become (in network parlance) "Breaking News," with images that are sickeningly familiar to us all. Unfortunately, television coverage focuses on violence and action more than politics and peacemaking.

Image #1

People are running. Ambulances are arriving. Squadrons of bearded men wearing the vests of emergency personnel are on the scene looking for bodies and body parts. It is the aftermath of a suicide bombing. The crime scene is confused. We hear a body count, which is certain to rise when everyone is accounted for. The event seems beyond rational explanation, the work of mad people. The horror is numbing and infuriating at the same time.

Image #2

Tanks roar through a Palestinian camp. Planes streak overhead. We hear the sounds of war, of bombings, and occasionally we see people running through the streets with bodies being lifted into ambulances. From time to time, there is a sound bite from some often-unintelligible and unidentified victim. Images this week have revolved around the escalating violence and Israel's invasion of Arafat's compound. We rarely see what happens to ordinary people.

Image #3

A meeting of Israel's cabinet. Ariel Sharon is sitting like a bullfrog, sometimes scowling at the cameras. This is a photo-op, a staged few seconds of footage before the actual meeting begins. Later we learn what did happen with voice-over narration explaining why government leaders say they must retaliate. Occasionally, a government spokesman is heard briefly. He is denouncing Arafat and demanding an end to terrorism.

Image #4

Palestinians are marching through the streets. A few men are holding a flag-draped coffin. There is chanting and singing, and talk, when we hear it, of martyrs and the need for revenge. The scene cuts to images of young people throwing stones and soldiers firing guns.

Cut to: Washington A State Department official or senior government leader denounces the violence. Indicts Arafat and suicide bombers. Announces no new initiatives.

Cut to: The U.N. Security Council Who appeal for a ceasefire. Men around a table raise their hands to support one motion or another. No one refers to the decades of unimplemented resolutions.

Day after day, night after night, the same imagery, often offered up without much information of context or explanation.

I can hear Americans saying: "There they go again." "When will they ever learn?" "How horrible!"

And: "What else is on?"

On Sunday night, Easter 2002, it was *The Ten Commandments,* a film that many take as literal history. "Behold the will of God," says actor Charlton "Moses" Heston (now the gun-supporting president of the National Rifle Association). Perspectives about this conflict seem shaped by images. Many supporters of Israel refer to films such as *Exodus,* chronicling the formation of the Jewish state, or *Schindler's List,* which exposed the horrors of the Holocaust. The Palestinians identify their battle in Third World terms, like the guerilla uprisings depicted in the Battle of Algiers. On each side, histories of oppression and dispossession fuel anger and righteousness.

Media analyst Eric Alterman, writing on MSNBC.com, has a point when he speaks of the coverage in terms of "competing narratives." He writes, "Both sides inflict inhuman cruelties on one another. Both sides blame the other for forcing them to do so. . . . In most of the world, it is the Palestinian narrative of a dispossessed people that dominates. In the United States, however, the narrative that dominates is Israel's: a democracy under constant siege."

A ROLLER COASTER OF IMAGES

And so it goes, a roller coaster of endless conflict and conflicting images. The American public often tunes it out or turns it off, in part because little of the coverage encourages viewers to get to know why the conflict continues or to become more empathetic to the people caught in the crossfire.

It is hard to find dispassionate discussions or even dialogues among the warring parties. The pundits on each side talk past each other, each clinging to "facts" and political demands. The Israelis want security, but their policies tend to have the opposite effect. The Palestinians demand justice but seem unable to contain their violent "martyr" brigades. Ideas for a breakthrough are rare to find in a television discourse suffocating from bluster and sloganeering.

It is no wonder that many of us have moved this issue in our minds from a problem that can be solved to a mess that can only be managed—and badly at that. Particularly on U.S. television, coverage rarely offers information on ways to resolve this conflict. Positions on every side harden when viewers are only offered familiar information that is only challenging or insightful. The truth is that there are many proposals—plans for ceasefires and peace—on many tables. And more agreement than you might think with the principles enunciated in meetings at places like Taba in Egypt or even from the Saudis' recently in Beirut.

All have been covered, but the chronology of the events is hard to keep straight. Example: The Israelis say Arafat backed away from a peace proposal at the Camp David meetings that President Clinton convened between him and then–Israeli Prime Minister Ehud Barak. The meetings were reported widely here because they took place in the States, but remember, the dominant image had less to do with substance than symbols—like Barak and Arafat kidding around about who would go through the door first. And then, the stories about Chelsea Clinton being present. As Bill Clinton acknowledged later, no written proposals were on the table at Camp David. It was only later, at a follow-up meeting in Taba, Egypt, that the two sides got specific and came close to agreeing. Since those meetings took place overseas, they rated less U.S. airtime.

Finally, the rug was pulled out from the under the process when Barak was replaced by Sharon, who has never seen a peace agreement he likes—or, from another point of view, when some Palestinian factions chose terrorism over compromise or coexistence with Israel. I haven't seen any television news reports or documentaries that explained this. In the absence of explanation—and it is a complex issue—we are left with easily manipulated perceptions that lead to simplistic assessments, such as that Israel wanted peace but Arafat did not. Or vice versa.

Time and again, voices of sanity are neglected, as if the two old men, Sharon and Arafat, are the whole story. They are not. There is a large peace camp in Israel with many sensible and responsible voices in the Palestinian community. With war escalating, many of these have been muted, just as criticism of the U.S. "war on terror" was stilled in the environment of a national security emergency. These third parties and critical movements have rarely had much of a media megaphone, although the recent activism by foreign NGOs—the so-called Internationals—have become part of the story, and this involvement can't be totally ignored. Few critics, however, get a chance to frame the issues or structure the debate on television. In a sense, many media organizations, by allowing the governments to define what is at stake, promote the worst possible outcomes. When people don't know there are alternatives, they don't fight for them. And they are not being told about them.

ALTERNATIVES DO EXIST

What can the media do? For one thing, they can consider adopting the tactics and goals of peace journalism. Mediachannel.org has featured many proposals originating from Reporting the World, a British association of journalists led by television journalist Jake Lynch. These specific and sound ideas demonstrate that "blood and guts" stories can be presented from a different perspective—one that plays up the views of other actors, such as the United Nations, Israeli peace camps, independent analysts, and leaders of Palestinian community groups who have been working to build a viable alternative to the likes of Hamas and Islamic Jihad.

This came out clearly in one of the conferences that Reporting the World sponsored on these issues. More than fifty top journalists and experts took part. As one of their reports explained,

One key issue was the understanding readers and audiences may form of the reasons for the violence, and how this arises out of "framing decisions" about what to include in reports of the conflict. Are there certain explanations that prevail by default? Or do they result from choices made by journalists? Is all the responsibility of ill-intentioned leaders, or an expression of 'ancient hatreds' welling up from within? Key contributor Lyse Doucet of BBC World recalled that peace actions were generally ignored by journalists in favor of "running off to the front-line"; but that meant "we never probed why the violence was there in the first place."

Clearly, the situation in the Middle East is a tragedy with deep roots and a complicated history. It is not black and white, and it won't be readily resolved.

My question to my colleagues is this: Are we inadvertently helping perpetuate this cycle of violence, or can we do more to transcend its terms, structure our own dialogues between the parties, and help audiences understand the imperative of finding just solutions?

And to the public and politicians: Please speak out against the growing violence against journalists on both sides, as well as Israel's announced intention to bar media from the current "closed military zone" of Ramallah (and in support of those brave war correspondents who at the time of this writing are ignoring these orders). We need to know what is going on. The situation is bleak enough without adding a media blackout, which is often a cover for human rights crimes.

Tips for Covering Conflict
From Reporting the World, Jake Lynch[*]

MIDDLE EAST MEDIA BIAS

1. Avoid portraying a conflict as consisting of only two parties contesting one goal. The logical outcome is for one to win and the other to lose. Instead, a peace journalist would disaggregate the two parties into many smaller groups who are pursuing many goals, thus opening up more creative potential for a range of outcomes.

2. Avoid accepting stark distinctions between "self" and "other." These can be used to build the sense that another party is a "threat" or "beyond the pale" of civilized behavior—both key justifications for violence. Instead, seek the "other" in the "self," and vice versa. If a party is presenting itself as "the goodies," ask questions about how different its behavior really is to that it ascribes to "the baddies"—isn't it ashamed of itself?

3. Avoid treating a conflict as if it is only going on in the place and at the time that violence is occurring. Instead, try to trace the links and consequences for people in other places now and in the future. Ask:

* Jake Lynch is a correspondent for Sky News and the *Independent,* based in London and Sydney. He is a consultant to the POIESIS Conflict and Peace Forums and coauthor of *The Peace Journalism Option* and *What Are Journalists For?*

- Who are all the people with a stake in the outcome?
- Ask yourself what will happen if . . . ?
- What lessons will people draw from watching these events unfold as part of a global audience?
- How will they enter the calculations of parties to future conflicts near and far?

4. Avoid assessing the merits of a violent action or policy of violence in terms of its visible effects only. Instead, try to find ways of reporting on the invisible effects—for example, the long-term consequences of psychological damage and trauma, perhaps increasing the likelihood that those affected will be violent in future, either against other people or, as a group, against other groups or other countries.

5. Avoid letting parties define themselves by simply quoting their leaders' restatement of familiar demands or positions. Instead, inquire more deeply into goals:
   - How are people on the ground affected by the conflict in everyday life?
   - What do they want changed?
   - Is the position stated by their leaders the only way or the best way to achieve the changes they want?

6. Avoid concentrating always on what divides the parties, the differences between what they say they want. Instead, try asking questions that may reveal areas of common ground, and try leading your report with answers that suggest some goals may be shared or at least compatible, after all.

7. Avoid only reporting the violent acts and describing "the horror." If you exclude everything else, you suggest that the only explanation for violence is previous violence (revenge); the only remedy, more violence (coercion/punishment). Instead, as a way of explaining the violence, show how people have been blocked and frustrated or deprived in everyday life.

8. Avoid blaming someone for starting it. Instead, try looking at how shared problems and issues are leading to consequences that all the parties say they never intended.

9. Avoid focusing exclusively on the suffering, fears, and grievances of only one party. This divides the parties into "villains" and "victims," and it suggests that coercing or punishing the villains represents a solution. Instead, treat as equally newsworthy the suffering, fears, and grievance of all sides.

10. Avoid "victimizing" language, such as "destitute," "devastated," "defenseless," "pathetic" and "tragedy," which only tells us what has been done to and could be done for a group of people. This characterization disempowers them and limits the options for change. Instead, report on what has

been done and what could be done by the people. Don't just ask them how they feel; also ask them how they are coping and what do they think? Can they suggest any solutions? Remember, refugees have surnames as well. You wouldn't call President Clinton "Bill" in a news report.

11. Avoid imprecise use of emotive words to describe what has happened to people.
    - "Genocide" means the wiping out of an entire people.
    - "Decimated" (said of a population) means reducing it to a tenth of its former size.
    - "Tragedy" is a form of drama, originally Greek, in which someone's fault or weakness proves his or her undoing.
    - "Assassination" is the murder of a head of state.
    - "Massacre" is the deliberate killing of people known to be unarmed and defenseless. Are we sure? Or might these people have died in battle?
    - "Systematic," as in raping or forcing people from their homes. Has it really been organized in a deliberate pattern or have there been a number of unrelated, albeit extremely nasty incidents?

    Instead, always be precise about what we know. Do not minimize suffering. Reserve the strongest language for the gravest situations, or you will beggar the language and help to justify disproportionate responses that escalate the violence.

12. Avoid demonizing adjectives like "vicious," "cruel," "brutal," and "barbaric." These always describe one party's view of what another party has done. To use them puts the journalist on that side and helps to justify an escalation of violence. Instead, report what you know about the wrongdoing and give as much information as you can about the reliability of other people's reports or descriptions of it.

13. Avoid demonizing labels like "terrorist," "extremist," "fanatic," and "fundamentalist." These are always given by "us" to "them." No one ever uses them to describe himself or herself, and so, for a journalist to use them is to always take sides. They mean the person is unreasonable, so it seems to make less sense to reason (negotiate) with them. Instead, try calling people by the names they give themselves. Or be more precise in your descriptions.

14. Avoid focusing exclusively on the human rights abuses, misdemeanors, and wrongdoings of only one side. Instead, try to name *all* wrongdoers and try to treat equally seriously allegations made by all sides in a conflict. Treating seriously does not mean taking at face value, but instead, it means making equal efforts to establish whether any evidence exists to back them up; it means

treating the victims with equal respect; and it means presuming that the chances of finding and punishing the wrongdoers are of equal importance.

15. Avoid making an opinion or claim seem like an established fact. ("Eurico Guterres, said to be responsible for a massacre in East Timor . . .") Instead, tell your readers or your audience who said what. ("Eurico Guterres, accused by a top U.N. official of ordering a massacre in East Timor . . .") That way, you avoid signing yourself and your news service up to the allegations made by one party in the conflict against another.

16. Avoid greeting the signing of documents by leaders, which bring about military victory or cease-fire, as necessarily creating peace. Instead, try to report on the issues that remain and that may still lead people to commit further acts of violence in the future. Ask what is being done to strengthen means on the ground to handle and resolve conflict nonviolently, to address development[al] or structural needs in the society, and to create a culture of peace?

17. Avoid waiting for leaders on "our" side to suggest or offer solutions. Instead, pick up and explore peace initiatives wherever they come from. Ask questions from ministers, for example, about ideas put forward by grassroots organizations. Assess peace perspectives against what you know about the issues the parties are really trying to address. Do not simply ignore them because they do not coincide with established positions.

The Arab Worldviews: U.S. Alternative Journalism

Fatemah Fatag
Al Ahram Weekly Online (Cairo, Egypt):
December 13–19, 2001

t's highly sophisticated, but is it truly free? As the mainstream U.S. media continues to beat the drums of America's "war on terror," Fatemah Farag investigates the implications for press freedom and finds islands of dissent.

Swimming Upstream

"It was the speech that clung to the ears, the link that tingled in the blood; U.S.A."

John Dos Passos, *U.S.A.*

What do we make of the "U. S. of A."? What speech is it that clings to our ears and molds our perceptions? Is it that of the six-pack-Joe, Hollywood, apple pie, and the "American Dream," all gift-wrapped in red, white, and blue? Or is it something else—something much more fragile and complex; heart-warming, yet heart-rending, like the men and women drawn up in John Dos Passos' 1948 novel *U.S.A.*

Ironically, the mainstream media in the United States has not only succeeded in creating a monolithic image of what Arabs are (to put it in bottom-line terms: crazed mullahs leading American-hating, bloodthirsty mobs); it has also succeeded in projecting a subversive, equally monolithic image of what Americans are—arrogant, racist, and brutal imperial masters who hate anything not American. These images are reinforced by both the actions and policies of the American establishment and our very own media in the Arab world.

It is the frustrating cycle of misperception. In an outburst in his daily column for Mediachannel.org (a nonprofit alternative news source with 840 global partners offering "critical takes" on media performance), Danny Schechter wrote: "Hello Arab World: not all Jews are Zionists or supportive of Ariel Sharon and his gang of ministers. Why don't you know that? I know why. No one ever tells you. Not your media and not ours. Dissenting views, and peace perspectives are filtered out, marginalized and silenced. That is why the conflict in the world is becoming jihad vs. jihad, Bush vs. bin Laden."

And why can't we hear the voices of dissent coming from within the United States? Rory O'Connor, president and CEO of Globalvision New Media (which produces Mediachannel.org), told *Al-Ahram Weekly,* "The United States is a large, disparate country with many people and many viewpoints. . . . [however] finding them and amplifying them can be exceedingly difficult. Thus, the problem with the U.S. media system is not that there isn't room for many viewpoints, opinions and conflicting content; it lies more in the fact that mainstream distribution is tightly controlled by a few, huge, centralized corporations."

And while we constantly focus on how we as Arabs bear the brunt of the current state of media affairs, we never take time to heed the fact that many Americans suffer equally. "What is surprising and maddening about trying to express alternative viewpoints in the United States is that there are so few places to put them," complained Wallace Shawn, writer, actor, and director, in an interview with the *Weekly.* "In New York City, this huge cosmopolitan meeting-place where I live, I hear an astonishing variety of opinions expressed every day by individuals, but there are only three newspapers, each one of them offering in one style or another the consensus attitude [in this case pro-war/establishment]. So each of the individuals I meet feels isolated, as if he alone has an alternative view, when in fact there are enormous numbers of people who do, but their views are not reflected in the newspapers, much less on television."

Last February, and on the occasion of the inauguration of Mediachannel.org, no less than veteran anchor Walter Cronkite noted: "I have been increasingly critical of the direction that journalism has taken of late, and of the impact on democratic discourse and principles. . . . I am deeply concerned about the merger mania that has swept our industry, diluting standards, dumbing down the news and making the bottom line sometimes seem like the only line. It isn't and shouldn't be."

Hence, the importance of the development and growth of alternative media sources within the United States—generally self-defined as news and information sources that set themselves apart from the mainstream by being politically opposed to the conservative, corporate agenda and by operating without corporate conglomerate dollars. "While only seven companies control most of the major media outlets, there are many local outlets, magazines of opinion, ethnic news sources, independent publications and a growing proliferation of independent Web sites offering diverse perspectives," Danny Schechter, executive editor of MediaChannel.org, told the *Weekly*.

The alternative print category includes magazines (e.g., *Mother Jones*, *In These Times*, *The Nation*, and *The Progressive*) and newsweeklies like *The Village Voice, Boston Phoenix,* and *LA Weekly*. Many of these have online components. In radio, there's National Public Radio (NPR), although even this is now considered by many devotees to have become more mainstream, as it is now largely funded by megacorporations. Other radio stations include the Pacifica Network (five stations) and "micro-radio," small, local radio stations that often have no official license. The television category is the weakest, with only the Public Broadcasting Service (PBS) counting for much in the way of viewership—and again, like NPR, it is hardly alternative anymore because of corporate underwriting.

As for the Internet, Tate Hausman, managing editor for AlterNet.org, drew the map for the *Weekly* as follows: "There are literally hundreds of very small, online magazines with small readerships—lipmagazine.org, yellowtimes.org, ironminds.com to name a few. These operate with almost no budget and have only online presence." Hausman set larger, more influential online magazines, like Salon.com and AlterNet.org, in a category of their own, saying that these have higher readership—AlterNet has between 15,000 and 20,000 individual visits a day. These sites also post pieces by their readers and link[s] to articles from other sites. Wrapping up, Hausman adds: "Then there are the independent media centers such as indymedia.org, a semi-successful experiment in unmediated media. Anyone who wants to publish a story or photo on the site can do so, without any editing or journalistic standards."

A cursory search on the Internet of these and other outlets transports the visitor to another world: Articles by Noam Chomsky, Alexander Cockburn, Arundhati Roy, Robert Fisk, Tareq Ali, as well as lesser-known figures like Nigerian activist Oranto Douglas and Palestinian poet Soheir Hammad, to name only a few, are readily found. Their absence is conspicuous in the mainstream media. These articles are provocative and cheeky—not very "newsworthy" in mainstream terms, as they often deal with the fate of developing nations in the "new world order" and offer a variety of antiwar takes. The slogans of alternative outlets are worth something in themselves: CounterPunch "Tells the facts and names the names." My personal favorite is DemocracyNow Radio: "Resistance Radio: the exception to the rulers."

Hausman described the alternative media world of the United States to the *Weekly* as "very complex and robust, but limited in reach." Of course, money—or the lack thereof, to be more precise—is a major constraining factor. "You know about the *New York Times* and CNN because they have gigantic budgets and advertising revenues. No alternative media sources can ever match their budgets," Hausman said.

But not everything can be measured in terms of quantity, and as Hausman himself pointed out, "Our audience is much more engaged in civic life than the average media consumer, and so we have an influence far beyond our relatively small audience."

Of all the mediums of alternative news, the Internet is the most easily accessible and, therefore, the medium growing at the fastest rate, especially since September 11. AlterNet, for example, has seen its readership grow by 300 percent since September 11, Hausman said. "Many more people are seeking out alternative information, and the Internet is the easiest place to go for that information."

But what kind of foreign coverage can the alternative media provide? Hausman points out that the reason U.S. coverage is weak is because "covering international affairs well is a very expensive endeavor. The mainstream papers don't do it because it isn't cost effective, and the alternative media simply can't do it because they don't have the resources." He went on to add, "What alternative media can do—especially online media—is to collaborate more with media outlets in your region of the world [the Middle East]."

And so AlterNet is working with foreign journalists and media outlets to re-present news and opinions from abroad. Globalvision has launched the new Globalvision News Network, which includes perspectives from outside of the United States. Globalvision's O'Connor argues, however, that while the Internet is part of an answer, it is not "the answer." He said that issues that pertain to other media, particularly the "branding" by huge communication conglomerates and their "choke-hold" on mainstream distribution, "are as important, if not more so, in the Internet space as they are anywhere else."

"For example, our company has two Web sites—Mediachannel.org and gvnews.net—where we offer international voices and views not in the 'mainstream' of American media," O'Connor said. "But supporting these sites and getting people to know of their existence and how they can be accessed is a major and ongoing challenge to us, as with all independent media sources in the U.S."

And while the constraints on freedom of expression continue to be tightened within a general environment of fundamentalist and crude patriotism, it is hoped that this, "if anything, will give us more articles to write, as we remain watchdogs over government abuses," says Hausman. "Unfortunately, it often takes a crisis like September 11 and the war in Afghanistan to make people appreciate and seek out alternative information. But along with the restrictive environment, the counter-culture of independent news and opinions will continue to grow. In fact, it may turn out that the more restrictive the government and mainstream media become, the more effective and important the alternative media will become," he suggested.

Alternative media may be one of the few areas that have the potential to subvert the myths constructed by "the establishment" and help create a new awareness of what "U.S.A." also stands for. In the words of Dos Passos: "Mostly, U.S.A. is the speech of the people." As it should be.

Counseling Journalists
*Gerti Schoen**

A handful of journalists are sitting in a soulless seminar room at Columbia University in New York, and they are trying to do some role-playing. Robert Wiener, who has worked as a reporter for over forty years, is struggling for words. He has reported about serious fires and the uprising of the Intifada in the Middle East. As he tries to describe an execution he had covered in Texas last year he pauses. "I still think about this man," he says. "That was heavy for me."

Wiener originally came to the three-day seminar because he wanted to offer emotional support. The Dart Center for Journalism and Trauma (dartcenter.org) had put it together to help reporters who have been traumatized during events like the World Trade Center attacks. When he found himself in the role of the one being counseled, he had to make an effort to get rid of the self-imposed image of "the cowboy who goes out there and faces the evil."

"A lot of journalists believe they are not allowed to be touched by what they are reporting about," says David Handschuh. He puts up his leg—it's in a cast. Handschuh, a photographer for the *New York Daily News,* has been dealing with traumatized reporters and photographers for three years. Since September 11, he is one of them. "When I saw the debris of the falling towers coming at me in slow motion, my first instinct was to bring my camera and shoot. But something in the back of my mind said: Run, run, run!" He was rescued by firemen and got away with a

* Gerti Schoen is a freelance correspondent for German media. This article was written for the weekly *Die Zeit.*

multiple fracture of his leg. Ever since, he has been one of the forces behind the Dart Center Ground Zero in New York, the second office of the institute, which is headquartered in Seattle. As of January there will be more seminars; freelancers and foreign journalists are also invited to take part.

"For most people it is important just to talk about it," says Handschuh. But with all the deadline pressure, a lot of New York journalists didn't take the time to think about their own feelings. "People need the permission to feel hurt," says Elana Newman, a psychology professor from the University of Tulsa, who is the director of the new center. And that would also go for all the reporters and editors around the world who—even from a distance—were constantly exposed to the horror of these images. "I know a photo editor in Michigan who looked at thousands of these pictures," says Handschuh. "She is thousands of miles away from Ground Zero and spends an awful lot of time crying."

During the last three years, many American media companies have started to offer counseling for staff members who have been exposed to traumatizing images. One of the first to do so was the (Oklahoma City) *Daily Oklahoman,* which covered the terrorist bombings in its hometown over several years. Television stations in Denver followed after the school shootings in Columbine. Opportunities for group therapy have been implemented in all of the bigger publishing houses in New York, including *The New York Times* and *The Wall Street Journal.*

But it is not so much the editors Handschuh worries about. It is the freelancers, the photographers and foreign correspondents who are not part of the newsroom and who he would like to see get out of their isolation. Journalists, he thinks, can counsel each other. "We know how to listen, how to ask the right questions," he points out. That is why all the participants in the Dart Center seminars are counselors and counselees at the same time.

"Policemen, firemen, volunteers—they all had to go through a debriefing, where they talked about their feelings, when they left Ground Zero," says Elana Newman. "Only journalists believe they don't need that." It is all about the macho attitude most newspeople like to show.

Robert Wiener may need some more convincing. "I don't know if many people can bring themselves to participate in such a training," he says. "It is a bit like falling from the horse and you get back up and ride off. Instead of sitting down, have a drink and just go home."

On Asking for Help

Chris Cramer, president of CNN International and honorary chair of Newscoverage Unlimited at the Dart Center for Journalism and Trauma, was briefly held hostage in 1980, while working for the BBC, during a terrorist attack on a London embassy. He spoke with German journalist Gerti Schoen on December 4.

> *Gerti Schoen (GS):* Why is the topic of post-traumatic stress disorder (PTSD) more urgent than ever?
>
> *Chris Cramer (CC):* The events of September 11 have produced a huge number of reporters that were confronted with horrors that their war correspondents colleagues have been confronted for years. My personal view is that we have a new group of people called "urban war correspondents," who may well be affected by what they cover, and as employers, we should understand that.
>
> *GS:* Did the war in Afghanistan gain new dimensions in that respect?
>
> *CC:* The war in Afghanistan may well draw a new line here in terms of danger. My view is that the media generally have taken a long time to wake up to the fact that they might be affected by what they cover. Last week the New York police department instructed all of its staff to undergo counseling. Here we have a police force that understands that people could be affected by unpleasant events. There is now a real revolution among the media in America and overseas and Britain who are

beginning to understand very slowly that employers should provide voluntary services for their staff and you don't have to behave in a macho way. You don't have to cover ten wars and go back and take drugs or drink yourself to death. The army, the navy, the air force accepted this years ago and responded in a much more intelligent way. But you know that this issue is very controversial, and there are many people who believe I am talking garbage.

GS: CNN has developed guidelines for people covering wars. What do they look like?

CC: CNN as well as the BBC and a few other media organizations have guidelines for operating in hostile areas, and we have guidelines when it comes to the likelihood by being affected by PTSD. We don't deploy people to war zones unless they have been to hostile environment courses, which are freely available in Europe and America. We make sure that our people travel in armored vehicles. We moved these vehicles into Afghanistan. Other things are protective clothing—that means helmets, goggles. That equipment has been used for some time now. And the journalists understand that we don't expect them to take unnecessary risks, that no story is worth getting killed for and that it's always possible to go down a road the next day.

GS: What are those courses in hostile environments like?

CC: Certain organizations design the course with the media. They simulate war conditions—you being taken hostage, you being attacked and shelled. They simulate the type of conditions you might find yourself being blindfolded, being thrown in the back of a car. These are scary courses and very real, and they saved a lot of journalists' lives over the years.

GS: Should there also be guidelines for regular disaster and police reporters?

CC: It is possible to be affected by fires or accidents. Police and fire brigades routinely offer debriefing. As far as journalists are concerned, it depends on the individual how much you are affected. You may be affected even by a court case that involves a serial killer—it is not unusual to be affected just by sitting in court. We have voluntary confidential courses, and if you want to use them, then use them. Don't feel you are a wimp or weak, we understand that this may happen to you. We provide counseling services for staff and their families.

Fast Forward to Summer: From the News Dissector's Weblog

*T*his book starts with the coverage of September 11. It was months before the coverage began to change and open itself up to critical views. By summer, the sense of crisis has all but abated. Anxiety levels were going down; vacation season had begun. Osama bin Laden had all but disappeared from television, with the exception of reports of an occasional sightings and the periodic threat. That old standby Saddam Hussein was being groomed to replace him as if the terror war needs a demonized enemy to slay. The flags were back out for July 4, America's Independence Day. In my neck of the woods, it was a day of renewed high security with New Yorkers who were braced for the worst.

Let's fast forward to some of my typical weblog entries later in the year. I began my weblog by waving the flag—my way:

July 4

Hip Hip Hooray

"We hold these truths to be self-evident. . . ." Those are the words that begin the Declaration of Independence, which Americans celebrate today with backyard barbeques and hot dog eating contests. The winner of last year's contest in Coney Island, New York, revealed this morning on CNN that he eats nine pounds, or three heads, of cabbage to stretch his stomach before the event, which makes for some media yuks. Is this not like athletes' taking steroids, I ask you? (But no one else is.)

Some Truths from Molly

Over on MSNBC this morning, complete with a new set and frenetic format (set off with new *whooshing* sound effects), there was a pause on a no-news morning for an interview with someone I hadn't seen on the air since September 11 (with the exception of an C-SPAN appearance). The folksy, left-populist columnist Molly Ivins was live from Texas, who offered some homiles about the importance of dissent to democracy, something the programmers over at the newly rebranded "America's News Channel" need to try to practice. She reminded us that it is precisely at a time of threat and anxiety that we tend to do damage to our own freedoms. The newscasters has just cited a new study that says more and more Americans are willing to sacrifice their freedoms for more security.

To this, Ivins reminded us of a saying, "America, right or wrong. When wrong, it is our job to put it right." In her interview, she felt the need to assert that she too is patriotic and that she writes a column each July 4 to express her love of America. At that, the anchors, who spoke of their newscast as a "show," wrapped up by saying "Left or right, we all love America."

Cue the marching bands.

July 5

A Bosnian View, an Israeli Perspective

Yesterday, by chance, I sat at a pool alongside Bosnia's ambassador to the United Nations at a Fourth of July party in New Jersey hosted by Jeanette, my weblog editor. He expressed consternation at (but not criticism of) the U.S. position—he is too much of a diplomat for that—suggesting that it is much ado about nothing.

And speaking of that speech by President Bush on the Middle East, here are some media comments—by way of Israeli's brilliant commentator Uri Avnery—that show increasing backbone:

> Everybody praised this fine speech. Prime Minister A. lauded the style, President B. commended the fabric, Sheik C. admired the collar. And I saw only a naked emperor.
>
> Everybody knew, of course, that it was a stupid speech, perhaps the most silly ever uttered by an American president. But who will confront the leader of the world's sole superpower? Who will bring upon himself the wrath of a man that possesses such frightening power, while voicing such inanities?
>
> A twelve-year-old would have been ashamed of presenting such a composition to his teacher. The assumptions are baseless, the general picture resembles a caricature, the conclusions are ridiculous and the parts contradict each other.

It says that the Palestinians must choose their leader in a free, democratic election, but that they are forbidden to elect a leader not approved by Sharon and Bush.

They must establish a democratic, liberal, pluralistic and multi-party system, including separation of powers, independent courts and transparent finances. For that purpose they are commanded to accept the assistance of America's allies in the Middle East: democratic Saudi Arabia, pluralistic Egypt and liberal Jordan. Financial transparency like in Riyadh, separation of powers like in Cairo, independent courts like in Amman.

The establishment of this ideal system is a precondition to any peace negotiations. In Europe, such a system was achieved after a struggle of hundreds of years. In the Arab world, it does not exist anywhere. Arafat is the only Arab chief of state who was chosen in free elections, under close international supervision, personally overseen by ex-President Jimmy Carter.

Where Do Israelis Stand?

While we are on the topic of Israel, Gila Svirky offers an analysis of some recent public opinion data that suggests that most Israelis want to make a deal. I thought this was fascinating since most of the U.S. media coverage portrays the Israeli people as uncritical supporters of the government and overwhelmingly hostile to Palestinian demands.

One of the best kept secrets in Israel is that most Israelis are fed up with the occupation, and just want to get out.

According to June's findings by Mina Zemach, Israel's foremost pollster, 63 percent of Israelis are in favor of "unilateral withdrawal." In fact, 69 percent call for the evacuation of "all" or "most of" the settlements.

Mina's numbers are corroborated by everybody else: The Peace Index of Tel-Aviv University's Tami Steinmitz Center found that 65 percent of Israelis "are prepared to evacuate the settlements under a unilateral separation program."

A poll commissioned by Peace Now a month earlier revealed that 59 percent of Israelis support immediate evacuation of most settlements, followed by a unilateral withdrawal of the army from the occupied territories.

Here's another "secret" revealed by Mina Zemach: 60 percent of Israelis believe that Israel should agree to the establishment of a Palestinian state as part of a peace agreement.

Is this too much good news all at once? To temper it, here are a few more findings by Mina Zemach: 74 percent of Israelis say that Sharon is doing a good job and 60 percent believe that the Israeli army should be allowed to attack the refugee camps in Gaza.

To quote Mina Zemach's closing remarks (at a lecture I heard her give in Tel Aviv yesterday, sponsored by the New Israel Fund), "Similar trends appear on the Palestinian side in surveys conducted by my Palestinian colleagues. Both sides want their leaders to be very aggressive, but most are willing to have a peaceful, two-state solution."

If this data from Israel totally contradict the central media frame that defines the conflict as all Palestinians versus all Israelis, there was some data I reported on a week later from the United States which shows American public opinion far more even handed on the issue than the Congress and that most media accounts suggest.

Survey Finds U.S. Public More Even-Handed Than Congress

And what is the U.S. public thinking? Here's a survey I just received but haven't seen reported in the press:

> A survey released today finds that last week's Congressional resolutions proclaiming unequivocal support for Israel in its struggle with Palestinians are out of step with the American public. Most Americans believe that the United States needs to be even-handed in the Israeli-Palestinian conflict, while only 22 percent believe it is actually doing so. Fifty-eight percent say the United States is taking Israel's side.
>
> In the poll of 801 Americans by the Program on International Policy Attitudes (PIPA) 58 percent said that both the Israelis and the Palestinians are equally to blame for the current situation in the region. Majorities favor withholding current aid to both Israel (61 percent) and the Palestinian Authority (63 percent) if they fail to agree to a ceasefire and return to the negotiating table.
>
> Contrary to the resolutions passed by Congress last week, only 17 percent of Americans see Israel's conflict with the Palestinians as part of the war on terrorism. The public also shows low levels of support for Israel's recent military actions in the West Bank. Sixty-three percent of Americans supported President Bush's call for Israel to withdraw and, if it does not, 52 percent favor telling Israel not to use U.S.-provided weapons there.

Paying the Piper

Despite surveys like this, many in Congress want to reward Israel and further subsidize the costs of its military campaign. Reuters reports:

A U.S. House of Representatives panel appeared set on Thursday to approve another $200 million in aid to Israel after the Bush administration convinced lawmakers to also provide $50 million in humanitarian aid to Palestinians. The House of Representatives Appropriations Committee will likely add the new funds to an emergency counterterrorism funding bill after receiving "verbal approval" for the move from the White House, a committee spokesman said.

Leaked War Plans

The New York Times reported on a new leaked document that claims to be a Pentagon war plan for Iraq. Fox News, as big a booster of that war-in-the-wings as there is on the air, suggested without explanation that it may have been leaked deliberately. Reported the *Times:* "An American military planning document envisions tens of thousands of troops attacking Iraq from the north, south and west in a campaign to topple Saddam Hussein." A Fox military analyst suggested that this plan is nothing new and, while targeted only at Saddam, is unlikely to win hearts and minds among the Iraqi people. He also intimated that it was this type of planning that recently led to a top general's resigning. That is some more intrigue for you.

July 6

Years ago, when Lyndon Johnson ruled the roost at 1600 Pennsylvania Avenue, CBS news anchor Walter Cronkite came on the air to question his policies and practices in Vietnam. Cronkite, then considered the "most trusted man in America," was clearly not part of the rabble (which included many of my friends at the time) who were often heard chanting "Hey! Hey! LBJ! How many kids have you killed today?" He was the paragon of establishment thought, and he had just begun to turn against a war that started with high approval ratings and ended with almost none. "When he lost Cronkite, we knew he lost the country," some of his aides said at the time.

The "Imperial Presidency" Has Arrived

Some tremors of this type are beginning to be heard within the higher reaches of the press corps. What began as mere questions or asides are becoming more strident and bold. The latest dissenting commentary along these lines comes from senior White House reporter Helen Thomas, now a columnist for the conservative Hearst newspapers but nonetheless a veteran of many White Houses and many wars, who has the sense of history that many of her more junior colleagues lack. Helen knows the rules and has played by them for a half-century. But now she is seething, and she has let it rip:

The imperial presidency has arrived. On the domestic front, President Bush has found that in many ways he can govern by executive order. In foreign affairs he has the nerve to tell other people that they should get rid of their current leaders.

Amazingly, with Americans turning into a new silent majority and Congress into a bunch of obeisant lawmakers, he is getting away with such acts. . . .

The list of the president's self-empowerment moves grows almost daily and will continue unless the Supreme Court calls his hand.

Did I say Supreme Court? Forget it. Not with this court. It handed him the 2000 election, and it would probably cite some World War II decisions that allowed the government to violate citizens' civil rights, especially those of Japanese Americans, in the name of national security.

Equally blatant examples of Bush's arrogance of power are in his foreign policy. What right does he have to tell Yasser Arafat that he has to go or to tell the Palestinians they cannot vote for Arafat in coming elections? Bush's speech could have been written by Israeli Prime Minister Ariel Sharon. Although he speaks of his compassion for the suffering Palestinians under Israel's military occupation, Bush is tightening the screws by making it clear he will deny them any aid unless Arafat is deposed. . . .

Bush is due for a reality check. . . .

Afghan Vice President Slain

Just as the United States is trying to apologize its way out of the recent bombing of a wedding that took between forty and 140 Afghan civilian lives, depending on whose figure you accept, there has been an assassination of the country's vice president and minister of reconstruction. CNN reports, "Gunmen have assassinated Afghanistan's deputy president Haji Abdul Qadir, government sources have confirmed. Haji Qadir and his driver were killed." This morning CNN surprised me by interviewing Eric Margolis, a deputy foreign editor of the *Toronto Star,* author of a book on the war in Afghanistan, and fierce critic of U.S. policy.

He explained the significance of this assassination in dire terms, pointing our that Qadir was a key operative for the United States in Afghanistan ("bagman" is the term he used) and the only member of the majority Pashtun tribe in a government dominated by ethnic minorities. Margolis knew him and his brother El Haq, who had been hung by the Taliban on a covert mission in Afghanistan before that government fell. He says this is a grave setback to the Kazai government, as he was a key political player and CIA advisor.

I was surprised that Margolis was on because he comes from outside the Washington foreign policy establishment, and he does not buy its pro-administration consensus. Example—his recent comments on President Bush's speech on the Middle East:

Bush, a man untroubled by deep thought or irony, had the chutzpah, as New Yorkers say, to urge Palestinians to adopt Scandinavian-style democracy, while telling them they cannot re-elect Arafat, who was elected in a fair vote by over 80 percent of his people—rather better than President Bush, who slid into office thanks to court orders and voter exclusions in Florida. As for corruption, Arafat's thieving PLO cronies look like the homeless compared to Bush's mega-crook pals at Enron who financed his election.

July 10

When I was a kid, I used to spend Saturday mornings in the neighborhood theater, mesmerized by movies warning of impending disaster. *The Day the Earth Stood Still* is one that comes to mind. Now I don't have to leave my home to get scared about imminent threats. The worst was the disclosure earlier this month that a football-stadium-sized asteroid came within seventy-five million miles of earth. Did you hear about it? We could have been goners was the implication. They are not blaming that one on al Qaeda. Not yet.

Earlier in the week, there were fears that terrorists would use ambulances to carry out attacks. This morning *The New York Times* says authorities are on the alert for fuel trucks that could be rammed into synagogues. In Las Vegas, an Arab man reported overhearing a cell phone conversation suggesting that the casino city would be attacked on July 4. Enter the media and the FBI. The guy failed a lie detector test. The mayor wants to prosecute him. The telephone caller says all the press attention caused him to confuse his story.

"At What Point Do You Get It?"

On June 19, Chris Hedges of the New York Times profiled a New York area man, John Wheeler, a crusader against government lies and deception, who says that citizens have to stop being scared and, instead get prepared, if all these terror threats are true. "We are Jewish. It is Germany. It is 1938," he said by way of analogy. "At what point do you get it? ... A lot can be done in terms of preparedness, but citizens have to begin asking pointed questions. Failing to prepare the public for a terrorist strike, including discussing what to do and forming detailed emergency plans," he said, "would be criminal."

I thought about this yesterday after an early morning snafu in the New York subways when someone said a "package" was being investigated. The system was shut down, but no one told us what to do or where to go. There could have been panic and chaos if there really were a real threat. Earlier in the week, I heard that emergency personnel were staging a chemical warfare drill in Yankee Stadium. But then I later saw nothing about in the press. The lack of a serious and organized attempt to inform and organize the public suggests that all this talk of war is revealing total incompetence among officials who are busy reorganizing the bureaucracy yet doing nothing to prepare people. Oh, well ... what did I expect?

And so went the news and my weblog tracking through the hot months of July and August. All of these columns remain available online.

* * *

PARTING SHOT

This part of the book ends where it begins, in South Africa on the eve of the first anniversary of September 11. I am here covering the U.N.'s World Summit on Sustainable Development, where passionate debate among governments, businesses, and NGOs has defined a new heavily compromised and politicized global plan of action on issues like economic development, climate, poverty, and the environment. It has also defined the continuing differences among nations, peoples, and the many stakeholders in the process, as a growing chorus of activists continues to rail at the injustices in our world and the gaps between rich and poor, men and women, and the divides that remain to be breached.

I was at the conference covering the issues and the coverage, filing reports for World Link Television (a satellite channel based in San Francisco) and watching the nearly 3,000 journalists who were reporting on the events. The United Nations had mounted an impressive media operation to accommodate the small media army that occupied a vast basement pressroom at the conference center housing this first Earth Summit of the new century. The South African press was loaded with stories and special coverage. CNN International and the BBC had fielded teams to pump out news from the front lines of this important international gathering, which was being boycotted, to the chagrin of most of the attendees, by the U.S. president, George W. Bush.

What the delegates in the hall and the activists in the streets did not know was that the American media for the most part was also boycotting the events. The CNN channel that provided Charlayne Hunter Gaults' well-informed reports was not seen in America. On the last day of the global event, I received an e-mail from the media columnist of the *Toronto Star*. She told me she had been watching the cable nets in the United States and found almost no coverage.

Once again, Americans were being kept in the dark. No doubt, many saw the heckling and jeering of U.S. Secretary of State Colin Powell by delegates and activists, but the issues and the background was not being shared.

The journalists, who a year ago had written about why "they hate us," are silent now. The media is back to news as usual and business as usual. A year has gone by. What have we learned? What will we do differently when, as is expected, the U.S. government moves on to its next war in Iraq and the one that is sure to follow?

Are there more September 11s to come?

Stay tuned.

PART TWO

Monitoring Media and Promoting Democracy

The World of Media and Media As a World

Visual coverage of the events of September 11 was as riveting as the unbelievable images it conveyed. Answers also came fast and furious to questions of "who," "what," "where," and "when." It was the "how" and, even more difficult, the "why" part of journalistic inquiries that, perhaps understandably, was not as well explored, as television reached for its cast of familiar pundits who often turned out to be as confused and predictable as they were jingoistic. What became hard to find after September 11 were places to go for news in which the broader dimensions of the story about the terrorists' attack on America were unfolding. There were, of course, in mainstream media questions asked—and answered—about who was responsible, how the acts of terror came to be, and how the nation's defense and intelligence agencies missed signals. Often, though, the level of indignation coming out in these interviews exceeded the depth of good information and analysis provided.

As a way to respond to what we perceived to be a vacuum, Globalvision launched its own online news network prototype (gvnews.net) for a more diverse, global syndication effort. By using this vehicle, we were able to offer stories from news outlets throughout the world. It became our way of bringing information and views of local sources—and often-unheard voices—to audiences more accustomed to the narrower range of Anglo-American news.

Our news network provides a panoply of "inside-out" coverage (for example, coverage about Pakistan is written by Pakistani journalists instead of Americans) rather than the conventional "outside-in" international approach. On a given day, our lengthy collection of stories—linked for reader convenience—can include reports from Interfax Russia, the *Kashmir Times,* Middle East Newsline, Islam Online, Iran News, the *Moscow Times,* the *Times of India,* Mandiri News, Israel Insider, and Radio Free Europe. We call ourselves "context providers," and we are turning a collection of stories into a news product that we hope news companies and websites will acquire to complement existing wire service reporting as a way of offering more and deeper sources to their readers.

Our initiative emerged as a response to media trends that over the years have shortchanged the public, and in turn, eroded our democracy. While Globalvision is not alone in rejecting the dumbing down of news, we are trying a practical and credible way to counter the pervasive withdrawal of international coverage by networks and newspapers. Yet it still surprises me to learn how many in the media business don't appear to recognize the scale of this problem.

Long before September 11, my colleagues and I had become alarmed by the consequences of America's media-led isolationism as it fueled citizens' ignorance about the rest of the world. And we could read about how this absence of engagement through public communication led the Indian writer Arundhati Roy to suggest that Washington's foreign policy was the consequence of the power of the U.S. media to keep the public uninformed. "I think people are the product of the information they receive," Roy writes. "I think even more powerful than America's military arsenal has been its hold over the media in some way. I find that very frightening. Just as much as America believes in freedom at home, or [. . .] free speech, or the freedom of religion, outside it believes in the freedom to humiliate, the freedom to export terror. And the freedom to humiliate is a very important thing because that's what really leads to the rage."

Agree or not with Roy, it is hard to deny that most Americans are confused about why "they" would afflict such terror on the freedom-loving "us." "I think most Americans are clueless when it comes to the politics and ideology and religion in [the Muslim] world and, in that sense, I think we do bear some responsibility," *Boston Globe* editor Martin Baron told the *Los Angeles Times'* Shaw. "In consequence, we are not only less informed about what's happening in the world but about how others see us."

This situation prompted Globalvision to create this news network of international reporting. Our motives for acting arose from both our personal

interest in trying to draw more attention to the plight of the world's dispossessed and in our company's interest in
tapping into a forgotten niche that
might serve as a lucrative business
opportunity. For fifteen years, we had
mostly focused on producing "inside-
out" television programming about a
changing world. Now, thanks to the
Internet, there is a distribution channel
to add international content to an all-
too-limited global news mix.

> "There are laws to protect
> the freedom of the press's
> speech, but none that are
> worth anything to protect
> the people from the press."
>
> — MARK TWAIN,
> author, 1873

Our interest is not in criticizing coverage for its own sake. We are not media
bashers. We present the information we do as a way of offering constructive
approaches to improving coverage. For example, Mediachannel.org carries work
by a British-based group called Reporting the World (reportingtheworld.org)
whose work shows how coverage of the same news can be told from a perspective of conflict resolution (they call this the "peace journalism" approach) just as
easily as it can be conveyed through the prism of "war journalism," with its
emphasis on bombs and body bags.

Also, we try to offer strategies and information that will help journalists
counter our largest media failure—the lack of a context that will allow news consumers to gain clear understanding of the background issues and clash of interpretations. Because our readers are able to look at so much coverage by news
outlets in other countries—many of whom report on the same story on a given
day—they are able to see for themselves the cultural biases and parochialism that
often deform news coverage. While diversity—although important—is not
a guarantee of accuracy, it does add another layer of context and, we hope, a
larger perspective.

Because of the reach of the Internet, many diverse sources of information
are now available. But despite all the choices, well-advertised major media
brands remain the primary source of news and explanation for most citizens.
This presents a problem since the crux of these debates—the impact of past U.S.
covert operations and oil interests, for example—fly below the radar of most
mainstream media outlets. And mainstream media offers a lack of dissenting
perspectives.

Media has a major role to play in reminding us of the ways lives are
entwined and futures are interconnected worldwide. The shocking events of

September 11 and the response to them call our attention to the deeply institutionalized failures in foreign policy, defense strategies, the work of intelligence agencies, and, yes, the U.S. media. We can call on others to fix the former, but only journalists can improve the media institutions we work for and rely on to strengthen our democracy. For too long, news organizations have failed to do this. They can fail no longer.

Mediachannel.org and Other Ways to Change the World

HOW DO WE CHANGE THE WORLD?

How many times have I (we) heard this question? For a political person like myself, it is a question that has always been with me and all of those who follow the muse of activism or are driven to the challenge of engaging with the times and the institutions around us. Many of us who have spent lifetimes battling for social justice and economic fairness have debated that age-old question: "What is to be done?" We are consumed by thinking about how our passions and commitments can best be channeled, what approach can have an impact, and which method can best foster change. This is usually a debate engaged in mostly by activists, inside and outside of movements and institutions.

Occasionally, challenges to the media system are reported on—although all too often, media critics are dismissed as conspiracy theorists, media bashers, or just plain "nuts." Yet today, this pattern of "critic denial" seems to be changing for reasons that have to do with the experiences so many professionals are living through in a changed media marketplace. At last, influential voices within the press are part of a discourse that has, until recently, largely been consigned to the campus and margins.

I am a journalist—by choice, by experience, and by inclination. I observe. I report. I explain. And I look for outlets to tell stories and pursue investigations into issues I care about.

This book is an outgrowth of a life in process. It is about challenging the media system from the inside. It is much more than my personal story because I am part of a growing community of independent media makers, editors, producers, and activists who are fighting for a more democratic and public service–oriented media and who believe that challenging our increasingly monopolized media system is essential to promoting change in the world.

This book details one relatively new way to confront a powerful constellation of corporate forces: the use of the Internet to help forge a larger movement for media reform and accountability.

WHEN YOU ENTER THE MEDIA WORLD, IT ENTERS YOU

I've spent half of a lifetime chasing stories about problems all around the world, running up impressive frequent flyer tallies along the way. As a writer and a television producer, I tried to use media outlets of all kinds to reach audiences with news and information that was not readily available. In that work, I tried to fuse the concerns in my head with the passions of my heart. I was fortunate to be on the front lines of many stories of international interest. Sometimes that work took me to faraway places. In many instances, I found myself with unique access to newsmakers and breaking stories.

But I soon recognized that a deeper problem was much closer to home. It was the problem of how to get real news of the world into a media system that was increasingly shutting it out. As reporting and producing such stories quickly became easier, disseminating them became more difficult. Thanks to new technologies, a new means of digital production became affordable, but the means of unsanitized and uncensored distribution was not. I came to see that one major source of "my" problems and our political culture was right next door.

And, as a media maker and critic I was part of it.

The media world I had joined surrounded me—physically, psychologically, and metaphorically. For years, it was a world that I identified with, living and working within, first as an "underground" alternative journalist, then as an employee at big media outfits, and later in an independent media company. All along I remained a compulsive media consumer, reader, and viewer. I made media, and I felt like I "ate" media, endless amounts of it. This intellectual diet nourished my curiosity and fed my need to know. But like many people aware of how news is collected and some say "manufactured," that diet became less filling as I became more conscious of its limits and more critical of its unspoken agendas. I soon began spending less and less time producing for media and more time writing about insidious media trends of all kinds. Not surprisingly I soon found my own life and work affected by them.

It is often true that when you enter any profession, its values and outlook enters you. This is certainly true of the media world. As you take on its assumptions, logic, and culture, you begin to reflect its worldviews. For me, this media world is now also a *physical* part of my environment, surrounding me in the neighborhood in which our company has been based for a decade—Times Square, in the middle of New York City, which proudly calls itself the capital of the world.

From where I sit (physically, not figuratively), it is clear that market forces are the driving forces. Times Square was once known for shows, sleaze, and sex. For nearly a century, it has been the Great White Way with its bright lights and titillating attractions, but much of that has been transformed as overt sleaze gave way to a more corporatized surreality with big media companies at its center.

Just outside the window from our Times Square office, investment banker Morgan Stanley's giant billboard pulsates around the clock, and like the city that never sleeps, it electronically chronicles every important trade, deal, and currency fluctuation in the world. It is a scorecard of the world's winners and losers, offering Dow Jones news, Reuter's financial information, and Bloomberg reports. Stare at it for more than a few minutes, and it is dizzying. Its function is to impress, not to inform, to project financial power and the band of big business. Its presence underscores how the world has changed, ticking off globalization's "progress," or lack of it. The winners and losers are digits on a moving screen. There are no human faces, no sense of the social and economic consequences behind a blinking parade of endless deals and developments.

Then, as you look around, from one building to another, the glue attaching big media to big business becomes apparent. Just a block away, down the street, Rupert Murdoch commands his Orwellian News Corp and rightist Fox News channel. Down the street, Viacom, home of MTV, VH-1, Nickelodeon, and now CBS, once considered the "Tiffany Network," stares across the Square at the German conglomerate Bertelsmann's tower and ABC's *Good Morning America* studio. The new Reuters Tower went up kitty-corner from the new Disney building, next door to the Warner Brother's store and in clear view of NASDAQ's showplace, complete with its own television studio. (NASDAQ is a virtual operation with no trading floor—just banks of computers, dressed up in this location to appear to be a real exchange so that reporters can use it as the backdrop or set for their stand-ups.) Scholars who write tomes about media concentration need only distribute a map of this ten-block area to illustrate what it looks like physically.

CONSUMPTION TRUMPS CITIZENSHIP

Tourists, and those who have come to hustle them, can get their news fix in the form of a headline hit parade from three sources (but all have the same stories). They can stand in the street and become mesmerized by ABC's multicolored "bulletin board," the original *New York Times* "zipper" now run by Dow Jones, or on the giant NBC Panasonic television screen a few yards to the right. There it is, the hour-by-hour digest of what these companies think we should know, all compressed into a few words and punchy phrases. For a few seconds, you feel part of a larger world, but to see it, you have to look up (but not touch). It's there, but not really there. It keeps you in touch with chaos and celebrities, but it distances you from them all at the same time. Taken together, this media mecca is not about educating citizens about the world, but informing us of their dominant place in it. It is an obscene display of the iconography of media presence and impact. It is the media environment. Its real message: consumption, not citizenship, is what matters.

The physical proximity of financial trading rooms and World Wrestling Federation restaurants, as well as ads for news companies next to slogans about "Being Bullish" is also quite blatantly a commercial for how ever-expanding media octopi serve certain economic interests. It is not surprising that there are now at least five channels focused on business and market watches and none on labor.

The global economy relies on their marketing reach, with many of its finely tuned components closely interconnected. When tech stocks collapsed in the fall of 2000, other parts of the economy went into a tailspin. Media companies began to lay off hundreds and thousands of employees to placate a nervous Wall Street that views cost-cutting as a sign of smart management and on the road to reviving the stock price. In mid-June, it was announced that as many as one hundred thousand jobs have been lost in the media sector. Has this had any effect on the quality of what they are selling? For the answer, one must borrow that lovely phrase from Bill Clinton's solution to the problem of gays in the military: "Don't ask; don't tell."

THE UNTHINKABLE: EMPTY BILLBOARDS

As I write in the spring of 2002, the unthinkable has come to Times Square. Billboards that once demanded two-million-a-year rentals go begging. They have become advertisements for themselves and the reality of economic decline—just white blotches like some conceptual art piece.

A knowing anthropologist from another planet or culture, studying these signs and symbols as the hieroglyphics that they are, would understand a great deal about the forces shaping modern America. For starters, they would see the centrality of media in stoking our global commercial culture. It is only by ana-lyzing the coverage on a daily basis that one spots the patterns and formulae that offer cultural insights. Our hypothetical "outside expert" might recognize that what often looks like information for the masses is really there to serve the upper classes. This conclusion is made in the sense that the needs of ordinary people are focused on far less than the conflicts and achievements of the people at the top of the pecking order, in the highest circles of economic, political, or celebrity "power." Our imagined onlooker would also be able to note the visi-bility and endless promotion of media "brands" that are far more alike than they are distinctive.

They would also recognize the effects of the ideology it has fostered, even if many on the left and the right do not fully appreciate its full impact in depoliti-cizing public awareness or the primacy of challenging its power. That is not totally true: the right has made influencing media a priority, opting to take it over rather than just criticize it. Many on the left do not deal with it much at all, as if exposure represents a form of contamination. How many among us say proudly "I don't watch TV" as a gesture of personal protest. (One group tells its followers, "Don't watch TV; it will rot your brain." Another sells bumper stick-ers that say "Kill Your Television.") Yet such a unilateral cultural withdrawal often cuts progressives off from understanding the ideas and information that shapes the consciousness of younger people.

It is also sadly true that philanthropists of the right put media at the top of their funding agendas while more liberal philanthropists, who are often better endowed (i.e., richer) leave media funding for last, if it is on the list at all.

It was in this environment that I began to shift my own career from a pro-ducer of programming *for* this media system into more and more of an analyst *of* this media system. I became an outsider-turned-insider who was, decades later, back on the outside. I had joined the media to spotlight the problems of the world, and I realized that I was unintentionally contributing to one of them. I made the media more of a subject for personal scrutiny and an arena for activism.

My first book, *The More You Watch, the Less You Know* (Seven Stories Press), chronicled my experiences and offered up from the trenches a view of a televi-sion system that gives viewers the illusion of choice inside a texture of same-ness, a smorgasbord of formularized programming, and predictable formats.

At first, I fancied myself a defector and network refugee turned radical critic. I soon discovered that the library of media-critical books is voluminous. The shelves of journalism books are filled with the recollections of media man-darins with stories of this or that company's betrayal of journalistic tradition. Many express views in their memoirs that they conceal in their work.

I was especially surprised that on the day my book came out, Walter Cronkite, once the "great god of American News," and a television anchorman who always struck me as the paragon of the establishment, gave a speech at a convention of radio and television news directors that was a straight out attack on corporate media that made me sound, well, er, moderate! (Today, Cronkite is an advisor to the Mediachannel.org. His views appear in the front of this book.)

It was clear then that just publishing jeremiads against the media was not enough. The industry was getting worse despite all the slings and arrows fired its way, from Hollywood films like *Network* to Broadway plays and critical essays. Words alone would not slay this beast, if it could be "slain" at all. Action of some kind (plus organization) was what was needed.

ENTER MEDIACHANNEL.ORG

I opted for fighting fire with fire, by creating a media channel to monitor all the other channels, to focus on covering media just as it covers and miscovers so many aspects of news and pop culture. Envisioning such a channel is far easier than launching one. At first, I wanted to do it on television, but it soon became clear that a media channel on cable television would be unaffordable, and even if it weren't impossible to create, getting on the air at all would be hardly ensured, even if you had the money. (Launching a cable channel these days costs in the neighborhood of $100 million dollars.) Carriage would also be a long shot, given how few companies control access to cable television and how closed it is, for the most part, to controversial content. No media corporation would likely carry it.

If television was out, what was in? Access to radio was also shrinking. That left only the Internet, where the cost of entry is far lower, but where many other problems present themselves. Creating a website is easy, but the type of site I envisioned would have to be more ambitious. We needed one that would allow us to network with groups worldwide who work on media issues. We opted to create a supersite, or what is known in the "Internet space" as a portal that can offer diverse content from many sources.

Since our idea was contrarian to the core (if not, downright adversarial), our methodology had to be as well. At the outside, we decided to go "dot.org," not "dot.com," to make Mediachannel.org a public interest, not-for-profit site as opposed to a commercial enterprise. In that period, in 1999, we were considered foolish for even thinking that way because it seemed as if every kid out of business school was being showered by Wall Street with $50 million IPOs for every imaginable Internet scheme. (Many of which, of course, later crashed and burned because business cycles could not and would not be abolished by false projections or fiat.)

We opted for a website structure that could aggregate input from affiliated organizations, as well as feature original content, including the columns featured in this collection. Mediachannel.org was what we ended up with. It soon became a hybrid: a newspaper, magazine, interactive chat room, resource center, and network all in one.

We decided to offer a blend of media news, opinion, personal accounts, research studies, activist reports, arts coverage, and debates about the nature of the media system and how it might be changed. Resources include thematic special reports, action toolkits, forums for discussion, an indexed directory of hundreds of affiliated groups, and a search engine constituting the single largest online media-issues database. We concerned ourselves with the political, cultural, and social impacts of the media, large and small. Mediachannel.org exists to provide information and diverse perspectives and inspire debate, collaboration, action, and citizen engagement.

We affiliated with the already well-established One World online network in England (oneworld.net) that focuses on environment, development, and human rights, so that we didn't have to reinvent the wheel technologically and so that we could keep our costs down. One World provided us with its software templates so that we could get up and running quickly. It also provided us with a global distribution platform. In turn, we based our servers in England, immediately making it an international project. We soon discovered on our own what has worked so well for so many larger media companies: the economic benefits of being synergistic.

It should be noted that our web "architecture" is built around a proprietary, database-driven, "cold fusion" system, in contrast to the open-source technology adopted by many other alternative websites, like indymedia.org, that offer up a more user-friendly system where every reader can be a reporter, usually without any editing or adherence to journalistic codes. The newer systems permit more spontaneity, its advocates say, and more radical reporting. Our systems are clunkier, true, but when one writes about media and for media, one has to try to ensure accuracy, and perhaps that precaution restrains more anarchistic interventions. In that respect, our site was forced to be more conservative in look and feel but not necessarily in content.

The other aspect of all this formatting is that we had to be conscious of the technology available to the user. Not every computer, especially in the developing world, can receive the latest state-of-the-art graphics and multimedia that may look good but take a long time to load. "What's cool" in New York may not necessarily be accessible in Bangladesh.

GOING GLOBAL

For us, the Internet offered the type of distribution platform that independent producers yearn for: relatively free and unfettered transmission worldwide. For a company like Globalvision, this was a way of realizing our goal of globalizing content and reaching audiences in other continents.

We had always considered the media issue, like so many issues, as an international one. But before the Internet came along, there were few ways small companies could report on it in those terms in a timely fashion.

We were hardly the only media company to recognize in our interdependent globalized world, as CNN did early in its existence, that the idea of "foreign news" was obsolete. CNN banned the word "foreign," replacing it with "international." The new world order demanded such an international approach.

As we began to move into the web, new global media companies were already there and consolidating in the global marketplace put in place by globalization. Their self-styled "New Economy" was built on three pillars: global trade, global capital markets, and global communications.

All three are interconnected, although to many activists battling this trend, the focus is only on global trade agreements, and occasionally, companies like Nike or Shell Oil. It seemed as if the activist movement was unaware that the crucial role played by global media combines in promoting the ideology of globalization and advancing the interests behind it. Magazines like *Forbes* were not shy about calling themselves a "Capitalist Tool," but others were less explicit about their function and priorities, hiding behind clever slogans and populist advertising. For example, for many years, MTV claimed to be leading the youth revolution while cultural commentators like Tom Frank of the *Baffler* and others have explained how such corporate marketing co-opts and perverts radical impulses among youth.

As the media globalizes, exposing and critiquing the media system in global terms is essential. If a global movement is to be built to challenge its impact, as in "globalization from below" taking on "globalization from above" (or in Jeremy Brecher's words, "the global village resisting global pillage"), we need to hear from and learn about the experience of others in countries that are usually outside the U.S. media discourse.

As it turns out, many other countries still offer more diversity in their media outlets than the U.S. outlets do, in part because of well-funded public service broadcasters like the BBC who still promote a culture of quality programming and have the budgets to sustain it. As someone who attended graduate school in London, I realized years ago that we in the United States could learn a thing or two from the best practices and examples of broadcasters and journalists elsewhere. Coverage of global media trends can help fertilize activism in the United States as well. It is always an uphill battle to get people to fight for better media if they have never experienced it—or realized what better media even is or could be. Mediachannel.org set out to share this type of global media information and connect journalists and activists worldwide.

HOW WE CREATED THE SITE

New projects require investment of funds and energy. They are expensive to launch and operate, although the costs of doing business on the web are lower than in traditional media. For obvious reasons, not-for-profit ventures are rarely attractive to investors. Where would the money come from?

Without a funding base of readers to appeal to—like the *Nation* or *Monthly Review* has—we had to put our hopes and our fate in the hands of foundations. We were well aware of how easy it is for those of us who want to be independent to quickly become dependent on their largesse. Going this route is hardly ensured—or sustaining over time.

Fortunately, perhaps because of our fourteen-year track record as recipients of foundation grants ("beggars in suits," we called ourselves), we were able to unlock generous support to get up and going from the Rockefeller Foundation, Open Society Institute, Arca, Reebok Human Rights Foundation, Puffin Foundation, and most recently, the Ford Foundation. Behind each of those commitments was months of proposal writing, follow-up calls, meetings, and more meetings.

You never know how much work goes into raising money until you try it. Of course, if you are well endowed to begin with and can invest in a fund-raising and development staff, generating support can become easier and more routine. When you don't, it's much tougher. The sad truth is, "Those that have, tend to get."

You quickly learn that fund-raising itself is also a business. Working it takes time—time taken away from other priorities. I am a journalist who wants to be writing and producing, not soliciting. And yet, in projects such as Mediachannel.org, everyone becomes a de facto part of the fund-raising effort.

Most news organizations separate all business and editorial functions. They pride themselves on the "wall" separating the two functions. When that wall is breached, editorial compromises invariably follow. So in principle, one would prefer not to mix the two. Yet, small companies cannot often afford the infrastructure that permits a complete separation.

I soon had to put my "funding hat" on!

ALL PRAISE TO THE ROBBER BARONS

The good news is that we were successful in the first round of foundation-grant seeking—and so, contradictions and irony be damned, let us praise the great robber barons of an earlier time for their craftiness and generosity! That old monopolist and protagonist of the workers John D. Rockefeller might be twisting down under was he to learn how his fortune is being dispensed.

The bad news is that no one foundation ever gives you what you really need. So that forces you to reach out to many different sources to get enough in the bank to fund a budget, hire a staff, and pay the bills. Also, alas, you usually can count on support for only one year at a time. It is easy to see how the need to keep the money pump going then twists priorities and the allocation of staff time and resources.

I know I am not the only one with this complaint. An old buddy of mine, now in Congress, tells me that every day he is forced to spend hours fund-raising—"dialing for dollars," he calls it. We all know about how obsessive money-raising distorts our political system. Well, here in the wonderful world of indy media, we have similar problems.

The foundations know this, too—which is why they have increasingly taken on the trappings of venture capital funds. Maybe it's the market logic of our times seeping into every crevice of public life, but most now insist their grantees become more businesslike. Also, many funding organizations who are willing to give you money don't really want to have you knocking on their doors again and again.

So they insist they you come up with real business plans to avoid overdependence on their support. They quiz you with questions that quickly come to resemble the Spanish Inquisition, about how you are going to start capitalizing your own venture. Suddenly, noble proposals and sometimes fuzzy-wuzzy or politically oriented ideas (i.e., "We want to raise consciousness and promote revolution") are being evaluated through the hard lens of monetization.

Their message is this: If you want to stay in business, you have to be businesslike and operate in a way that can sustain the business. Decentralized, affinity group–like structures do not impress them where process is more important than product, as is common in parts of the NGO world.

THE MEDIACHANNEL.ORG STRATEGY

Globalvision was already a business, and we ran it like one. If we weren't a business, we couldn't have survived over sixteen years while producing programs rarely considered commercially viable. My own experiences in the movements of the sixties convinced me that only this type of structure could sustain a media venture like ours over so many years.

We have shaped Mediachannel.org as a public–private partnership—or in the words of Jonathan Peizer, the thoughtful technology chief of the Open Society Institute, a dot.com–dot.org fusion between our mission oriented non-profit work and business strategy.

Luckily for our new media company, we found progressive investors in Europe, where there is more openness to projects critical of U.S.-dominated media culture. Those investors brought in, first as an advisor and then as the chairman of our board, James R. Rosenfield, the former president of CBS. Soon Walter Cronkite was invited to join us as an advisor, along with other respected media personas. The investors recognized that aggregating content and affiliates could help legitimize the company's commercial plans for a new global news syndication service and provide a base for further potential collaborations. They put their money where their convictions were. They wanted to do well, and they also wanted to do good.

The investors also introduced more businesslike approaches, which we hope will lead to a better chance for survival. (By 2003, as the larger economy has slid into decline, these prospects are hardly guaranteed.)

SHOULD YOU TAKE CORPORATE MONEY?

After considerable debate, we decided to try to reach out for corporate under-writers—a decision based on that understanding once attributed to the American bank robber Willy Sutton who, when asked why he robbed banks, said simply, "That's where the money is."

The corporate world is where the money is, in today's world. And we decided to see if we could attract some—without compromising our mission. We were very mindful of the risks and dangers of moving in this direction. All one has to do is look at American public broadcasting to see how a reliance on corporate underwriters seemed partially responsible for keeping PBS so bland and tepid. At the same time, we realized that there are companies who profess social responsibility in their mission, who might be supportive. We were, of course, insistent on ensuring our editorial independence.

As a result of our outreach, one leading transnational corporation is already on board, and others are in discussions with us. Many have public relations departments led by former journalists who are supportive of our critique and want to help. We realized that many companies want to reach the opinion lead-ers in the audience we are developing. In addition, we are working on a number of revenue-producing modules of services that we intend to introduce.

This is all part of trying to generate a multiplicity of revenue streams. Mediachannel.org sought to appeal to a variety of audiences, and our hope was to attract support from a variety of sources. Are there potential contradictions and a minefield of possible conflicts with this approach? You bet. But what's the alternative? Where will the money for independent media come from? Ultimately, our supporters have to bank on our integrity.

THE MANDATE AND METHOD: BUILD A NETWORK OF AFFILIATES

We then tested our idea by inviting media-related organizations to join as affiliates. Affiliates have no obligations, but they do agree to allow us to offer their content on the Mediachannel.org site. This is achieved via technology so that readers and users can, with a simple click of a mouse, visit the affiliate site and become familiar with what they do and have to say.

We started with fifty groups. By January 2003, we topped 1,000 affiliates, making Mediachannel.org the largest online media issues network in the world. (*Monthly Review* is an affiliate, along with the *Nation, Mother Jones, In These Times,* and many progressive organizations and their counterparts in other countries.) Some of these affiliates simply saw us as another distribution platform for their websites; others participated more actively. The public, too, soon responded, with an average of several million hits a month. A survey we sent out received an 18 percent response. We found that we are reaching a diverse audience, with half outside the United States. We confirmed that a substantial number either work for media companies or study or teach the subject. At the same time, a large portion of the readers who come back day after day and week after week—we redo the whole page weekly on Wednesdays, but update news and features during the week—are a cross-section of web users of all ages and backgrounds who hear about us in the press or through links on other sites. The site is growing. More affiliates join weekly.

Why are they coming? We would like to think because Mediachannel.org positioned itself with a broad, multipronged mandate, offering a wide menu of content and services.

Here's how we describe our offerings:

- Mediachannel.org is a primary source for news, information, and opinion about the cultural, political, and social impact of global media, including print, broadcast, film, video, music, the Web, and independent media.
- Mediachannel.org educates, engages, and inspires citizen involvement by providing a well-marketed, professionally designed, and accessible online forum

for debate and discussion of the key issues regarding the media, as well as by posting action alerts for events sponsored by affiliated sites. Its online community encourages individual engagement in media issues on a global scale.

- Mediachannel.org is a growing global network of media reform, research, and professional organizations, facilitating the sharing of contacts and information to help make their work more effective; the site's directory of affiliates is the most comprehensive resource of media-issues organizations now online.
- Mediachannel.org is a gateway to media arts news and resources; it showcases major new works using the latest web technologies.
- Mediachannel.org pioneers innovative uses of the web to make news and information about the media available from the widest possible variety of qualified sources, ranging from original source documents to news dispatches, feature articles to opinion pieces, while coordinating efforts among disparate media issues organizations to develop original content.
- Mediachannel.org is designed to be a state-of-the-art, world-class news site. Mediachannel.org organizes all of this material in an intuitively accessible manner to make it easy for the site visitor.

A great deal of internal debate and planning went into deciding what resources we should offer and how the site could play a role beyond its being a content provider.

At this writing, resources include the following:

- A journalist's toolkit: created for journalism classes or school newspaper projects; also provides online writing and research tips valuable for any student.
- Global news index: links to hundreds of local newspapers worldwide; organized by region and country.
- Affiliate directory: the index to Mediachannel.org's global network of organizations and publications.
- Book corner: books for journalism, media studies, communication, or cultural studies curricula, with excerpts, reviews, and quick links to buy (purchases support Mediachannel.org).

THE MEDIACHANNEL.ORG MISSION

Mediachannel.org has focused its mission around four key challenges: the challenge to understand what is happening in the media today; how those changes are affecting our politics and inspiring resistance; the role and impact of alternative media and new forms of independent media activism; and finally, the relationship of the "media question" and media activism in a larger political context. What is all of this independent media energy, online and off, contributing to radical politics in an age of globalization?

There is no one set of politically correct answers to these challenges and questions. Instead, there is struggle for independent media to remain vital while sustaining itself financially, for new forms of media to grow and old forms to be renewed, for new generations to develop communication skills and forge new platforms of expression.

All of this is playing itself out in exciting ways in countries on every continent, confronting different types of obstacles ranging from traditional government censorship to new high-tech surveillance and filtering; from terror and repression aimed at courageous journalists to corporate pressures and self-censorship imposed in subtle and not-so-subtle ways.

These are the issues that Mediachannel.org explores on a daily and weekly basis. They are also the subjects for debate in our interactive forum and weblogs, in addition to what I write about in a column drawn from my own research, experience, reporting assignments, and interactions with media insiders at conferences or media events.

DEFINING MEDIACHANNEL.ORG'S ISSUES

New York University's distinguished media scholar Neil Postman often asks audiences, "What is the problem to which you are proposing a solution?" Ours is all around us. Just turn on a television set, radio, or in many instances, open a newspaper in America, and you find problems to which Mediachannel.org and its affiliates propose solutions. Such problems include media mergers, the "dumbing down" of news, and the global expansion of media cartels promoting the same formats and formulas worldwide. Our landscape has changed. What are the implications for journalism? For democracy? Where can we find real news about what's happening in and to the media globally? How can we encourage media consumers to sharpen critical skills, discuss and debate news coverage, and promote media accountability and reform? How can we connect those concerned about improving and renewing the media with one another, across borders, so that they can work together more effectively?

With fewer than ten transnational conglomerates dominating our broadcasting systems; with only twenty major companies effectively running the majority of our newspapers, magazines, web portals, film studios, radio stations, and book publishers; with market values firmly in command in the media in the West and influencing changes in the developing world, we are witnessing the commercialization of public space, a crisis for independent journalism, the denigration of ideas of public service, and the weakening of our political culture.

While these issues are most acutely felt in the United States, the "American media model" is now influencing broadcasters and news companies worldwide. Across the globe, public service broadcasting is being cut back, and diverse media sources are at risk. The media system has gone from being seen as the salvation of democracy to a global problem that threatens it. In many countries, the media arena has become a stage for contest, conflict, and debate.

How can we inform the public at large about what's happening in the media world, and why they should care about it? Where can we even talk about these issues since the media itself rarely puts itself under the scrutiny it reserves for others?

There has been no one place to turn, no easy-to-access credible source of diverse perspectives that brings together media news, criticism, education, arts, and proposals for enhanced citizen involvement. There has been no way for groups promoting socially responsible media practices to interact globally.

Hundreds of organizations and thousands of individuals are engaged with these issues. Some are online. But they don't necessarily know about each other, or how to connect, or how to best use the Internet to promote their work.

As desktop multimedia increasingly becomes a major communications platform, its technology and global reach lends itself to exciting, dynamic ways to build communities of concern, to focus attention on international problems, and to prompt action within the media industry by voices of conscience outside and inside the powerful media businesses that shape so much of the national and international public discourse.

In many ways, Mediachannel.org has sought to become a response to the homogenizing pressures of globalization in which giant transnational corporations spread their tentacles from above, prompting a desire for more networking and resistance from below. The global Internet technology makes possible an instant form of interaction across borders and boundaries. And while it has not yet penetrated into every village in the developing world, it has been widely adopted by media organizations in virtually every country. It is the fastest growing technology in the history of the world, with its own set of problems and limits. And just as it is used by the dominant corporate world to market its dreams and products, it is also being used by organizers of every ideological stripe to build new structures for communication and resistance.

MY ROLE AND THE COLUMN

I am the executive editor of this small ship, steering through often-turbulent waters with a tiny team of web-savvy professionals. We only have a small staff of editors, producers, and managers. There are differences among us in attitude and age. Sometimes I feel like I am being tolerated as an old fart who still clips newspapers and buries himself with print publication, or "dead trees" as they call them. When they want to know something, they hit the search engines. When I am looking for information, I first ferret through the piles of media mulch on my desk. Our styles may be different, but our goals are shared.

I am also a columnist, writing under a *media nom de guerre,* "The News Dissector." In some ways, that is how I chose to "brand myself" as a media personality first, affixing a catchy nickname to raise my recognition factor when I was an on-air newscaster on a Boston radio station for a decade. It is also part of who I am. Unlike many more sober, traditional progressives who write in more mainstream academic or journalistic styles, I have always opted to inject more personality, punch, and subjectivity into my work. I guess that's what I learned back in the insurgent 1960s from my onetime political running mate Abbie Hoffman, who realized that in a culture dominated by personalities, it didn't hurt to become one, especially if you want a megaphone. His Marx was Groucho; his Lennon was John.

I know this approach may be dismissed as an ego trip by some, or somehow regarded as being less than "serious," because folks on the left, by training, often have academic orientations where "objectivity" is more highly prized than more stylized and subjective writing. I have always found that, by personalizing feelings and analysis, one can be more effective. I was always drawn by that revolution sought by Emma Goldman (I was born on her birthday) in which dancing and fun had a big role to play. Humorlessness was part of the reason the "old left" so isolated and marginalized itself. I think one can write in a personal way without being regarded as a simplistic "diarist" or pedantic diatribist. I deliberately set out to write a column that ranged from examining single issues in depth and reporting on events for and about the media. I am a big believer in "participatory journalism," a journalism of involvement.

In my case, my status as a media veteran, having "been there and done that" as a reporter, news director, and producer in commercial media, qualifies me (I hope) to comment knowledgeably and credibly on media developments. Reporting on personal confrontations with media moguls and conversations with media makers, in my view, enhances that credibility and makes the writing livelier.

THE NEW MEDIA (DIS)ORDER

We are all living in this new media order that seems to be changing every day as new technologies render old ones obsolete. No one alive is blind to this drama. There are hundreds of television channels and hundreds of thousands of websites. There are wireless phones and mobile devices that provide e-mail access. There are satellite dishes the size of dinner dishes and phones that can fit on a watch like the ones the comic strip hero Dick Tracy used to wear in the Sunday papers I grew up with.

I am on my seventh computer in twenty years. Many of my friends replace theirs yearly. Software is constantly being outdated. I use more phones than ever, but I always seem to be one model and gadget behind. Many of us are like that, running to keep up and stay abreast of the latest techno toys.

Most media seems to be morphing into other media in a great mush of convergence, with radio stations available through cable modems and with newspapers that have more color in them than television shows. Massive investments have been injected into industries that have reshaped the way we communicate and for many of us, the way we buy, look for information and stay informed about the world. Billions have been invested into mergers and acquisitions that have bolstered the bottom line of investment banks and produced unprecedented levels of concentration of media ownership. All of this has affected what our children see and know, what issues politicians discuss, and the larger environment in which political activists operate.

Media is everywhere and everything seems to be media. And yet behind it all are new corporate configurations that are, in the words of Marshall McLuhan, "pervasively invisible." Who is in charge? Where does it all come from? How does it get here? And does it matter?

Of course it does, but just who is in charge doesn't really deal with the key issues that media activists committed to deepening democracy see.

THE FOUR KEY ISSUES

There are four principal issues or questions that this book explores and that I treat in different ways in the diverse columns collected in this book. They revolve around an axis familiar to activists of all types: the dialectic of power and resistance, the conflict between dominant structures and those suffering under them. In the case of the media, it is harder to make the case that people are being totally oppressed by its relentless ideological pounding. After all, you can always turn it off . . . or can you? As I argue, it's not so easy to live outside the media's shadow in a country so drenched in a media-mediated culture.

Our focus is not abstract at all. We report facts, not just deal with theories. We examine relationships and alliances. But we also offer diverse opinions, mine among them, about how to make sense of the fast-moving currents of capital shifts and deal-making in the dynamic media sector. We deal with questions like these:

1. What is happening within the media today? What are the "economic pressures" driving media decision makers? What are the results of growing concentration of ownership?
2. What is the nature of the media debate? Who is fighting who over what? How does the public relate to media issues? And which group or groups are contesting these issues? How does this play out in society? What forms of activism are emerging?
3. What is the alternative media today, and what impact does it have? Does the alternative media—NGOs, websites, independent radio, and the like—provide a real alternative to the mainstream media? What opportunities are there for them, and what obstacles? What role is the Internet playing?
4. How do developments in the new media activism relate to a larger political context? What does an alternative media culture have to contribute to radical politics today?

As part of an effort to discuss the political significance of the changes underway in old media and the challenges represented by the new, let me touch on these issues and introduce the Mediachannel.org columns that speak most directly to them.

THE ISSUE OF OWNERSHIP

Media concentration is an issue that has been part of the American media debate from the early days of the republic. Many were shocked back in 1983 when Ben Bagdikian, once the ombudsman for *The Washington Post* reported in his book *The Media Monopoly* that ownership was concentrated in just fifty companies. At the time, his findings were mostly dismissed by his colleagues as "alarmist."

Writer Mark Derry notes: "now, after the frenzy of mergers and acquisitions in the '80s and '90s, a PlanetMedia run by 50 firms looks almost democratic, as the number of transnational firms who dominate the global media system has dwindled to nine." (It has dwindled even more *since* he wrote, with AOL Time Warner's becoming the number one media company in the world.) "Why should we care? Because, according to some critics, these global media giants are sacrificing journalistic quality and ethics on the altar of shareholder returns.

MBA's with no experience in—and little love for—journalism are downsizing news divisions and upping the fluff-to-fiber ratio in order to boost profits. Ominously, some corporate parents are meddling in the newsroom, slipping product placement into news shows and censoring investigative reports that bite the hand that feeds."

This is the institutional context we find ourselves in. It is a new arena of media power that is made difficult to challenge or contest. Why? Because regulation, a process usually designed to encourage public input and participation, has largely given way to privatization, permitting media companies to operate only according to market strictures with little accountability.

This leaves few venues for debate in which political constituencies can publicly assert their interests, or even attempt to influence the discourse. For most media companies, serving the public interest, an obligation once mandated by law, has been "redefined" and is now considered as giving the public what it is interested in. And, of course, media companies cultivate that interest through their offerings. Media moguls then rationalize their programming decisions in terms of "giving the people what they want."

Clearly, many viewers, readers, and listeners do not want what the media companies think they do. Evidence for this disinterest can be found in the growing tune-out of prime-time offerings and the overall drop in television viewing. New shows flop far more often than they succeed, despite all the focus groups and market research spent on designing shows that will pander to the public. As many blockbuster movies fail as they do succeed. Fusion of art and commerce has always been combustible, with the "best and the brightest" media executives often left with egg on their faces. Unfortunately, the failure of one tabloid shock-show just leads to a new one's debut. The "Dream Factory," as Hollywood is called, follows the dictates of other manufacturers, pumping out products that are usually not needed but using advertising to stimulate consumer demand.

THE MEDIA RESISTANCE

A resistance to media power is emerging in a number of forums and directions. Organizers of the Media and Democracy Congress held in San Francisco years ago started when 600 activists showed up. A year later, a follow-up meeting in New York drew twice as many participants. Most agreed on what was wrong, but there was no consensus on joint action. It is still difficult for radical media groups with different sensibilities, styles, and priorities to work together.

Some activists have been targeting media companies. There have been protests at television stations, including Rupert Murdoch's Fox News channel, by democrats outraged by that outlet's right-wing partisanship. There have been mass marches against the National Association of Broadcasters convention in San Francisco led by the local media alliance's fighting for rights for microbroadcasters. Groups like Fairness and Accuracy in Reporting (FAIR), People for Better TV, and Citizens for Independent Public Television have been mobilizing their members through forums and letter-writing campaigns. Media-critical think tanks like the Center for Media Education and the Benton Foundation hold conferences and produce policy proposals. There is a Minority Media Council and law firms engaged in crafting challenges to FCC decisions. The Mediachannel.org policy center has more than sixty participants. Hardly a month goes by in media centers like New York, Washington, and Los Angeles without forums, conferences, seminars, and meetings discussing aspects of the media problem.

Less visible is how these issues are contested *within* the media industry, where fights over what's ethical and not in addition to resistance toward corporate pressures goes on every day. Regularly, trade publications and media industry gossip websites report on denunciations of media practices by insiders, and professionals' being fired or quitting for refusing to get along by going along.

Publishers at leading newspapers have likewise denounced cost-cutting and layoffs in their industry. They have protested the way their company's bottom-line needs are undermining their journalistic mission. In June 2001, I spoke with Rick Kaplan, who left CNN as its president eight months earlier. He told me that CNN had been making a 40 percent profit for Turner Broadcasting, but that wasn't enough for AOL, the new owners. They took over, soon laying off 1,000 people. What happened? Ratings and profits plummeted.

Overseas, the battle lines are different because public broadcasting is being challenged by market-minded managers from within and threats of privatization. Over 100,000 people rallied in Prague to defend their public television when journalists went on strike. There have been other protests in Russia, Bulgaria, and Finland about similar issues, but not on the same scale. The Czech protests were the largest since the days of the Velvet Revolution in 1989.

THE INDY MEDIA EXPLOSION

As big media merges and converges, there are companies, my own among them, who see new opportunities to offer underreported and unreported "news not in the news" to underserved audiences. Funding and investment for these projects is hard to find, but potentially profitable niches are there, as is the technology, to meet needs that the system by its incompleteness, misses or denies.

Alongside the emerging protests outside and inside the media world, a new generation of media activists is launching new websites and publications in flurry of creative activity. Just as the Internet is used to spark and help organize mass mobilizations like the ones in Seattle, Independent Media Centers are documenting what happens and reporting on the issues, arrests, and plans of the global justice movements with state-of-the-art technology.

The indy media movement now has thousands of participants, contributing to hundreds of websites. (See Indymedia.org for a list of sites.) They are nowhere close to replacing mass media, but they are building support.

In June 2001, there was a report that the FBI seized an e-mail list from Independent Media Center in Seattle with a million names of recipients of indy media bullets and alerts. That's a lot of people. The costs for their media making and activism are relatively low—and the impact high at least in the activist world. They face the same problems other indy media outlets face—a need to become more credible, attract funding, and market their products. As I write, these institutions are young, and they need help in institutionalizing themselves and training the largely volunteer base. The energy and enthusiasm that can sustain them can burn out just as the thousands of underground newspapers of the 1960s did.

While the indy media groups relish in their antibureaucratic forms and belief in decision making by consensus, it often leads to a very time-consuming process, that older people, or others used to more traditional top-down hierarchies, are impatient with. This generational divide may make it difficult to build alliances with unions or other groups.

Although the Internet is becoming more accessible and easier to afford, there are still digital divides that need to be overcome. Poorer communities often don't have access. Ditto for many working people and their organizations. A recent survey in the developing world found that 40 percent of those asked said they had no time or interest in going online. The digital divide is often an economic divide too, in a world still deeply divided on class, ethnic, and racial lines.

The Internet also leads to more individual relationships with media, which can undercut the type of solidarity and organizational activism that most movements are built on. The web is a one-on-one media, while television and films are often group experiences. This troubles some critics who complain that too much Internet-based activity isolates people from friends and communities.

THE THREAT TO THE INTERNET

In 1999, only 6.7 percent of the world's population used the Internet, with more than 201 million users, although these figures are multiplying rapidly. While this reach may be relatively small in absolute numbers, it offers a chance to reach a not-insignificant audience with alternative information of all kinds. A 2001 Press Freedom survey found that the "trends in freedom of the Internet are mixed. Perhaps surprising, many traditionally authoritarian countries now permit unrestrained use by citizens while several of the most democratic states (like the United States) attempt to impose restrictions in the name of protecting national security and public decency."

The threat to freedom on the Internet comes from both governments and corporations. In the United States, one danger is posed by the consolidation of internet service providers (ISPs). AOL and three other big ISPs control the majority of Internet traffic and could in the future regulate who has access. Countries like China are building their own Internet filtering systems to keep out ideas they don't like. In some instances, U.S. companies have sold them the software to implement their censorship schemes. It would be wrong to think that the relative freedom on the Internet will last unless users organize to defend it.

The forces of co-optation are very slick and seductive. Increasingly, what starts as an alternative finds itself forced by the logic of the marketplace to commercialize its content. That is what happened to online magazines like Salon.com on the Internet and film festivals like Sundance.

THE MEDIA MOVEMENT AND THE PEOPLE'S MOVEMENTS

Strong media movements can help build larger people's movements. Skilled media makers are needed to inform and inspire and help advocacy groups market their ideas to the mainstream. There are many dangers and limits, of course, but the energy, creativity, and determination of those who care about media will help renew movements for change.

Years ago Marshall McLuhan called media the message, or was it the massage. If you, like me, are tired of being massaged by its message, join us in doing something about it.

One World under Media*
The Media We Share Shapes Our Lives—It Can Be Great . . . But Not Always

All of this happened in January and February of the first year of our new millennium, 2001:

- In the Philippines, 150,000 people converged on the center of Manila to demand and then win the ouster of a president. It is later revealed that their protest was made possible through the dissemination of text messages on mobile phones, marking the first political transformation triggered by a digital revolution.
- In China, the Falun Gong spiritual practice, though banned by a repressive regime, used beepers and the Internet to mobilize its faithful to resist a crackdown on religious freedom.
- In Prague, 100,000 people rallied in the largest outdoor assembly, since the Velvet Revolution that toppled Communism, to insist that the Czech Republic's public service television broadcaster serve the public and guarantee independent journalism.
- In Davos, Switzerland, a small church is outfitted as a television studio for a night for an unofficial video "space bridge" dialogue between powerful attendees at the World Economic Forum and activists at the "counter-Davos" World Social Forum in Puerto Alegre, Brazil. The amateurish broadcast illustrates the vast gulf that exists between the two "sides" in the debate over globalization.

---

* Written for *Tribute Magazine* (Paris)

- In Washington, television network executives are hauled before a congressional committee investigating alleged election-night mistakes by news forecasters. Clips of on-air "projections," which in retrospect seem absurd, are shown.

All over the world, and on every continent, people are plugging into new media and old, often using it in bold, interactive, and imaginative ways. Communication systems that were once just thought of only as a one-way source of consumer enjoyment are now points of contact. As billions of e-mails rocket through cyberspace daily, millions of us are tethered to technologies that years ago seemed unimaginable, except in the pages of science fiction.

Who can say that their lives have not been touched if not enriched by the penetration of the octopi of this media system? Surely, this is a form of "progress" that has quickly been adopted and just as quickly been taken for granted.

At the same time, as this multimedia system consolidates and grows more powerful, it becomes more than a transmission belt for the "issues" our respective countries struggle over. It has, in its own way, become an issue in itself, an arena for debate about such weighty concerns as how to erode a digital divide that is spawning separate worlds of information haves and have-nots.

Our communications technologies have indeed made the world smaller by altering most traditional concepts of national borders and by influencing how decision making happens in the public sphere. This impact is global, not just national or local. The United Nations now sponsors an annual World Television Forum, inviting top media executives into chambers usually populated by diplomats, almost as if the locus of power has shifted from the political sphere to the corporate one, from the public to the private. The U.N.'s interest is how to encourage media institutions and news agencies to highlight concerns such as hunger, war, peace, and development, which the world organization addresses. Clearly, politicians need the beneficent eye of media perhaps more than the media needs them.

The corporate world is also reaching out even as branches of it invest heavily in media and technologies. Increasingly, global and regional forums on economic development focus on how to introduce and utilize communications systems to further their own agendas. I have reported for several years on how the corporate summit that convenes annually at Davos makes a special effort to cultivate journalists and editors as well as other opinion leaders.

Perhaps that's because it is increasingly recognized that media and communication systems play a key role as core components in the spread of economic globalization, in addition to the interdependence it promotes on virtually every level, including the virtual one.

At the same time, disputes about the credibility and responsibility of the media itself is now on the global political agenda as ordinary people increasingly find ways of becoming media makers as well as media consumers, putting an end to what has been a passive, one-way relationship. Computers now offer software that enables people to make their own videos; the Internet allows access to a plethora of sites and ideas; the global penetration of wireless technologies and widespread use of cell phones hold out the promise of bringing broadband fusions of video and audio services to remote communities that currently lack electricity.

Travel (as I have recently) around the world—from Japan to Johannesburg, from Milan to Munich—and you see how fast these technologies have globalized and how widely they are utilized. A car passes with four people, each babbling into a cell phone. *The New York Times* columnist Tom Friedman predicts that peasants in Africa will soon have their own "palm pilot"-type personal organizers even if they only live, as many do, on a dollar a day.

The television system we have grown up with is changing rapidly, as digital technologies replace analog ones. Suddenly, hundreds of channels are now available to people who could originally access only a handful. New screens—flat, gigantic—turn living spaces into movie theaters. Almost every big city projects news now on walls and public spaces, from Times Square to Piccadilly Circus to the Ginza in Tokyo. When something "important" happens anywhere in the world, the headlines ricochet globally within minutes.

Increasingly, irrespective of national differences, the same news from many of the same sources gives us all a rather similar frame of reference, even as interpretations of that news can vary from place to place. Culturally, the impact goes deeper. Thanks to Hollywood films, fashion magazines, and a global music business, film stars, fashion models, and rock icons now have global followings. This promotes a cross-pollination of rhythms, celebrities, and fads.

It all sounds exciting (and it certainly can be), but there are drawbacks. Communications "progress" can become a double-edged sword. On the positive side, satellites and television images and the Internet bring the world together with new markets and a faster exchange of ideas, transcending ideological and cultural boundaries as well as physical borders. This is the "global village" ideal realized through a communications revolution that's been credited with also promoting economic progress.

On the darker side, there's the fear of global pillage, of media giants promoting a homogenization of consumer culture, even an "Americanization" that threatens to erode the integrity of diverse cultures. In response, some countries erect barriers and retreat into nationalism and chauvinism. The war in the Balkans, for example, began as a media war of hostile propaganda between Serbia and Croatia, and it later burst into a shooting war. In countries like China, state controls over media and the Internet have orchestrated cultural revolution-type clampdowns on dissenting speech and popular movements. At least twenty countries are committed to regulating and limiting Internet access and freedom.

Professor Benjamin Barber, a respected scholar of democracy, sees this media conflict as an extension of, and unintentional promoter of, a deeper cultural and political polarization, pitting forces of modernism and a fundamentalist reaction. Media is often at the heart of the clash, even as it occasionally reports on it. He notes that every day the same newspaper presents conflicting images of a world that is simultaneously falling apart and coming together at the same time. Our front pages, for example, carry screaming headlines about wars, disasters, and instability while the business section reports on mergers and growing business synergies, as well as the convergence of technologies. (That is until the economic decline accelerated.)

The spread of global media often has the capacity to drive political agendas in ways that make politicians more reactive than they should be. All too often, decision makers, military planners, and office holders find themselves reacting to the issues and images hyped by the twenty-four/seven cable networks. I have heard the U.N. secretary general, Kofi Annan, speak of CNN as the sixteenth member of the Security Council because the stories it broadcasts often influence the aid and peacekeeping priorities of the world body. In truth, our politicians in democratic governments often have more pressures for accountability for their decisions than media organizations. In many countries, revolutions are fought for control of the television station. Control of the media is widely perceived as essential. In Russia, for example, the emergence of independent television networks has been an anathema to the political elites who have sought to control them through legal and illegal means.

In many places the media is more than a marketplace; it is a battleground for a context over freedom of expression, which is key to democracies. Hundreds of journalists are still at risk and often on the front line of that never-ending fight. Each year, many are killed and imprisoned for doing their job in countries like Iran or Sierra Leone. It seems clear that media freedom puts a check on the behavior of rogue states who clamp down on human rights and democratic rights. It is often the only force capable of preventing the excesses of overly centralized rulers and corrupt politicians.

Ironically, this media world can abuse its authority, too, and become a threat to democracy, not just its guarantor, and not only in countries where media is rigidly state-controlled. The dumbing down of the news is sadly pervasive in Western countries, where it underinforms as it diverts attention away from important problems. Its dramatic images penetrate our minds as well as our living room. Sensational stories often drive commercial media agendas to the detriment of more serious fare. Television writer Larry Gelbart has taken to calling television "a weapon of mass distraction." It may not be as deadly as weapons of mass destruction but it can deaden the impulse of people to participate in civic affairs.

The developing world is worried about the impact of all this, and it is worried about building its own media capacity and infrastructure, as well as training journalists and trying not to be left behind. It's significant that India has become a world software center. (At least 25 percent of Microsoft's key employees are from India.) Jordan is building its own Silicon Valley for the Arab World while the African American musical personality Quincy Jones is working with South Africans to build a similar infrastructure in Capetown. In poor countries like Bangladesh, a cell phone company has grown out of the Grameen Banks' efforts to promote development through microcredit lending. Australia has an Aboriginal TV network while Kapapo Indians in the Amazonian regions of Brazil teach videomaking to their youth as do Canadian Indian tribes in the Arctic zones. All are determined to represent themselves and now document their own traditions and aspirations.

All over the world, new strategies are emerging to permit developing counties to survive in the new media jungles, sometimes as ants do among the elephants, and at other times as emerging players in the media marketplace. No one can predict with certainty where all this going—but it is safe to say, it is not going away.

Who Sets the Media Agenda?

LEIPZIG, GERMANY, MARCH 2000

This was the heart of the old East Germany, its center of ideological training as well as a transportation hub for rail traffic heading east. One of Europe's most beautiful train stations has been rebuilt just across from my hotel, partly as a shopping mall crammed with global brands. It is one showcase of a reunified Deutschland, with billions invested to beautify and businessify what had been a crown jewel in the old state socialist order. A picture of orchestral conductor Kurt Mazur is exhibited on the inside; posters of Madonna are plastered on the outside.

The station is fronted by Leipzig's Ring Road, where ten years ago, in the heady days of the 1989 revolution, 100,000 people marched peacefully against the old regime. It was a resistance movement bigger than the one in Berlin, if not as well covered. In those days, cameras operated by the feared Stasi secret police monitored the population. The cameras came down when the Wall did, but now some are back up, this time to monitor drug dealing and troublemaking among street kids hanging out in front of the station.

There's a lot more that needs to be monitored, including the revival of aggressive neo-Nazis like the ones who stomped and murdered an African immigrant in Leipzig a few months ago. On the day I arrived, Germany's interior minister banned Blood and Honor and its junior arm, White Youth, two Hitler-loving hate groups (although banning them, many fear, may just force them underground). The day before I arrived, two German newspapers reported that the government has undercounted the number of people murdered by like-minded thugs. Since reunification, they count ninety-three victims, far more than the official tally of twenty-six. These crimes have received lots of chilling media attention overseas, too much for the taste of locals, who say that it distorts the reality of a place where extremists constitute only a tiny, if troublesome, minority.

It is certainly unfair to tag all Germans as unreconstructed haters. But the activities of this fringe unfortunately continue to shape a distorted image of Leipzig in the world at large. Frankly, as a foreigner myself and as a member of a certain ethnic persuasion that perished in the Old Germany, I was a bit anxious about traveling here but pleasantly relieved when my fears about the place were not realized.

MEDIA AND POLITICS

A few blocks from the hotel, up café-lined Nikolai street, there's a another brand of monitoring underway at the office of MEDIA TENOR, a professional media monitoring organization and a Mediachannel.org affiliate. I had been invited to a MEDIA TENOR international conference on agenda setting, or how the media and politics interact to define the issues that the rest of us focus on and argue about. The company is led by Roland Schatz, a dynamic, socially responsible, young German entrepreneur, who decided to base his operation in this city's beautifully rebuilt old town, just across the street from the University of Leipzig, which has a tradition of media analysis going back to 1690, when the world's first media studies thesis was published.

MEDIA TENOR now has offices in six countries, and representatives from all of them were in town to talk about their work and findings. Many of them work as "coders," analyzing news stories, sentence by sentence, to detect biases and dissect the way information is structured. Their work offers content analysis but also a deeper assessment of the meaning of the data. Their company seems to have two goals: to build a successful business and improve media performance. They even give awards to media outlets with the best practices.

They have just launched an innovative finance site on the web that examines the work of industry analysts and financial journalists who influence, often inaccurately, a company's share price. Some of their many findings are published and available online, while others are produced confidentially for powerful clients such as Lufthansa, DaimlerChrysler, BMW, and Allianz Insurance, which need reliable information about how their companies and products are being treated in the press. A few of MEDIA TENOR's clients sent executives to the conference, as did all of Germany's major political parties.

This event was a long way from the Chicago Media Watch teach-in I wrote about previously, which drew only like-minded outsiders who hate the mainstream media. Some of those folks were discussing how to understand agenda setting so that they could learn to use the media more effectively. As we learned, agendas on different issues can be set by different players—who are usually maneuvering to frame issues their own way. The politicians want to be in the lead, but increasingly, their options and media access are determined by the media itself or by nongovernmental players including NGOs and the corporate sector.

I soon learned that media and politics interact here in a quite different way than in the United States. Europeans have yet to be "Americanized" for a number of reasons, including the presence of well-financed, noncommercial public broadcasting outlets with large audiences that set a standard that elevates national political discussion. Years ago, Germany invested billions in public television; ARD, their main public channel, has just turned fifty. There is also an active political party system that interacts with journalists in a more intimate way.

Barbara Pfetsch, a Berlin-based media scholar, explained the differences in a paper offering a detailed comparative analysis of the norms of media agenda setting in the United States and Germany. The Germans have a politically motivated communications culture enriched by ideological debate that goes on between well-established mainstream parties from competing traditions—including socialists and Greens, who now form a governing coalition. In contrast, she depicted the United States as a political system dominated by a media-driven commercial system and weak parties, where ideas and real differences are minimal and cleave to the center. (Hedrik Hetzberg makes the same point in the current *New Yorker,* arguing that "the United States doesn't really have a two-party system because the Democrats and Republicans aren't really parties" but shifting coalitions.)

In both countries, there is interaction between the media and politics, but the values and orientations of the actors are different. The media system in Germany is far more politicized. Political success is defined by how the parties and their programs are received. "In contrast," explains Fetsch, "a media-oriented political communication system is concerned only with favorable media coverage and the unspecific support for which the media public is surrogate."

THE MEDIA PUBLIC

Let's underscore her insight: The public in the United States is not seen as "the people" but rather as a "media public," conditioned by media, educated by media, and in many ways misled by media. The political actors then utilize "media logic" to influence this media public. "This approach implies techniques of political marketing, looks for strategic target groups, sees voters as consumers and offers a symbolic product which is constructed and marketed," she argues.

"Constructed and marketed!" Yup, that about sums up the presidential-election ritual in the United States. There you are: I had to come to Leipzig to get a more precise handle on what is happening in my own country.

And yet this German audience was fascinated by the presidential campaign, continually asking me for my prediction on the Gore–Bush showdown. Over a cup of chai at Coffee Culture, a local Starbucks clone, one researcher told me that this is a matter of collective self-interest, not just curiosity. "Whoever wins," he explained, "will have his finger on that red button, and that worries us in Europe a lot." Another said that since so many Americans don't vote, maybe the rest of the world should be allowed to participate because what the president of the world's only real superpower does, or doesn't do, directly affects everyone on the planet, whether Americans care or not.

If the media sets the political agenda, they can also set counteragenda that promote a rejection of politics. Saying one thing and doing another is nothing new, of course. Just recently, it was revealed that major media companies that said they opposed marketing violent products to children actually did just that, according to government findings. There's a logic to depoliticizing the audience in an industry where stimulating consumers is far more important than educating citizens. If entertainment programming produces higher ratings and revenues, why not cut back on politics? Thus, the self-interest and lack of democratic accountability of those at the top of the media system translates into political programming that has a low priority and receives less airtime.

Data was introduced to show how media cynicism produces unimaginative coverage, which in turn encourages public apathy. Studies by the "Vanishing Voter" project at Harvard University partially explains the declining level of voting as a function of the loss of engagement by individuals in all phases of the political process. This is seen correctly as a threat to the future of democracy in the United States, and, if true, can be blamed in no small part on the media itself. Ironic, isn't it, that freedom of the press, which enjoys constitutional protection because it was perceived as the guardian of democracy back when the republic was founded, is today actually helping to undermine democracy?

What can be done to resist the trend? Political scientist Stephen Coleman of England's Hansard Society, based at my old alma mater, the London School of Economics, was very forthright in insisting that the purpose of media criticism must not be limited to "lamenting what's wrong." "What we need," he said, "is a public agenda to set it right and promote democratic accountability." He pointed to the way government regulation is used in Britain to support public-service networks and ensure a modicum of social responsibility by broadcasters.

He then laid out an agenda for what democratic media should be. In his view, they must be accountable and transparent, but they must also be *seen* as accountable and transparent—and they must do so in a way that builds public confidence. Second, media should promote a plurality of views, and they should offer airtime for alternative discourse and access for a range of views. Finally, they have to encourage debate and public deliberation on the issues of the day, which requires that media inform people about issues and choices, not just assume personalities.

Coleman noted that the British government has now invested over two billion pounds in a new online, Internet portal, United Kingdom Online, to encourage the type of civic involvement in government that is increasingly missing in the media. He stresses the importance of building and sustaining a vibrant political culture in an era of mounting media fragmentation. Coleman places his hopes on encouraging more online interactivity at a time when the very concept of citizenship is moving toward voyeurism and passivity.

These issues were raised and debated with the participation of media monitors from Germany, England, the Czech Republic, the United States, and South Africa. What became clear is how much research is needed on the impact of new media and the changing nature of old media. MEDIA TENOR's research is showing how powerful private broadcasters are in influencing public broadcasters to become more like them, to focus more on crime and sensation, and less on politics and ideas. The data they so carefully compile is beyond dispute. I came away with the sense that despite national and regional differences, reforming media is a prerequisite to energizing democracy on a global level.

At the end of the conference, Richard Gaul, head of communications at BMW, suggested that to test how agenda setting works, the conferees should think about an agenda they might be interested in establishing. He proposed they consider ways to recast the city of Leipzig in a new light, as a community that looks forward and is not trapped in a totalitarian past. His provocative and constructive challenge did not go unanswered.

Roland Schatz's idea was to link the city to a new global initiative helping the millions of AIDS orphans worldwide, to show that Leipzig cares about people. That thought led to another: to encourage the town he loves to become Europe's "Capital of Compassion" and mobilize its resources to assist children of the AIDS pandemic whom the world seems to be abandoning. Leipzig will work with the Global Action for Orphans campaign, launched by the FXB

Foundation. If this campaign works, Leipzig could potentially "get by giving"—and build a whole new image in the process.

Right now, because of the fanaticism of a few, Leipzig, once known as the home of Johann Sebastian Bach, is being portrayed as a center of skinheaded, neo-Nazi killers. The image is wrong and devastating. But what to do? Can a new agenda reframe the city's image in the public eye? If anyone can do it, thirty-five-year-old Roland Schatz can, as a man whose grandfather quit a job as a newspaper editor rather than serve the dictates of the Nazis. Since the age of twenty, he has been writing and publishing about news and newsmakers. Following the example of his own father, also an editor, who stood up for his independence and refused to write what his publisher ordered him to, he will stand up for his beliefs.

Media Monitoring

MEDIATENOR.COM

Day after day, more than 150 analysts (coders) all over the world scrutinize each contribution in the major German, Czech, Canadian, English, American, and other daily and weekly newspapers and monthly journals, as well as in television news and magazines.

Sentence by sentence, the analysts ask themselves what topics, from what originator and what source did the journalists select for print or broadcasting. Following a catalog of criteria—established in cooperation with the universities of Mainz, Munich, Leipzig, Berlin, and the partner institutes in the International Media Monitor Association—the contents of the media are subject to a scientifically approved analysis. This offers the opportunity of measuring—beyond personal opinionating—what concerns the media and what does not.

In Germany, for instance, passages referring to Germany's economic and social situation, political values, the image of the former German Democratic Republic and German reunification, the European Union, the "Third Reich," companies and trade unions, as well as new technologies, are analyzed in the greatest detail.

Example: Contribution Analysis

Euro-Start a Success

Frankfurt. The introduction of the Euro was celebrated with a party at the Frankfurt stock exchange. Jacques Santer, president of the EU Commission, talked about . . .

Firstly, this article is analyzed with respect to the technicalities of its publication: on what page is it and in what position on the page? With or without photo? And from what press agency, if any at all? Then the topic (Euro) and the place of the action (Hessia) is encoded; thereafter, the personalities or organizations involved are documented.

Example: Passage Analysis

If a Grand Coalition in Germany is going to lead to a dilemma, it is most probably not going to be decided in a head-to-head race between the Social Democrats (SPD) and the Christian Democrats (CDU/CSU), but depends in the end on the results of the smaller parties: the Greens, the Liberals (FDP) and the Socialists (PDS) will decide on Sunday night.

Information about politicians and parties is analyzed sentence by sentence. What is the topic? Who is the source of the information, and what is the evaluation of the political actors? The example contains information about the election chances of five parties and about the possibility of a coalition between the SPD and the CDU/CSU.

The international MEDIA TENOR Institute publishes a research report on a monthly and a quarterly basis, presenting a survey on media trends. The data exclusively shows the information given by the media—it does not show, however, what those concerned really said or what action they really took. This means the following:

- For journalists, the reports of the leading media decide the importance of a specific topic. What is the opinion of those leading media? MEDIA TENOR is not only able to show media trends, but it can also pinpoint topics that were neglected by the media.
- For scientists, the ongoing contents analysis produces a wealth of valuable data. How does specific media communicate certain topics? MEDIA TENOR offers its research results to academic institutions for further analysis.
- For politicians, only through the media is it possible to engage the wider public with a specific argument; therefore, which arguments can be communicated through which media? MEDIA TENOR reflects on the priorities and preferences of the media.
- For managers, a company's media image can become an existential question. How can managers recognize trends in branch reports early enough to react adequately? MEDIA TENOR offers important leads for successful company communication.

AGENDA SETTING

The influence of the media on public opinion is still subject to dispute. Do important topics influence the media, or does the media influence important topics? MEDIA TENOR compares up-to-date research in contents analysis and public opinion research and thus contributes to a deeper understanding of how agenda setting works. (See agendasetting.com.)

About the Contributors

D ANNY SCHECHTER grew up in the Bronx and graduated from DeWitt
Clinton High School, where he edited the high school newspaper. After
receiving a bachelor of arts degree from Cornell University in 1964, he
became a civil rights worker and community antipoverty organizer. In 1966, he
was an assistant to the mayor of Detroit on a Ford Foundation grant. Between
1966 and 1968, he studied at the London School of Economics, earning a mas-
ter's degree in political sociology in 1968. From 1970 to 1977, he was the news
director, principal newscaster, and "News Dissector" at WBCN-FM in Boston,
where he won two Major Armstrong Awards and a national reputation for innovative radio journalism. He was honored with a Nieman Fellow in Journalism
at Harvard in 1977–1978. His television career began as an on-air reporter in
1978 at Boston's WGBH and has since included stints as a producer at CNN as
well as eight years as a producer for ABC's *20/20*. Since 1987, he has been executive producer of Globalvision, a New York–based television and film production company he cofounded. Mr. Schechter has one daughter and lives in a New
York City loft with his eight-thousand-album record collection and an Apple
computer that is always nearly out of memory.

At Globalvision, he produced 156 editions of the award-winning series
South Africa Now, coproduced sixty-two editions of *Rights & Wrongs: Human
Rights Television* with Charlayne Hunter-Gault, and directed eleven films on
social, cultural, and political topics. (The films are listed at Globalvision.org.) He
has also produced and directed many other television specials and films. His
writing on politics, current events, and media issues has appeared in leading

newspapers and magazines, including the *Boston Globe, Newsday, Detroit Free Press, The Village Voice,* and *Columbia Journal Review.* His first book, *The More You Watch, the Less You Know: News Wars, (Sub)merged Hopes and Media Adventures* was published by Seven Stories Press in October 1997 and reissued as a paperback in January 1999. *News Dissector—Passions, Pieces and Polemics, 1960–2000* (Akashic Books, 2001) is drawn from forty years of writing on politics, current events, and the media. He is also the author of *Falun Gong's Challenge to China: Spiritual Practice or "Evil Cult?"* (Akashic Books, 2000), and he served as editor on *Hail to the Thief: How the Media "Stole" the 2000 Presidential Election* (INNOVATIO Verlag, 2001).

He is the editor of Mediachannel.org, the world's largest online media issues network and Vice President for News at the Globalvision News Network (gvnews.net).

ROLAND SCHATZ studied philosophy, economics, history, and political science in Fribourg, Switzerland, and Bonn. He is the founder of INNOVATIO Publishing Ltd. The company focuses on media monitoring, organizational development, East-West relationships, culture management, and new methods in education. Roland Schatz teaches communication and strategic information management at the Universities of Berlin, Bonn, Leipzig, and Prague.